CONSULTING DEMONS

CONSULTING DEMONS

INSIDE THE UNSCRUPULOUS
WORLD OF GLOBAL
CORPORATE CONSULTING

LEWIS PINAULT

HarperBusiness
A Division of HarperCollins*Publishers*

HarperCollins books may be purchased for educational, business, or sales promotional use. For information please write: Special Markets Department, HarperCollins Publishers Inc., 10 East 53rd Street, New York, NY 10022.

FIRST EDITION

Designed by Jackie McKee

Printed on acid-free paper

Library of Congress Cataloging-in-Publication data has been applied for.

ISBN 0-06-661997-1

00 01 02 03 04 ❖/RRD 10 9 8 7 6 5 4 3 2 1

For My Wife, Sasha,
Whose Love, Perception and Courage
Restore and Fulfill My Dreams

We can judge our progress by the courage of our
questions and the depth of our answers, our willingness
to embrace what is true rather than what feels good.

—Carl Sagan

CONTENTS

ACKNOWLEDGMENTS

For helping me to envisage and realize an ambitious and daring work, I thank my editors Adrian Zackheim and Edwin Tan, and my agent Ethan Ellenberg, for resounding confidence and support from day one. Working with this team of newfound colleagues, I enjoyed as creative and challenging an adventure as I have ever experienced in consulting, science, and the law.

For the many whose stories are enfolded in this narrative, and the thousands more who complete untold, impossible feats of stamina and delivery in the consulting business every day, I give tribute to the sacrifices made, and extend to them, and especially their families, my greatest compassion. My views of the choices they have made and the consulting industry aside, I was there, too, and have only the highest respect for their energies and intelligence.

AUTHOR'S NOTE

The people and events portrayed in *Consulting Demons* are real. Only a few individuals who figure in these pages, however, people such as Dr. James Abegglen and C. K. Prahalad, are today reasonably well known worldwide beyond management consulting circles. Many of the individuals that feature in this book are here simply because they were my colleagues and acquaintances and had the hapless fortune to share my adventures. For the most part, these people were my fellow sufferers in the relative anonymity of the day-to-day consulting world. Given the circumstances, I have elected to protect the privacy of many who appear here by changing their names. For the readers' convenience, names that have been changed are placed in quotation marks the first time that person is introduced.

PROLOGUE

"Lying, cheating, stealing."

"I beg your pardon?" responded the professional, and in the circumstances, annoyingly alluring, Japanese woman poised on my hotel room sofa. I glanced at my watch: we still had twenty minutes left.

"Let's explore your feelings about what some would say is the darker side of this business."

"*Kurai tokoro?*" Dark places? Her retreat into Japanese was clever, I reflected. I knew this woman understood the sense of the question perfectly well, and that she was simply buying some time to think, or better yet, understand where I wanted to go with this. Was I a good guy? A prude? Did I want a knowing answer that would wink at questionable practices? Or did I want a flat declaration that she would sell her soul for a taste of the joys and evils of the consulting life?

She was right to hesitate. A brazen appetite for skullduggery would not go over well with our more sensitive clients. But by now, even the clubbiest of the boutique management consulting firms was no place for the squeamish.

I knew my recruiting interviewee, "Kumiko"-san, was among the Harvard Business School's best and brightest. Here at the Embassy Suites Hotel in Cambridge, she was the twelfth candidate I had interviewed that day for Gemini Consulting's just-opened Japan office, where I was the newly installed manager. Kumiko was doing well. She had not flinched at my *gaijin*–talking dog trick (vanilla white-guy foreigner fluently speaking Japanese). Her handling of the last test business case (conducted in Japanese, allowing no excuses for weak problem-solving) was imaginative, for what was basically more a cash-flow than strategy exercise. In responding Kumiko had strained both my language skills and my less remarkable accounting talents, and had given life and entertainment to a sample problem I usually found terminally boring. Now she seemed ready to brave the English portion of the interview.

I determined to be hard on her.

"Let's discuss a few situations that might be politely described as gray areas."

I went over to get a refill from my third pot of coffee that day. The Embassy Suites are brilliantly designed for intimate business meetings: each tiny suite has a small living room area decorously screened off from the bedroom, and a mini kitchen and bar perfect for marathon sessions like these. This was high recruiting season, spring 1992, and virtually all the suites were booked out by consultants from Gemini and a dozen or so other consulting firms. Conveniently for recruiters and candidates alike, those who were soon-to-be awarded their master's in business administration could just march down the corridors from one firm and interviewer to the next until their destiny was determined. This still seemed an unusual venue to me, though, and I was acutely aware that we were next to my bedroom. I had probably spent too much time in Tokyo, I reckoned. This setup would be unthinkable in the more frankly sensual Japan, but was no doubt viewed as safely sterile here in my harassment-conscious homeland.

"How about we start with lying," I continued. "Let's say we have a chief executive who wants to really shake and revitalize his organization. He asks us to paint the most dire possible picture of his own company's competitive position, to thoroughly frighten his management team."

I settled back into my miniature armchair. Kumiko rearranged herself subtly on the sofa, the first I could recall her actually moving. There seemed to be an extra tension and alertness about her, enhancing her overall attractiveness.

"Well, presumably the CEO is the paying client," she began without hesitation, "and we should aim to fulfill his wishes. We should do a thorough competitive analysis, learn everything we can about how scared they should really be. If there's enough material to be legitimately worrying, I suppose we would just emphasize those facts, let them speak for themselves. If, on the other hand, we find that they really enjoy a superior position to all their current and foreseeable competitors, we should show that to the CEO, definitely, even if it's not what he wants to hear."

Kumiko paused, appearing to reach a decision. I marveled at her English, the product of private high school in the States and an English major at Tokyo's famously internationally minded Waseda University.

"If their position is good," she continued, "and the CEO knows and understands our research showing this to be true, but he—or she," Kumiko smiled briefly, "if he still wants us to deny this comfort to his own employees, that's the CEO's business. Then it's our job, I would suppose, to select those facts that would create the most useful concern. We would not, I think, want to actually manufacture false facts, but we could be pretty selective, for the greater cause of raising the energy levels and revitalizing the company. Of course, there are probably a dozen ways that this kind of demoralizing strategy might backfire. You—we—presumably get paid to not only create anxiety, but also to harness it, no backfires allowed."

Oh, she was good, I thought. I interpreted her reply to mean she would indeed falsify information as needed, but that she knew better than to say so. Kumiko had been a summer-intern at one of Gemini's key competitors, McKinsey, by many measures the leader of the consulting industry. She claimed to have spent her summer with them crunching data, but she had clearly picked up enough about consulting culture to hazard some good guesses. She was shopping us for better money, more control, and faster promotion prospects, and was now well on her way to an offer. Even as she spoke I began to picture her role on one of our new, large-scale revitalization projects.

"Stealing, then," I parried.

"Competitive data?" Kumiko asked. "No, I don't think so. Not the kind of thing the client would like us to get caught at, either, I imagine."

"Yes, but how about this. We go to a client's competitor, and *tell* them we represent an undisclosed competitor. We agree to give away a lot of goodies, nuggets of information, in the course of discussing areas of mutual interest. We say we want to share thoughts about the results of a recent customer survey, for example, which we'll give them. But all the while, we're actually looking for just one or two juicy bits of critical information, which, carefully, we raise as a casual question of side interest."

Ah, I could see signs of an internal struggle.

"I must admit I find it hard to believe any company would agree to such a meeting."

"For now, trust me that they do."

"Then, I suppose," she offered with returning confidence, "if it does not occur to them to suspect deeper motives, they deserve the consequences." Kumiko brightened. "I'm not sure I would call it stealing."

"No one does. Okay, that just leaves us with good old cheating."

"What about sex? Or is that what you mean by cheating?"

Now it was my turn to be startled. Dismissing my initial reaction that this might be some kind of a challenge or even a come-on, I convinced myself this was a joke.

"Sex?" I laughed a little uneasily.

"You know, with clients, with their competitors? For favors and advantages."

"Um, programmatically, no, no sex, not that I'm privileged to know about. I think that would be pretty much up to the individual consultant, and the desperation of the moment."

I was surprised to hear the defensive tone in my own voice, and determined to take back the initiative.

"No," I went on, "I mean to explore what many would say is cheating a client out of their money. Going in to do one thing with a client, and systematically expanding the initial task into perceived needs for more consulting work."

I thought I saw a hint of disappointment in Kumiko's eyes. These were not standard recruiting questions, but rather tests of conscience—or for the absence of one—for seasoned managers and partners. Why was I burdening her with this, she seemed to ask. Or was it something else? Had I missed some important gambit?

Whatever I saw was momentary. She replied lightly and easily, "I thought that was how the business worked. Get in, find or invent more problems, sell more. Move on when the well runs dry."

A warning knock sounded against the door. Time to write up Kumiko's evaluation ("strong recommend") and get ready for the next recruit.

"Yes, well, indeed that is how the business works," I admitted, feeling a bit foolish as I closed out the interview. Drawn to Kumiko as an anonymous confidant, maybe something more, I recognized an urgency to fill an undefined but growing void in my life. There were issues here I needed to discuss with *someone*, but I would need to find a less dangerous sounding board than attractive recruits.

ABOUT *CONSULTING DEMONS*

CONSULTING CLIENTS ARE RARELY AFFORDED THE CHANCE TO SEE HOW a consulting company sees them. Indiscretions over drinks, mid-level cross-hirings, or the stress of desperation to close a new sale may offer the occasional flash of insight. But a clear view of how consultants of every rank serve precise, critical roles in creating and nurturing an institutional organism, a colonial consulting creature designed to thrive on the identification and manipulation of client weaknesses, is quite carefully kept from the client's line of sight. Even within consulting firms, an increasing segmentation of individual roles, and an emphasis on growth by acquisition of unknown smaller consultancies, helps ensure that many consultants themselves have only an incomplete picture of their company's client-consuming dependencies.

Alongside the machinery of this systematic anti-client bias, there is a startling but equally well-hidden reliance on bright, accomplished people operating well beyond human capacities. Finding that a lifetime of doing things well and thoroughly will no longer serve their professional needs, consultants quickly learn to make do, to stretch, pilfer, pad, and deceive as required by the impossible demands of their work. Over time, the more jaded consultants come to believe that this is in fact just what the client wants, that the appearance of controlled solutions, at the right time, can be more

1

important than any actual fix. Compounded guilt and cynicism combine with the highest sustainable levels of personal and professional stress to make the business of consulting an unusually vibrant display of human flaws and failings.

A high-level purpose in my writing *Consulting Demons* is to examine this dichotomy, to show that consulting is both better organized, for the wrong reasons, than clients are led to believe, and that the practice of consulting carries higher risks, based on simple human frailties, than few in the industry would care to acknowledge. Simply put, consulting is at its most organized, intimidating best when it is working to maximize its take from the client. Its key vulnerabilities, on the other hand, are rooted in using some of the most impressive people in the world to do too many questionable things too fast. The view I reveal here is thus not a flattering picture of the consultant-client relationship—nor certainly will it be true for all cases. But it is a story that I believe should be told, if only to alert current and potential clients to the way their trust, time, and money may be systematically abused by their consulting firms.

Few who can tell this story from the inside would choose to tell it. They stand too much to lose, in entrenched rewards and industry reputation, if not by more forceful retribution. I am deeply compelled to share this story, however, both by compassion for the many who meet harm by way of this business, and by a desire to encourage and celebrate the talents and accomplishments of all those who escape consulting's destructive attractions. I expect more of these revealing stories will inevitably surface, and if I play a small part in encouraging that to happen too, so much the better.

I aim also that even people who have never given a thought to consultants or consulting will find a tale of broad significance here. Consulting behavior is increasingly driven by, and itself nurtures, global competitive forces that are fast redirecting the course of daily lives everywhere. Consulting's great weaknesses—its pretended expertise, human and political ruthlessness, and self-justifying problem-making, all in the headlong rush to greed fulfillment—are, to me, symptomatic of the global corporation's own real and potential failings.

I hope to contribute to an understanding of what a management consultant is. Despite twelve years among the best in the industry, in half as many firms across the world, and a final, successful ascent to a choice partnership, I find that this question still defies a simple and honest answer. The fact that this is so, I believe, says something about the course and conduct of the consulting industry itself, and a great deal about those like me who defined their lives within its fuzzy, changing boundaries.

There is, of course, quite a menu of possible answers to the question of what a management consultant is: a problem-solver, a businessman's businessman (still no pretense of gender equality in this industry), a strategist, a knowledgeable expert, a ruthless defender of the bottom line, a seer, forecaster, or guru, a competitive-intelligence gatherer, a market geography specialist, a rallier and motivator, a message bearer, a sounding board, a CEO's friend and champion.

Like many consultants I have been perceived and promoted as all these things. Consultants can also be described as efficiency drones, headcounting cannibals, surface-skimming masters of pretense, spies and data fabricators, threat mongers and opportunists, hit and run specialists, experts in no industry but the promotion of their own expanded sales and well-being. That such descriptions are often rooted in the facts and reality of the consulting industry is central to what I relate in *Consulting Demons*.

Finally, a key personal objective in sharing this no-holds-barred review of my life in consulting is to hit the master's in business administration student right between the eyes. I imagine that few MBAs today are so soft-minded as to believe that consulting is an easy career, a guaranteed learning experience, or a sure-fire transition to rewarding positions in client companies. But having brought literally hundreds of new recruits into the consulting fold, I know that these, and far more bizarre expectations, can sometimes be the norm. If I can do a little to share the flavor of the adventure, and point up the possible benefits of considered alternatives, I will perhaps have done the greatest service of all.

At its heart, this book is the uncensored story of my life in consulting, of the dozen years I devoted to surviving, and ultimately succeeding, at least by the industry's standards, in this frenetically evolving business. My first two years at BCG Tokyo were handily followed by two more in BCG Boston headquarters. The staccato beat of the U.S. domestic travel required soon had me angling for a return to Asia. Offered a take-it-or-leave-it return to Tokyo to effectively handle the office library and fax queries, I ducked for a few months into a client's office at General Electric's Japanese factory automation joint venture, and re-emerged instead as a consultant for a small BCG spin-off, Jim Abegglen's Asia Advisory Services (AAS).

Or so I thought. The spin-off was about to be acquired by the MAC Group, together with another target, guru C.K. Prahalad's Change Management Initiative (CMI). The MAC Group had so far resisted its own acquisition by the fast-growing consulting upstart United Research (UR). Aware that UR was now enlisting the French software giant Cap Gemini Sogeti to help force the takeover, MAC, bowing to the inevitable, sought to quickly build up its buy-out cache by first acquiring a few gems of its own in Abegglen and Prahalad.

The new MAC-AAS-UR-CMI agglomeration was to be melded with Cap Gemini's information systems consulting team and ultimately its own parent's consulting interests, the Daimler Benz consulting outfit. The whole mess would go under the moniker Gemini Consulting. So I joined the MAC Group, and was merged into Gemini Consulting with everyone else in 1990. I started in Gemini's London offices, gratefully working principally CMI-derivative cases, while MAC and UR veterans fought for cultural dominance of the new firm. After a year in London, Gemini moved me to Tokyo again, where I was promoted to manager and took a lead role in preparing Gemini's expansion into Hong Kong and Singapore. Ultimately Gemini's expansion plans stalled, but I decided to stay in Southeast Asia, working as a freelance for Gemini and others, finding a home for a while with Arthur D. Little, and flirting with BCG again. While working on a large Gemini project in Hong Kong I was made a generous offer by Coopers & Lybrand, who were aggressively expanding into the consulting business in Asia, and I finally joined them, becoming a partner in their Hong Kong office in 1997.

Then I quit. As much as anything else, this book is implicitly about why I quit. But true to my imbued consulting instincts, below I tidy up this tale of ruthless and hazard-ridden progress into a simple chart, for convenient reference.

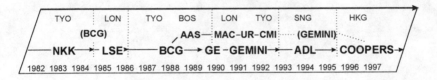

Though *Consulting Demons* is roughly organized to follow the chronology of my consulting life, along the way you will see I have inscribed a few memorials under the heading of *Consulting Demonology*, mini treatises on the real ins and outs of the business. These encapsulate a few of the more telling practices of the consulting cult, and taken together, these *Demonology* tracts comprise an unorthodox primer on the consulting industry. No firm will likely look kindly on the often unseemly secrets and rites I describe, but having interbred with more than the average share of consulting organizations, I am at least as qualified as most other practitioners of these arts to offer insights to these inner realms.

CHAPTER 1

CONSULTING AND ME

LIKE MANY OF THE INDUSTRY'S TOP ACHIEVERS, I DID NOT SET OUT TO become a management consultant, or even consider a business career, until well after college. Consulting recruiters value diversity and esoterica, founded on strong educational pedigrees, knowing that this is the stuff of staying a step ahead of one's clients, of engaging, entertaining, and when need be, duping them into a paying belief in new and unique perspectives.

Diversity and esoterica I had in spades. I grew up in Rhode Island in the boom years of the 1960's, when everything interesting seemed to be happening all at once, but somewhere else. The youngest of six children, I benefited from parents with a staunchly liberal, New Deal view of the world and social justice, and brothers and sisters engaged in every part of the causes of the time. Several of them would embark on academic careers, and all would at least try to live out of state if not overseas. Though working-class poor, my parents encouraged the gathering of new experiences and a high investment in education.

While most were caught up in one way or another with Vietnam, however, I developed an early and obsessive interest in the space program. More than anything else, I wanted to be a scientist astronaut, or perhaps an astrophysicist, and explore other worlds and solar systems. The moon landings seemed but a small first achievement, and between Arthur C. Clarke's *2001* and *Star Trek*, I had all the fuel I needed to imagine humanity's future role in space. A little weirdly, but telling for my interests in international space development then and today, my personal hero of *2001* was space-bureaucrat Heywood Floyd, not the odyssey-making astronauts, and the concept of *Star Trek's* United Federation of Planets intrigued me as much as any alien slug-fest featuring Captain Kirk.

I was fortunate to have my choice of colleges, and the Massachusetts Institute of Technology I hoped would in turn give me a choice of jobs in the space program. But the late 1970's proved a dismal time for space development. Much of NASA's energy and budget was then consumed by trying to get the intractable space shuttle off the ground, and I was angered to find American popular, governmental, and commercial interest in space at an all-time low. Midway through MIT I chose two new directions which I hoped would one day lead me to an engaging career in the use and exploration of space. I started an ocean engineering major and internship program and enrolled in a domestic year-away program at the University of Chicago, to take up intensive Japanese studies.

In ocean engineering I hoped to find the excitement and experience of exploration-driven technology development, something I planned to use when prospects for space development turned around. I loved the oceans, and inspired in part by Arthur C. Clarke's own celebration of both the oceans and outer space, I took up scuba diving and fully embraced my new medium. In Japan, I expected to learn something about large-scale project finance for civil engineering projects and hoped to tap that country's competitive strengths for application to space development, once the treaty law barring Japan's own space launches expired.

These were towering ambitions for a poor, struggling student, but I had blundered into the right time and place for combining engineering and Japanese skills. Harvard's Ezra Vogel, with *Japan As No. 1*, had just hit the best-seller lists, and study of Japanese management techniques would soon become an institutionalized fad. After Chicago I returned for two more years at MIT and cross-registered at Harvard in Japanese language, business, and government, finally finishing inpolitical Science at MIT so that I could combine credits in both disciplines and still manage to graduate, in 1982.

I had managed to squeeze in some fledgling German into my poly sci degree, and while waiting on job applications, I took up a United Nations scholarship to do a summer internship in technology transfer at the UN complex in Vienna, Austria. Days before I left for Europe, I was offered and immediately accepted an open-ended job with the Japanese steelmaker and shipbuilder Nippon Kokan, where I would become one of the conglomerate's first foreign professional hires. I arranged to fly directly from Vienna to begin work at NKK's shipyards in Kawasaki at the end of the summer.

My three years with Nippon Kokan were a key formative experience for me both personally and professionally, molding much of what would drive and sustain my later, largely unexpected commitment to consulting. Combining some of Japan's most challenging living conditions with exposure to one of the world's most stimulating urban cultures, all the while propelling me through extraordinary new responsibilities, in these years I became at once professionally confident and alive to Tokyo's many attractions, and desperately eager to find a means to enjoy them.

Like many of the traditional Japanese industrial giants, Nippon Kokan firmly believed in isolating its new male employees in bachelor dormitories, where conditions were spartan at best. The idea was to build a certain sense of equality and camaraderie, reduce any last pretensions to a private life, and encourage early marriage to company-approved spouses.

By and large this approach worked quite well. The pre–World War II Itanaka-ryo where I was assigned was infamous for dilapidated facilities, complete lack of heat or air conditioning through freezing winters and stultifying summers, and truly horrible food. We had one six-man *o-furo* bath for two hundred grimy shipyard workers, filled with hot water only every other day. I quickly learned to tolerate the blistering heat of a fresh fill of the bath, to avoid dealing with the floating scum that would quickly collect with the first few uses. Creatures of all kinds shared our quarters, from bats to horror-movie roaches and a lumbering sort of praying mantis–like thing I still cannot identify. Unaccountably, though most workers would not reach the dorm till nine or ten at night, the evening meal was always prepared by five in the afternoon and left out to get cold in cheap plastic trays. The newfangled cafeteria micro-wave was soon overworked, proving a popular means to drive insects out of cold rice, if you got the timing just right. Board-stiff starched sheets, atop straw mattresses, were the only protection against frenzied mosquito attacks each night. The dorm managers inspected rooms every morning, searching for everything from illegal space heaters to union literature—a bit of a challenge, no doubt, since most of the cramped, two-to-a-room quarters were hovels of old newspapers, magazines, and the remnants of treasured care packages from home. Women, of course, were strictly for-bidden, and I cannot imagine that any would have visited twice; my MIT fraternity life became a distant, painful memory.

There were two immediate benefits for me in sharing this lonely, wretched place with two hundred stressed NKK workers. The room and board was virtually free, and no one had the energy to speak to me in English. My Japanese became solidly fluent. Over time, I also realized that I had gained a certain respect; most salarymen leave their dorms after the requisite first year if they can. My three years at Itanaka-ryo let people know that I was either crazy, or had found that even when show-ing one of its worst faces, life in Japan was somehow worth living.

My initial plan was to stick with NKK for a couple of years, helping on some minor engineering projects, and then to return to graduate school. But NKK headquarters kept tabs on me, and became interested in my swift progress in Japanese. I was transferred to Tokyo headquar-ters and given a business analyst position in corporate planning, a slot usually reserved for mid-level managers. The thinking ran that a recent American college grad would have fresher ideas and better access about international projects in need of finance, at a time when NKK was desperate to diversify away from traditional shipbuilding.

This was great fun. By twenty-five years' age I was facilitating three investment projects of my own creation, including a pilot project for mining cobalt from subsea volcanic crusts, ocean drilling robotics, and a proposal with some of my old MIT professors for accelerating underwater construction of the English Channel Tunnel. I began to travel frequently to Hawai'i for the ocean mining project, and became fascinated by the various legal regimes proposed for developing and sharing the resources, knowledge, and benefits of the international seabed. For graduate school, I began to think about some combination of ocean law and science that might make me a practical expert in something that might later be highly applicable to the use and exploration of outer space.

I had to acknowledge that my business skills needed formal development, too, though, if I wanted to continue on this ocean-to-space development track. NKK put on some friendly pressure for me to take up an MBA, which was highly seductive. I knew I could barely afford going back to school again, and returning to Tokyo on an MBA's salary, courtesy of my sponsoring company, was very appealing. Most of my dating experiences in Japan had fizzled when the money inevitably ran out. Though I was more than reasonably attractive, I like to think, and had very high novelty value, a nice meal and a degree of privacy in Tokyo could cost me a month's salary.

It was about this time that I came to the attention of my first consulting company, the Boston Consulting Group. NKK's corporate planning department had hired a BCG Tokyo team for an organizational study, and it was not long before they noticed the Japanese-speaking *gaijin* with the nifty, well-budgeted projects. Soon BCG was suggesting that *they* sponsor me for an MBA, after a year working with them as a junior analyst. Somewhat in desperation, I took a long shot at potential independence from either NKK or BCG, and applied for a Fulbright Scholarship to complete a combined master's of science in sea-use law and marine science at the London School of Economics. Remarkably, I was awarded the all-expenses-paid Fulbright in short order, and I thought I had bought myself some time to think about how to hang on to my ambitions and yet find a way to afford a life of some indulgence in Tokyo, should I choose to return there.

It was at that point I was hooked into BCG and the consulting life. As detailed in these pages, the Boston Consulting Group made me an offer I could not refuse, and for the next twelve years I was fated to earn more and spend more in a life that grew very distant from my early ambitions. In the course of the success, of a kind, that I achieved in consulting, through a progression of different firms, I learned and exercised the industry's dirtiest tricks and most deceitful representations. On occasion, I also saw applications of consultants' skills and energies, often without support of their own firm, that brought real benefit to client companies and the lives of their employees.

But consulting is something more structured than a mere collection of the goods and evils that characterize any human enterprise. Consulting is an industry with very specific origins, marked by key evolutionary events and defining personalities, whose complex and expanded structure today is still a function of certain relentless brands of logic and cunning. My story in consulting happens to track not only to the industry's origins but also the people and mores that built and comprise its culture today. The first of my *Consulting Demonology* tracts is designed to help keep this complex of characters straight.

CONSULTING DEMONOLOGY, TRACT 1

CONSULTING COMPANY COVENS

1

The Bureaucrats of consulting are the most enduring, enjoying remarkable resiliency to consulting fads, low employee turnover, and the comfort of knowing that if there is a government tomorrow, they will profit from it. *Arthur D. Little*, the grandfather of all consultancies, perfected the extension of scientific analyses for industry to general business problem-solving. Born of MIT a century ago, and thriving with the onset of military-industrial mobilization in World War II, ADL was first to fill the ecological niche between science and industry, and has never strayed. Only the Stanford Research Institute *(SRI)*, and *Booz Allen & Hamilton* would successfully imitate their plodding and inexorably profitable style and approach, by structuring research-oriented, government-contract case teams to cater to the growth of the new West-coast electronics and aerospace industries, and the increasingly technologically enthralled Pentagon. A thriving home for Ph.D.'s and aliens working on visa extensions and security clearances, these are outfits that remain loathe to recruit young MBA's, preferring hard credentials and actual experience. Many Booz divisions have loosened this standard to accommodate international growth plans, but their culture, like SRI's, remains faithful to the glories of the grind, nicely captured in ADL's motto, "Knowledge at Work." Translation: for recruits, low pay, long hours, and the possibility of meaningful work; for clients, a habit-forming reliable bargain long on analysis and short on competitive thinking and imagination.

2

The IBM of Consulting remains McKinsey & Co., another first-in-the-niche, historically advantaged firm. Borrowing a favorite IBM refrain, McKinsey clients enjoy giving play to the myth that "no one ever got fired for hiring McKinsey." Where ADL played the government, McKinsey took the organizational lessons of World War II and gave them full rein in the private sector. By being the first to make extensive use of MBA hirings, McKinsey gave tremendous momentum to business school growth, ensuring pride of place at all elite schools' recruiting functions forevermore. To control the risks of youthful indiscretion and stupid mistakes, McKinsey consultants were carefully drilled in button-downed conformity of dress and manner, and then supplied with a still-growing library of how-to-consult manuals designed to cope with every contingency. One of the few firms to fully budget for comprehensive training at every level of the consulting hierarchy, McKinsey developed a strong pride in the total interchangeability of its consultants at any given level. By adopting an early policy of kind but aggressive outplacement, McKinsey has built the largest alumni network of any firm, ensuring a ready supply of potential clients for quite some time to come. While turnover is consequently high, pay at all levels has steadily defined the high end of the field, and the hard-to-get partnerships are the only ones in the industry approaching par with investment banking compensation and accouterments. Testosterone levels are high. Being able to count on two hands how many nights you slept at home in a year is a common brag. Promising but nonconformist talent is sent to the rural communes first: the path to the glam Tokyo office for an experienced, Japanese-speaking foreigner might be five years Cleveland followed by five years Osaka. For recruits, a painful life in the Royal Horseguards, with plenty of pay and a high reputation to spend a later day. For clients, a hardworking army of blinkered, manual-thumping know-it-alls, more likely than not to be right.

3

The Thinkers of Consulting. When you are not first in the niche, the next most successful survival strategy is usually living by your wits. In the 1960s, Bruce Henderson broke from a dalliance with ADL to form a research outfit that would ultimately become **The Boston Consulting Group**. By focusing exclusively on the strategy needs of top management, and in quick succession producing a series of breakthrough analytic tools that have long since entered the everyday parlance of business people the world over, BCG produced a low-cost formula for tapping large billings. Small, creative teams, applying radical, analytically informed insights, were able to charge high fees for a minimum of client face time. Graphically geared presentation preparation involved little textual documentation. With spartan offices, excellent research libraries, and first-rate art departments, BCG continues to produce some of the most beautiful proposals and presentations in the industry. BCG's emphasis on data gathering and scientific objectivity also helped make them the standard-setter for competitive research and intelligence gathering, making them an elite and powerful tool of industrial espionage for the clients who could afford them. A variety of daring firms attempted to follow suit, most now demised or acquired. BCG vice president Bill Bain's Bain & Co., founded in apparent spite for Bruce Henderson's reluctance to make way for Bain's leadership at BCG, got much mileage from offering the BCG product to Bain clients with mutually exclusive twists: five-year retainer contracts for both Bain and the client guaranteed no service or use of each others' competitors. Alas the resulting incestuousness would nearly become the company's undoing. **The MAC Group**, or Management Analysis Corporation, would try to emulate BCG's boutique success, cultivating Harvard Business School professors' pet research assistants to become expert financial strategists. In a controversial but mainly happy ending for MAC, their absorption as junior partner in Gemini Consulting would ironically see the lasting dominance of their influence and thinking. Like Bain, other BCG spin-offs would surface from time to time, usually not independently outlasting the whims of their founding officers, as with BCG Tokyo founder Jim Abegglens's **AAS** (Asia Advisory Services). For the recruit, the thinking strategy boutiques can be stimulating, fun, and egalitarian, with significant risks attending the more uneven business flow, relative lack of structure, and haphazard opportunities for professional development. Historically, the pay has been good, and at least at BCG, at times higher than anywhere else in the industry. Culturally, these firms can swing from intellectual arrogance to extreme angst and inferiority complexes. Where once McKinsey was BCG's foremost worry, the lack of a full-services, technology-nimble backstop to their strategy work increasingly defines both their weakness and uniqueness. For the client in search of competitive advantage through strategic innovation, the best choice remains BCG and its surviving close cousins.

4

The Operationalists of Consulting. First-in advantages and savvy can sometimes be countered by the dogged persistence of large numbers. Where the scientists of ADL, the organization men of McKinsey, and the innovators of BCG would not tread was the factory floor. Its very unseemliness no doubt accounts in part for the late ripening of this relatively rich consulting opportunity, but the detail and rigor required in improving manufacturing systems and processes required a depth of application and manpower that few firms could afford to wield. Hiring large numbers of operations-fluent consultants, fielding them for periods of sometimes years at one given client, and knowing what to do with them at job's end was a problem few firms cared to stomach. A.T. Kearney, the one-time partner of McKinsey, would adopt an operations and systems emphasis that led to key experiments in direct operations intervention and implementation. Michael Hammer's reengineering works fueled great interest in the area in the 1980s, helping accelerate United Research's power glide to consulting's highest growth territory of the time. UR had consciously structured itself to thrive on plain-vanilla, process-cost–reduction cases. By guaranteeing generous multiples of return on their fees, and eschewing high-cost MBA elites reluctant to get their hands dirty, UR was able to field huge teams on client sites across the United States, helping to trigger a downsizing craze which firmly fixed the public image of consultants as bloodletting automatons. United Research's implementation skills were directly folded into Gemini Consulting with the company's acquisition in the early 1990s. While few stand-alone firms now conduct exclusively implementation-geared assignments, more and more of the larger consulting firms have subdivisions that do. For the recruit inexperienced in operations consulting, the work can be an unfortunate combination of stress and drudgery, and seldom pays well. For general industry veterans looking for a chance to try consulting and enjoy some greater variety and freedom of action, the rewards can be high. For the client, a certain wariness would be healthy. Operations and implementation work is one of the most studied, high-stakes sales a consulting company can make, and the consulting company involved will work hard to set the measure of results to standards convenient to reflecting its own performance. Demonstrable savings and efficiency improvements will follow, but they may not be in the areas that matter.

5

The Networkmen of Consulting. The ever-diminishing circle of the traditional Big Eight Accounting firms, down to four or five at last count, is using a strategy of thriving through imitation with increasing success. Particularly in international markets, where these companies enjoy entrenched infrastructure, hard-won client relationships, and regional familiarity, **Arthur Andersen, Price-Waterhouse Coopers** and others of this select club are quickly gaining acceptance as consulting advisors in their own right. In many overseas markets, the differences among accountancies and consultancies is indistinct to begin with, an advantage the highly networked tax and accounting types are only beginning to fully tap. Arthur Andersen's sister company, Andersen Consulting, began a trend of migration to consulting through technology that has become one of the most important factors in future consulting competitiveness. Under extreme pressure to grow their consulting businesses, the strategic service arms of the former accountancies can sometimes produce sloppy, even desperate work, but for key client relationships ample oversight is usually brought in from the core of the house. For the experienced recruit, these can be high-paying if lonely opportunities, with ample running room and a chance to have defining influence; for the less experienced, they can be dangerous forays into the land of wasted time. For the client already anchored into a working relationship with an accounting firm, the consulting arms can be a relatively low-cost source of advice well worth a first try. But for the first-time user of a given firm's services, there is a real risk of inattentiveness, or of becoming the focus of unwanted attention from the accounting side of the house, attempting a cross-sell of their services.

6

The Technologists of Consulting. Survival of consulting firms in this new century will hinge on higher states of evolution and the creation and domination of new niches. **Andersen Consulting** has taken strong strides in this direction, reaching deep into its pockets to support systems technology, strategic services, and international expansion, especially in Asia, moving far past its origins in Arthur Andersen. It has explored alliances with Baker McKenzie, one of the world's largest legal firms, and, in what may be the major impactor redefining the niches available for survival, with strategy stalwart McKinsey & Co., sketched above. With these or similar alliances in place, Andersen may soon lay rightful claim to being the world's first all-function professional services firm. Determined since its creation a mere decade ago to outdo both McKinsey and Andersen, **Gemini Consulting** also remains a strong contender for establishing a world-class integrated, technology-as-strategy full-services entity. Combining the technical expertise of parents Daimler Benz and Cap Gemini Sogeti in operations and systems, and acquisitions in strategy, processes, and change management, Gemini's greatest challenge may be in creating a high enough degree of cultural integrity, fast enough to keep all its many powers focused on specific clients' needs and opportunities. For recruits, these new powerhouses run much risk of offering compartmentalized experiences. In *Star Trek* parlance, the experience is likely to be akin to being welcomed to the collective on a Borg cube, without the benefit of an insight to the hive mind. But with time and maturity the new evolutions of Andersen, Gemini, and a small handful of others may attempt to offer cross-disciplinary career ladders, specifically designed to cultivate multi-talented leaders. Without them, even clients with the largest appetites may not understand why they should engage the entire integrated complex. For clients, engagements with these firms will entail a substantial loss of sovereignty. Much of the client's own identity will be re-made in the course of interaction with these new behemoths, and the risks of an assignment's failure may run to the client's own collapse. But ready access to state-of-the-art services, across the full gamut of a company's needs and functions, is already emerging as a critical source of competitive advantage for the largest, most successful firms, and the most cost-effective engagements may be with the fully integrated houses. As seen in these pages, however, based on my experiences, few consulting firms will have matured responsibly enough to be entrusted with this power.

CHAPTER 2

THE RECRUITING MACHINE

TOKYO, SPRING 1985

My dozen-year diversion into management consulting began with "Harry Yoon," the head of the Boston Consulting Group in Tokyo during the years I first worked in Japan with the steelmaker and shipbuilder Nippon Kokan. Harry had heard about me from the BCG team working with NKK Corporate Planning, and though he knew that my department hoped to sponsor me for an MBA back in the United States, he discreetly requested I send him my resume.

Soon Harry proposed that I give some thought to spending a few years deepening my business skills and making great money before returning to graduate school. Harry's own resume and demeanor spoke the message I needed to hear: I am more like you than you are, and I know this is the business for you. I knew that Harry had gone to Caltech and taught physics in Taiwan. He had recently overseen construction of his Palo Alto home, which remains a favorite of architectural photographers, and staked a half interest in a now-flourishing San Francisco Chinese restaurant. Fluent in English, a variety of Chinese dialects, and Japanese, Harry is soft-spoken and elegantly slouchy. Relaxed and at home with himself, he is often and correctly described as a gentleman. If this guy could learn to like consulting, I thought to myself, so could I.

Harry would soon leave BCG Tokyo, and with him faded a good deal of the affable, high-caste culture that presided there. But for the moment I saw him as representative of a milieu where I was sure I could thrive: studied and intellectual, with the time, money, and sensitivity to find and enjoy life's grander adventures. Solving business problems would be child's play, and our clients would be privileged to gain from our higher perspective.

Harry explored my pedigree and interests, and made a persuasive case for there being little harm in sidelining my academic ambitions for a few years. He then turned me over to the other two resident partners, both Japanese. "Numata" was a study in arrogance—he would be shortly phased out, and even denied a small office while he took up teaching again. In at the start in the early 1960s, Numata had simply become too expensive for the firm to afford. But here he was at the height of his powers, and Numata chose to exercise my Japanese with a series of mind games and weird grammatical constructions. "Before you answer that, let's assume that I am you answering. How do you think I would answer, and how would that be better than your answer?" Strange, but I played along. Then I was turned over to "Kuroda": nervous, gangly, and a haphazard speaker of English, Kuroda was famous for his arcane insights and deep absentmindedness. I would later see that secretaries were always chasing Kuroda to the airport with his passport or tickets. He presented me an organizational problem he had been working on at NKK, taking furiously detailed notes as I struggled through the issues; by the interview's end I realized I had simply been pumped for information about my own company.

And that was it. I would make my way to London under my Fulbright scholarship, and begin a steady process of integration into BCG. On my way to England I stopped in San Francisco to visit Harry, and he made me a firm offer to start in Tokyo as soon as I finished my master's at the London School of Economics. He suggested that I take some accounting courses, and offered that he would set me up as an unpaid intern in the London office, so that I could learn more about what I was getting into. I could make my final decision when I finished my master's, I was pleased to learn, and hardly knew the ship had left the dock. The starting money was astonishing, three times what my highest paid fraternity brother engineers were making, and I settled into London and got very used to the idea of becoming a management consultant.

LONDON, SPRING 1986

My internship in BCG London involved occupying a beautiful Green Park office while doing my homework, suffering an occasional research project in the library, and attending luxurious training conferences in the English countryside. I also hung out with some friends from NKK, who had been recently assigned to my old company's trading office in London's City financial district. There I was a mascot, treated to green tea and the Japanese newspapers in the morning, and two-hour pub lunches and late-night mah-jongg whenever I could make it. My tutors at the London School of Economics were outstanding, and I really enjoyed my courses and Fulbright research, but the indulgences of business life began to sharply contrast with student and academic anxieties.

In London I occasionally heard rumor of big changes underway in BCG Tokyo. Indeed, one of the many small eruptions of the industry was at work in Tokyo while I was gone. A relative newcomer, an exemplar of those whose destinies surely could not have been consulting, had set it off. Raised in Japan and England, "Yoshi Morikawa" was the son of a Japanese diplomat. On the back of a fine Oxbridge education in history and languages, he had become one of Japan's leading international journalists. Morikawa's aspirations included leadership of Japan's Liberal Democratic Party, and in the land of the economic animal, there was a cool logic in his entering Harvard

Business School (HBS) in middle age, where he quickly set himself atop the class, graduating as a Baker Scholar.

Morikawa's first aim, within a year of graduating from HBS, was taking over the Boston Consulting Group's Tokyo office. While I was in London he entered the firm as partner, and successfully insinuated himself to become next in line for Tokyo's managing partner. In so doing he would become the first Japanese managing partner in an American consulting company in Japan. Chaos apparently ensued. Three bypassed managers promptly quit and took more than a dozen consultants with them. Three competing firms were thus spawned in short order—one of which still survives and at times out-performs BCG's overall Asian operations. Morikawa managed to outlive this debacle, but his official leadership of the office was put on ice. BCG brought in the most Prussian of its German partners, "Dietmar Hoffstetter," to instill discipline and control the damage where possible. But as "der Herr" had no experience in Asia nor with Japanese clients, real control soon settled into the hands of the still ambitious, largely able Morikawa.

Inevitably, one day Harry called me from his new assignment in San Francisco, and explained to me that Morikawa was now in effective control of Tokyo and Tokyo hiring—not himself and not Hoffstetter. Harry emphasized that I should therefore expect to hear from Morikawa-san soon, and that I should, by all means, humor him. In fact, I learned, Morikawa was on his way to see me in London, stopping over from an assignment on the Continent. Harry said he would stick by his offer but recommended that I win Morikawa over on his terms, and not invoke Harry to force myself on the new order. On a slow afternoon in the spring before I graduated, I got a call from Morikawa in the NKK London office, while my hosts were still in a bleary post-pub daze.

In rounded Oxbridge tones, but with very American urgency, Morikawa wasted no time letting me know where I stood with him. "Lewis, I understand you're interested in joining us, and that Harry may have already made you some kind of offer. Of course I need to see you for myself. I'd like to meet you for dinner tomorrow. I want you to pick the restaurant—which one you pick is part of the test. Leave a message at my hotel. I look forward to meeting you."

In a panic I shook my Japanese buddies out of their pub-lunch induced torpor. For months they had all been rooting for my taking up a consulting career. A crisis-management meeting was immediately called in the conference room. I loved these guys—this was just the kind of thing they lived for. We tried to review everything Morikawa might be looking for in a restaurant—sensible economics, good taste, and privacy? Or local culture, fun spiritedness, and a chance to let loose, see me drunk, and know that I knew how to enjoy life? Concluding that we had no way of knowing, I went with the NKK office manager's recommendation: pick the best, most expensive place possible that I would enjoy, and know that I would have a good time whatever the result.

And so it was formal dining at the Inn on the Park. It is the only time I have ever even seen, much less eaten in, a separate room dedicated to a caviar bar. Morikawa was late, and I was worried that if he did not show I would barely be able to pay for my own first round of drinks and appetizers. When Morikawa did arrive and was directed to my table in the bar area, he gave the restaurant a quick look, enigmatically commented "nice place," heaved into the seat, and without apology pressed his attack.

"Lewis I have three concerns. You don't have an MBA. Consultants have MBAs. Numata and Kuroda may have been easy on you, but I know from experience that no American businessman can really fully function in Japanese. And I've studied your file in detail, and the impression I get is that you do not have the slightest idea or target for what you'll be doing in ten or even five years." I looked carefully at Morikawa as he spoke. He was better dressed than any businessman I had ever met, and sleek with a few extra pounds from good living. He wore gold rings and cufflinks that on any other Japanese might mark him as a gangster. Knowing something of his high-life background, and seeing his appearance, I concluded he should be the last person to pronounce on fitting in with Japanese business culture.

I could feel myself redden. Nothing was worth this: people telling me that I have no long-term plans, particularly people who propose to rob me of those plans, really get to me. I looked around the room, gauging what kind of scene I might be about to make. Finally, in Japanese, I fairly exploded. "Since you seem to think I suffer from deficiencies in the language that you're too proud to speak with me, then no doubt speaking to you in it, whatever offense it might cause you, is a way to address the issue. Of course I do not have an MBA! I didn't *want* an MBA. I never applied to business school. I was thrilled to be made a Fulbright scholar and given the chance to study something I feel might actually matter. Long-term issues! My research is all about how to share humanity's greatest resources . . ." I stumbled, sensing the deep end ahead. "The high seas, Antarctica, the pyramids, the moon!" I stopped. This kind of speech sounds even more pompous in Japanese, and already I was dwelling on what life without the Big Money was going to be like.

Morikawa's generous face split into a wide grin. He barked some choice Japanese obscenities, slapped the table, and plunged into his caviar. He suddenly looked much more relaxed, as if he was about to have fun. Was he pleased with me for having spared him the task of weeding me out? "That's really great stuff," he fairly giggled, continuing in English. "Did you practice that or what? Hah, I don't really care ,you know. Your Japanese is terrific. Nobody speaks two languages perfectly at the same time, just keeping up with the telly is murder. That bit about the MBA? Forget it! They put me up to that question back at the office. Believe me, nothing you could learn there is going to be of much use in your work, I know." My work, I echoed to myself, feeling a great wave of gratitude to Morikawa already sweeping in. "We need to have some name-brand MBAs around, like me, just to keep the clients impressed. You'll make those MBAs do all the work in the end. I can tell you're great officer material. I like you! You've got passion. I don't have any idea what I'm going to be doing in five years, so why should you?"

Morikawa could see that I still had not caught up with him. I believe he knew more than I did that this was a turning point of my life, that I could either take one final step away and assert the righteousness of my heartfelt interests, or own up to my own sense of greed and need to belong. He moved along, familiar Americanisms beginning to assert themselves in his speech. "What a fantastic place you picked. I've never eaten in this place. This is unbelievable. Let's get some of those frozen vodkas and see what kind of damage we can do here. I'll make sure they keep a nice table in the dining room waiting for us." I began to munch, my brain on hold. "This is one of the best things about consulting you know, everything first class. You work hard, you travel everywhere, but we always stay in the best places, eat the finest meals, have the greatest exotic experiences. The clients all know it. But if they resent it they keep it to themselves, most especially when you're treating them to something out of their company's pocket that they'd never experience themselves."

A business that let you thrive on the flaunted waste of clients' money? He could not really be entirely serious, I decided, but I noted with a weakening sense of guilt that my interest was piqued. Morikawa saw this, eyed me meaningfully. "I suppose you'll be glad to get a nice place in Tokyo after living in that *dokushinryo* in Kawasaki." Morikawa pronounced "bachelors' dormitory" with the special disgust it deserves. "When you come back to Tokyo with us you should pick any hotel you want, stay for a month or so there, and take a good look around. Get the right place; we'll help you out." I was stunned. A month at the Imperial Hotel would weigh in at a substantial portion of even my *new* salary. I knew exactly where I wanted to live: a swank little neighborhood in teen-idol land in central Harajuku. "Can you tell me what kind of caseload the office has now?" I asked, and so embarked on my great consulting voyage.

It would not be my last experience being recruited into a consulting company, but by the next time it would be for a manager's position at Gemini, and from my own recruiting experiences by then I had mastered the ropes. Over time I would enjoy an exceptionally high hit rate as a consulting recruiter, both in terms of "target conversion" and "picking for retention." My advice for recruits trying to secure offers from the choicest firms, featured in my next *Demonology* tract, should also serve to alert the client to the traits most highly valued and carefully cultivated in the consultants who ostensibly work for them.

CONSULTING DEMONOLOGY, TRACT 2

THE ALCHEMY OF GETTING A (GOOD) OFFER FROM A LEADING CONSULTING COMPANY

1

Never admit to a long-held interest in consulting. Most consultancies, and older strategy firms in particular, are wary of anyone who has set out to be a consultant. With the exception of McKinsey, non-MBAs with other advanced degrees are welcome. Even for McKinsey an MBA with an industry-bound bent, unless you summer interned for them, comes across as persuasively healthier than the born-to-be-a-consultant recruit. Most experienced consultants are rightly suspicious of recruits who declare that their life's passion is consulting: at best it implies that the recruit will be boring to work with, and at worst it implies a dangerously shallow loyalty to the firm. The best catch is a nonintended recruit who will be forever grateful for the admission to the club.

2

Never admit to a future interest other than consulting. While your interest in consulting should appear relatively recent, your potential commitment to it should appear genetically disposed. A recruit's partner potential is included on many firms' interviewing guides, and any doubts about whether you might be around long enough can weigh heavily against you. Do not worry about demonstrating how loyal you will be to the recruiter's firm. Once you are in, securing your loyalty is the consulting company's problem, and one they will know how to control. Potential disloyalty to consulting itself, however, is a red flag. Demonstrating too strong an imagination about alternatives is another warning sign: "If I were not a consultant? Well, I've thought hard about setting up my own business, and I have the family resources to do it, but now might not be the time, and I'd like to try consulting for a few years first" is an almost guaranteed "ding" response. The recruiter knows how grisly the work can get and will not be encouraged by the thought that you might have a Plan B handy whenever the going gets tough. Demonstrating a deep need for consulting involvement, and evidencing an insatiable appetite for problem-solving, travel, and teamwork, is a much safer tack. Great greed and ego helps too. "I want to earn some very serious money and maximize my peak earning years potential, in an industry that's more stable than investment banking. I want to be in a position to influence the course of the top dozen of the Fortune 500," is the sort of response that almost always meets with approval.

3

Get the interview cases right. There *is* a right answer to interview case examples. Almost all interviewers use the same handful of example business problems to quiz hundreds of interviewees, and look at a recruit's response against their personal data base of other recruits' answers. Often the cases are drawn from personal experience, and the surest positive hit is to address the issues of the case just as the interviewer did. Whatever the interviewer may say to the contrary, there will be little interest in exposure of your thinking processes unless there's something wrong with them—and by then he or she is hunting for quotes to use in dinging you. Instead, ask a few meaningful questions that you believe will help you solve the case, and take notes (on your own pad, out of view, and never on a whiteboard unless you've got something conclusively spectacular). Take your time, give what you believe is the most sensible answer, and say as little more about it as possible. If you sense you got it right, just move on, you probably scored well. If you did not, move on quickly to another case (*ask* for one if you are certain you choked), or spend the time left to win your interviewer over in other ways. Sometimes you can bypass the case-testing process entirely by discussing from your own experience how you solved a problem you found interesting. It gives the interviewer a chance to ask questions that will make him or her feel intelligent and you look good, and as a result the whole interview can be less boring and more positively remembered.

4

Personalize every interview. Give each interviewer something unique to remember about you and share with the others who have met you. Over a three-day recruiting exercise each interviewer may meet several dozen candidates. Those that emerge from the blur in later review sessions are the ones people like to trade stories about. Anecdotes about business school professors, gaffs made by another cross-recruiting consulting firm, or outrageous indignities from your prior working experience can all help form the pastiche that for a critical moment becomes your remembered identity.

5

Probe the current caseload. The surest way to find a mid-level champion, and at the same time assuage higher level concerns about your incoming billability, is to find an upcoming or ongoing project you might join directly when you enter. A comment on your evaluation to the effect of "could use her on the AT&T case starting next month" goes much farther than dry analytic scores or appearance ratings. Even if you think you'd rather die than, say, help Philip Morris with its overseas cigarette distribution, this is not the time to take your stand if you really want in. It is unusual for an interviewer to share their current case projects with recruits for fear, among other things, that you will pass these comments on to the next consulting company you interview with. When offered a peek into what the interviewer is currently doing for a living, grab at the chance immediately. In many firms, clients are not billed, or are billed at steeply reduced rates, for the time of new consultants in their first three to six months on the job, justifying a bait-and-switch substitution of an MBA neophyte for an experienced consulting manager. For a consulting case manager this means free labor for the project, and maybe an extra weekend or two at home. The surest way to get your candidacy championed is to help a project manager believe you will immediately improve his or her professional and personal life. Sometimes project managers not in the recruitment rotation will join in just to prospect for their own cases, and it is best to be prepared to grab the chance when you see it. Afterward simply delaying your acceptance for a month or two can usually avert the more abhorrent mismatches with your real interests.

6

Multiply expenses and interviews. Most firms' recruiting budgets are very flexible, and top candidates that are taken aboard will sometimes have their hotel and meal expenses blurred into their first client assignment's budget if they can be put directly on to the start of a large case. There is a general awareness, however, of how many interview rounds; plane, meal, and hotel bills; and interviewer billing time is consumed by each candidate. Consulting firms' public denials to the contrary, there is a high reluctance to lose someone who's really run up the tab. At a minimum, if a borderline candidate has seen almost everyone, has no dings but maybe no champion or immediate case opening either, he or she will be passed on to another office for review, rather than lose the time and money invested, or worse yet risk that a competitor picks up the candidate. The moral is to keep showing up, extend your stays, ask to learn more about the firm, and try to schedule time over nice dinners, anything that broadens your apparent familiarity with the firm and raises the expense stakes.

7

Have fun, be fun. One of the few entirely honest comments that consultants routinely make to their recruits is that they look for someone they would enjoy being stuck on a dull trip with. There are many dull and trying moments in consulting, and most of them are associated with travel. Whether it's a ten-hour rental car ride through Ohio, a Chicago airport shutdown, or a thirty-hour flight to Delhi, you will get opportunities to know your colleagues better than most members of your family. Convince your interviewer that they would *like* to get stuck somewhere just for the chance to get to know you better, and you are probably halfway to a strong recommendation. Preserving a sense of humor is no small accomplishment in consulting, and sharing it with your colleagues goes a long way in initial acceptance and later, the choicest projects. Be aware, too, that with one of the highest divorce rates of any business, consultants' personal relationships are constantly in flux, and there is a strong chance that one or more of your interviewers is scoping you out with other things in mind. Photos often go with the advance resumes, and more than one consultant has signed on to the rotation just to meet a physically intriguing candidate. If you have an attractive photo, the reality is that attaching it to the resume greatly increases the chance of making it into the first-round invitation.

8

Know and support your champion. Every consultancy's evaluation form has a summary assessment to the effect of "strong recommend, weak recommend, weak reject, strong reject." A strong reject is almost impossible to overcome, unless the rejecter is a known jerk and you have two or more strong recommends. Getting a mix of weak recommends and weak rejects is fairly common, however, and can be equally useless to securing an offer. Just one strong recommend in that kind of mix can make all the difference, and it is critical to identify who you think is your strongest supporter, and to get him to take on the role of personally championing your case. This means getting to know him better, calling him at work and at home off the record, getting the details of the progress of your case, and getting your champion's help in setting up favorable further interviews. As unlikely as such actions might seem, it is done all the time: the champion cannot initiate contact, but the recruit can. For someone who has identified you as somebody they want on their case team, you are a competitive commodity. There are only so many open slots each recruiting season, and your champion will compete with his or her colleagues and their preferred picks to see that you get in—if you know whom to ask for the help and chase after it.

9

Know and isolate your detractor. You should also pay attention to who is likely to be your strongest detractor, particularly someone you think may be leaning toward writing you up as a strong reject. Remember this person's name, learn all you can about him and the type of work he does (including, however brazen it may feel, directly from him at the end of the interview), and with judicious care relate what an unpleasant experience you had with him to each of your more positive interviewers. Get the others thinking that this person did something to mess up your interview, setting it up so that your detractor is likely to be on the defensive about his or her evaluation of you in the common review session. Evaluations can be changed, and second rounds with a particular individual can be requested by both sides. Chances are that an interviewer on the defensive will be ultimately happy to join in the supporting chorus.

10

Get the best possible deal. Be prepared that the details of an offer will often be tested out on you before the offer is formally made. The obvious psychology involved is to get you to accept less while you are still of a mind to be wildly grateful to get any kind of offer at all. With the caveat that your champion may be preparing a final pitch based on your relatively low cost to the firm, this is a good time to stand firm. Research the company's salary, bonus, and benefit standards for each level, and set expectations just slightly higher; there is almost always room for some 15 percent slack. State flatly, now, your expectations for a sign-on bonus (up to 30 percent of first-year salary) and/or business school reimbursement (second-year tuition is reasonable). But above all else find out exactly what level you are being placed at, and, if you can afford it, forego extra goodies for a year or two higher level of intake. All entrants may be called consultants or associates, for example, but being tagged in the system as a second-year consultant or third-year associate can make large differences in your early salary and promotion opportunities. Your billing rate may be higher, but if your champion seems eager to use you immediately a higher billing category nonetheless, you may have a good chance to hit higher cash levels that much faster. Finally, for those contemplating assignments overseas, however intellectually or romantically appealing you may find foreign cultures and travel, never let the recruiting firm smell that you might consider an international assignment to be a privilege. Make the company pay for it. Americans particularly should be aware that far broader packages are routine overseas, and that U.S. citizens are often hired for their very ignorance of the standard goodies. A company car, full housing allowance, pricey social club memberships, and tax equalization packages are par for the course in many non-U.S. offices, particularly those in British Commonwealth or former British Commonwealth countries. Without these benefits six-figure salaries are suddenly seen for the real overseas weaklings they are.

CHAPTER 3

CONSULTING SPYCRAFT

TOKYO, SPRING 1987

IN THE MID-1980S TOKYO WAS PREPARING FOR ITS OWN MORE MODEST version of London's big bang—a wave of staged deregulations that would permit deposit, commercial, and investment banks; life insurers and property and casualty firms; and savings and loans and community development banks to overlap their products and services and leverage one another's customer bases and infrastructure. The ever-expansive Morikawa-san was eager to see to it that I cut my teeth on these cases, as a means of basic international intelligence gathering that would ready me for later, more intensive work geared for specific acts of espionage.

My first major client, "Koyo Life," was a traditional life insurance company, with a staid reputation for scale and reliability. Its enormous pool of financial resources backed one of Japan's largest *zaibatsu* business groups, the powerful industrial conglomerates that helped realize Japan's war ambitions, but it had never been free to pursue non-life financial ventures on its own. With deregulation, the firm would be free to invest in virtually any other financial institution, and its ambition was a whopper. "Pinault-san," Morikawa called me over to his suitably distinguished office. It never ceased to bother our ostensible country manager, Dietmar Hoffstetter, that Morikawa managed to arrange his office in subtle ways that left Japanese visitors with little doubt that Morikawa was in charge.

"I think I have an exciting case for you. You are exactly who we need for this." Morikawa invoked his most serious and professional demeanor, leaning forward over his desk, addressing me in high Oxbridge. Unfortunately, I never developed the Japanese business talent for letting it all hang out on a company drunk one day and then acting like nothing happened the next day at work. An unbidden image from but ten hours before—Morikawa charming a young Japanese woman lost in a fur coat, just to show he could, and then depositing her on me—was not easily dislodged.

"But you must keep this very hush-hush." I swore the appropriate oath. No problem, I thought. If I could keep the prior night's antics to myself, I could certainly hold some boring company initiative close to the chest. I had another secret that was more problematic. I had started dating the office receptionist and was fast losing my appetite for these all-night outings. But in the very Japanese culture of the office, unless I declared an intent to marry, my newfound interest would have to stay secret, and somehow I would have to balance Morikawa's continuing expectations for my good-time companionship.

"Do you know Koyo Life?" Oh no, I thought. Morikawa's right-hand man, "Shogo Okada," had had some role on Koyo for the last eighteen months, and no one working on it had yet to escape and find reassignment. No one talked about it much, but it was supposedly some personnel reorganization study. I could not picture anything more boring: rearranging insurance bureaucrats in one of Japan's stodgiest, most parochial companies, famous for a dim-witted lack of imagination and passive subservience to the needs and strategies of their greater *zaibatsu*.

Okada was doing very well by these institutional drudges: he was the first outside consultant the firm had ever hired, and they had bought a full-scale case team and kept them running on a one-year renewable contract—they seemed to have no sense of competitive consulting fees. Some university buddy of Okada's ran a small research department at Koyo and found Okada's assistance and renewed friendship a great excuse to hose away expense accounts on Ginza nightlife. Reputedly neither Morikawa as a senior advisor, nor Okada, as case officer, spent much time on the case itself, making fully chained slaves out of everyone else on the team.

"I don't really know them, no. I hear you've been doing some very high billings with them though," I ventured, hoping to sound respectful but firmly uninterested, if not dangerously ignorant.

"Oh yes. I think there's a lot more to come. This client could really make a great future for a young consultant."

Uh-oorah, uh-oorah, the Nazi air-raid sirens screamed. In a business where strength in general practice was still the key to career advancement and independence, getting locked into one client, however lucrative, could mean certain destruction. At best one might hope for late promotions, begrudgingly given for simply reliably bringing in the dough. Worse might be an eventual dignified exit of retirement to the client's firm in some dead-end, internal advisory role.

Morikawa assumed other causes for my apparent distress, and switched to a kindly spoken Japanese. "You know, it's always better just to chuck it up the night before, Pinault-san." The Japanese have a great onomatopoeia for this, *gero-suru*. Pronounced *geh-rowh*, the *geh* captures the gasped preliminary retch, and the *rowh* extends to sound out the release of fluids; a good rendering will leave you hearing the splatter on the pavement, I swear.

Off guard, I managed but a blank acknowledgment, and Morikawa pushed on, returning to English.

"It will be excellent to have you on this project. As I mentioned, it's a secret, but now that you are with us, you'll be glad. Here is the challenge. They want to buy a bank."

"A bank?" I faltered, "Buy?"

"Yes, not just a bank, a merchant bank, an investment bank. An *American* investment bank."

"I don't understand," I answered honestly, "how does a Japanese life insurer buy an investment bank?" Morikawa let me go on. "What American bank would let them do that? Some boutique house? What do they do with it? Just put money in, in the hopes of future returns? The risk would be huge. Surely they'd be better off putting their money in a thousand other places first. Have they ever done anything like this?"

"Oh, Lewis, I knew you would be interested," Morikawa fairly chortled. "These are good questions. Koyo will like you. You will see they really mean to do this; they have made up their mind. And they are not just talking about a boutique, no. They have done their homework, and they want a Smith Barney, maybe a Goldman Sachs. Not just a profit stake, they want Japanese staff on Wall Street. This is going to be the biggest financial news of the year, maybe the decade.

"You're going to help me out here. Too many people at Koyo have already made up their minds about this, and now they basically just want us to give them a shopping list and recommend some asking prices. They just want a little strategic advice, and then they will turn to other kinds of firms for the in-depth help on the laws, the accounting, the banking systems. I believe we should be able to do much more before we turn this over to anybody else.

"First, I want you to spend as much time with them as you can, at every level of the organization. Do a good number of interviews, find out what each middle manager and account executive really expects out of this kind of deal. Many will not know what is at stake, so I would like you to play the role of representing an American bank interested in a Japanese joint venture. That's why I want you to do the interviewing, you will look the part and help bend the rumors away from the truth. Think of it as a bit of Special Air Services work, in a good cause."

Perhaps Morikawa could see I was a little disappointed in the blatant, if creative, use of my mere Americanness. "And there will be many more important tasks for you on this assignment. Weren't you interviewed by quite a few merchant banks before you joined us? Didn't Goldman Sachs make you an offer? You must have some friends there now."

Once BCG had shown an interest in me, I had made a brief foray into investment bank recruiting, just to be certain, given my abandonment of school and space schemes, that I had optimized my money-to-pain-tolerance ratio.

"Sure," I confessed, "the salary was tempting, but not the narrow skill sets, the physical confinement, and the mind-numbing hours."

"See, these are already the things Koyo needs to know. I want you to go spend some time here and then there, in New York. Find out what it really takes to work and learn the game on Wall Street. I'm envisaging a complete report on this, a kind of road map to what it takes for a Japanese to learn the investment banking business. That's what they want to buy here, not a company, but a knowledge of how to work in this business. Your job is to find out if they can really do it or not. Catalog everything that it takes: know-how, access, stamina, the whole lot. Find some expat Japanese who work on Wall Street and find out how they cope. I'll get you some names. Talk to their American colleagues about them behind their backs. Are they respected? Do they really know what's going on?"

Though I found it hard to imagine such findings could be a real consulting product, I was hooked on the idea of schmoozing around Tokyo and Manhattan to absorb the investment banking lifestyle, without actually having to do any of the work. To get there, though, I had to start with the drones at Koyo, and the first of not a few lies in the name of greater consulting goods.

"You mean, an American bank would want to partner with someone like us, here in Japan?" It was not hard for me to feign a shared incredulity. Among my first interviewees was "Mr. Inoue," whose work seemed to involve no motion from a desk or human interaction whatsoever. His pear-shaped, ultra-pale body had long since conformed to a teardrop-perfect balance on his delicate chair, the bulges smoothed by a stiff vest, eyes well hidden behind thick lids and thicker glasses. He was in charge of distribution network analysis, and he was working on a design for Koyo insurance products that could be sold at bank teller windows, under the new umbrella of deregulation.

"Why?"

"Um, well, yes. This is just exploratory, but with the rules relaxing a bit we thought that this might be the right time to line up strategic partners, offer some new products, tap into some new capital and, um, resources." I let my Japanese flutter a bit—sometimes it helps to have stupidity masked by assumption of things lost in mismatched languages.

"I see." Inoue clearly did not. "But, of course, we have nothing to offer but problems. Our own distribution is all wrong, we can hardly access the market ourselves. I can't imagine our capital would ever lend advantage to a foreign partner—we'd ask too high a price in sharing our own exposure with our property and casualty partners, no one would really want all that earthquake risk. They wouldn't even know who they're partnering with! It's a mystery to me who we own and who owns us. We have no real manpower. Most of our employees are stringer sales ladies wandering around all the offices here downtown. We do all we can just to keep our new recruits entertained; training's basically a joke. Me, I'm the new product design team. The other members of the team are hiding, waiting for me to come up with something. So, how do you like working in consulting, anyway?"

That, of course, was code for "Okay, bonehead, you obviously don't know what you're doing, but we can talk about something else if you like; is it true consultants eat live sushi on the bellies of naked hostesses twice a week?" Clearly, it was time to beg. I suspected Okada was wandering about somewhere nearby, and he did not need to hear me regaling Inoue with lurid adventures, however much Morikawa might appreciate the fact that he starred in them. "You know, it's really my client's job to explain their interest; I'm doing them a disservice in even trying," I said, drawing little comfort from this near-truth. "What they sent me here for was to learn more about what a company like Koyo might gain from an American banking partnership. I don't want you to feel you're wasting your time, but if you help me to get to the issues as you see them from your side, I'm sure my client's management will be able to do a more focused job in explaining to Koyo's board how they would see the partnership work."

What garbage, I reeled inside: for starters, Koyo *is* the client. I began to picture Morikawa and Okada in unpleasant situations. A last hope: "You know, maybe you could join the guys and I some evening and we could talk about consulting, too."

Whether for reasons of mercy, boredom, or morbid curiosity, Inoue then and there became my key internal informant. He decided that I was, first, in need of an insurance education, and began by explaining to me the challenges of designing a properly linked, appealing insurance product that could be readily explained and sold at a bank teller's window. I got my first primer on actuarial science, and discovered that there was little that was new in life insurance, except for non–life insurance products. This is where Inoue picked up on the importance of understanding banking. "With deregulation, there are innumerable things we can do, expanding our existing portfolios in things like real estate, and achieving a real sophistication in new financial instruments, things that might let consumers and institutions buy an interlinked package of financial products and options, from just a few or even just one source."

"One-stop shopping."

"Yes," Inoue sighed with mysterious glumness, "exactly."

"Well, that sounds pretty exciting," I tried, thankful for the non-committal tone the Japanese lent the phrasing.

"Exciting if you're Mitsubishi Bank, or Nomura Securities. Exciting if you already have a sound, working knowledge of banking, with dozens of overseas offices and thousands of personnel who work the international markets every day. The problem with deregulation, for us, is what nobody wants to say: the banks will learn our relatively simple business practically overnight, long before we have a handle on theirs. We're going to be stuck with more risk than we should really handle. Our pension funds are supposedly the bedrock of the country, but we're going to be forced to carry some of the worst loans around just to stay alive. Deregulation's exciting if you like guttings, beheadings, and self-immolation. Your American banks should be talking to Japanese banks about how to stroll into the soon to be totally unprotected insurance market, not about the death wishes of a dinosaur insurer like us."

I tried to stay upbeat. "So the Japanese banks will be your new competitors. Well, what about learning banking from someone more sophisticated than them? Say an American Wall Street outfit?"

"Why should they teach us?"

"Buy them." I had taken the plunge. First I had lied to one of my client's employees to cover up who was after what. Now, I was betraying the client's trust about keeping what was going on under wraps, by raising the strategy as a fictitiously spontaneous idea. To close the loop, now I had to make it seem like Inoue's idea, so I would have something to report.

"Eh? Buy them?" A range of emotions swept across Inoue's face, a bit of light from the eyes escaping the heavy confines of Coke-bottle lenses. Mockery, hope, fear, and paranoia all seemed to collide. "Well, yes, of course, that might be possible, um, theoretically." Suddenly, suspicion: "Are you going to try to sell us your bank?"

"No, really, I can honestly tell you I have no bank to sell. I'm really a bit off the topic. But I think you have a good idea here. This could be a very revealing exercise, valuable to you internally and to our client, and to anything they might do together. Let's just go with what you've got: if Koyo *were* to buy an overseas bank, how would you do it, and why would you do it? What would you get out of it?"

And so we were off and running. Inoue detailed for me his wish list for an overseas bank. The emphasis was clearly on learning, as Morikawa-san had predicted, and Inoue had some fairly crisp ideas about how to do it, buying a controlling interest in a Wall Street firm with a strong asset management group, and infiltrating that group with a team of both experienced Koyo staff (such as they were) and new recruits specifically hired for the task. Clearly I had Inoue's interest if not his full understanding. By going around the company to Inoue's peers, and pitching this "thought experiment" as *his* idea backed by *my* (nonexistent) expertise, I also gained his trust. Soon we had a fairly fully developed model of what might be gained; I began to believe it might be Koyo's real salvation, and was anxious to report back to Morikawa-san and prepare a presentation.

My mentor, however, had other ideas. We were at a *robotakaya* in Roppongi, a country-style restaurant in the midst of Tokyo's most expensive foreign ghetto. The entire restaurant consisted of a large wooden bar surrounding several elevated open cookpits, at which sat, *zazen*-meditation style, several cookpit stokers. The stokers held paddlelike devices, affixed to ridiculously long bamboo poles. Upon shouted orders from the servers prowling the customer side of the bar, the stokers would take bits from the mounds of raw food surrounding them, shove them into the pits, and then, in an impressive display of muscle, precisely extend the results all the way to the ordering customer's place at the bar, on the precariously balanced paddles. There was much shouting going on all the time, lubricated by generous pourings of the house drink, cold sake in wooden serving boxes, constantly served to overflowing. "This is terrific material, very detailed," Morikawa shouted at me in English, "it seems you hooked them up to an intravenous caffeine vita-drink. This is very fast work for Koyo. I assume these are essentially your ideas."

I beamed back a gratified acknowledgment.

"You didn't tell them about the acquisition plan, did you," Morikawa asked. My heart fluttered. Before I could answer he immediately and angrily shouted for a refill of sake, and I very nearly jumped out of my skin.

In prepared denial I explained my thought-experiment gambit as carefully as I could, in the circumstances.

"Well," Morikawa went on, this is either very good or very bad."

I had been so wrapped up in schmoozing with the Koyo team that I had not kept up with Morikawa's own efforts on the case. I immediately regretted having left aside a cardinal rule of independent forays on big-budget assignments: the need for constant case team communication. I knew Morikawa had had some idea of what I was doing, but I had not thought to learn what he was doing, trusting he would descend from the heights at the right moment to tell me.

"You have got them voicing the right logic, and you have definitely speeded up the consensus-building process. Our case for emphasizing and selecting an acquisition based on learning benefits is strong. But Pinault-san, the idea is not to have middle management take over our ideas and go home. We have a living to make here. There are a lot of people on the board who would be very happy to say, 'Very, nice, thank you gents, we can handle it from here.' A lot of them are wondering why we are the ones doing this anyway, why not use their own accounting firm or banking consultants? Just nominate the right investment bank, give us a name, and you can go home, that's what they are thinking. But that's not what we want to do, is it?"

Just then a paddleload of food hovered in my face. Startled, I swatted at it, sending the edge of the platter cracking into the bar, and nearly tumbling the hapless stoker at the other end of the paddle into the cookpit. Bits of shrimp and onions skittered across Morikawa's sake ensemble and down the length of the bar.

"No, that's not what we want to do," I managed, after all the horrible apologies. The servers and cookpit men made as if it were all their fault, and free food and drink made their way to us. Morikawa seemed unfazed. Distracted and not a little bit frightened, I tried to struggle with the logic of what Morikawa was saying. Why not, after all, admit our job was done, screen for the right bank, and move on? The longer we stayed on the task, the greater the risk that something would leak or that our internal credibility would collapse, in all likelihood, if not because of my ignorance of the industry, because of

some future mismanagement by me of all the layered lies. I was looking forward to getting on to the Manhattan visits, getting down to a
nice shortlist of acquisition targets, and getting this case on the
résumé. My fear of being sucked up into the wake of the unstoppable
Morikawa-Okada juggernaut resurfaced: somehow Morikawa would
make this engagement go on and on, and I would never work on
another case.

We finally left to an embarrassing chorus of shouted thank-yous
and apologies. As we walked to the subway Morikawa outlined his
new plan.

"Here's the deal. They want us to wrap it up now and pick them
a bank. So what should we do?"

"Um, say we need more time?"

"Well, now you're going in the right direction. But that kind of
thing is not good for our reputation. If we want more time for the
case to run, and we are at risk of terminating because of the accelerating effects of our own—your—good work, what do we do? We
don't stall; we shouldn't risk the impression of bilking them. Now is
simply the time to tell them that they are all wet."

"All wet," I echoed in uncertain fascination. I began to feel very
out of my depth, and wondered if this was some kind of a subtle joke,
or another strange test. Maybe, I thought, I would simply never get
all the nuances of British English crossbred into the Japanese language.

"Wrong, exactly. Just when they appreciate how fast and effi-
ciently we work the smaller tasks, it's time to let drop that they need
a much bigger task. The best big assignments hinge on things they
have never invested time and energy in, the ones that leave them
completely unprepared. So now we tell them an investment bank is
simply a bad idea. When they ask us to nominate a bank, we refuse."

"Look, Morikawa-san, I'm sorry if I moved things along too fast
or made this too easy for them. And I'm sorry for that mess back
there. But I didn't mean to trash the case or to force you to raise the
stakes. Won't they just blow us off if we tell them they're wrong? And,

I mean, if they agree with us, we won't really have anything to do."

I realized I was missing my trip to New York already, and was angry at myself for having somehow screwed up my chances of going. But as I said this my wistfulness was quickly overcome by dread. No doubt there still would be some minor ongoing work, down in the ditches with the likes of Inoue doing detailed product design, a no-doubt fitting punishment for a meddling young consultant.

"No, look, I've been thinking about this. Maybe this investment bank buyout really *is not* a good idea. Gaining access to the things they want to learn on Wall Street is, in itself, a great idea, and your interviews help confirm that. But I am starting to think that the Koyo board is too caught up in the prestige of owning an American bank. When you think about it, it's an awfully expensive way to gain experience. And maybe there are some traps we don't know about: what if they get the bank and all the key staff disappears, or the Koyo staff gets walled off by other firms or even internally? What if there's some huge backlash from the American government or the Fed or the SEC? What if we wind up in some bidding war with another Japanese firm? No, you're right, you have forced my hand a little, but I'm thinking it's a good thing. Now we have the need and the excuse to tell them they're wrong. We're going to have to talk with Okada, and we'll set this straight. Besides, we're BCG," Morikawa laughed, "Clients like to hire us to be smarter than they are, so let's tell them they're wrong."

"So Okada's just going to say it's a bad idea in our next presentation? Um, is this after I present the interview results?"

"Oh, you'll present the interview results. And don't cancel New York, now you really need to move on it. No, for now, we're going to share the results but seed some of these doubts. Then in your trip to the States to sound out your buddies, I want you to really find out where they might get hurt, find every pitfall. Meanwhile, I'm going to work on some answers. I'll be catching up with you in New York. This is go-for-broke. We need to come back for the final presentation, and you'll start. You'll begin with the long list of banks you'll have interviewed, whetting their appetite; the board will be anxious to hear whom we've nominated. But remember, we can't really handle that direction anyway. We don't have the manpower, the tools, the expertise. Hell, at heart, I'm still a journalist, and you want to be some kind of Jacques Cousteau in space or something.

"So you'll give them all the bad news, all the things that can go wrong. They'll hate you—it's going to be a great experience for you," Morikawa chortled appreciatively. "They will look to Okada and me to make things better. But then I'll make clear that you've greatly influenced my feelings. Okada will present some of your research as his own based on further, concerned investigations. Finally, I'll tell them they should not do it."

Death wish, I began to think to myself. I got the sense that Morikawa was relishing this a bit too much. I also started to wish that some other consultants were hearing this for the record: my supporting role in what sounded to be a staged disaster might otherwise be my last.

"They might kill us right there," a delighted Morikawa seemed to speak my thoughts aloud, "but I don't think they will. I'll let the panic sink in for a beat, wait to be sure that at least some of them share our concerns in full. Then, of course, we'll have the answer, some alternative we'll come up with, and one that if we're doing our job right will require a big enough case team, but one with a focus we can handle, with many, many months of billing."

I was filled with admiration for Morikawa's cunning and chutzpah. He was not quite done with me yet, though. "You know, if they do kill us, it just cuts us off where you were going to leave us done anyway. And if they go for it, you can thank yourself for pushing me to it. Either way, I'll remember you for it."

I kept this gangsterland blessing in mind as I made the rounds in Manhattan. No longer a big budget, burn-the-high-octane-test-driving-the-Ferrari exercise, this was now a big budget, we'll-never-get-our-expenses-reimbursed-if-we-fail exercise in fear. Of course, it was hard not to have fun. I enjoyed taking out my former recruiters, fraternity brothers, and fellow Japanophiles at Goldman Sachs and other bastions of the Street, at all the institutions designed to impress, from private club lunches to imported-beach-sand-on-the-floor, tropical-theme dance clubs.

I also began to take to the work. Now that our intentions ran the other way, I could be looser with references to Japanese client interest in acquisition, and began to collect a wealth of detail. I learned that the Japanese already working on Wall Street as visitors for training purposes had consistently less than useful experiences. Typically, a visiting intern from Japan would wholly lack the language skills, aggression, and speed of technical precision required to cope with trading operations, and be unable to manifest the confidence, connections, and wholesome manners to be entrusted with anything meaningful in corporate finance. Interviews with these unfortunate visitors and their putative host teammates, who ostracized them, confirmed that very little real learning was taking place.

My fraternity brother at Goldman was a case in point. "Bill Cowan" graduated from MIT a year ahead of me. I knew him to be naturally bluff and foul-mouthed and generally free of any trace of tact. An aerospace major who spent his summers at the Chicago Board of Trade and discovered that commodities trading had more appeal for him than the human destiny in space, Bill was doing exceptionally well at Goldman and was featured in that year's annual report, a gesture the likes of which I knew I would probably never see in a consulting career.

"Oh, the Japs are here all the time. I don't know why they waste their time. Mostly, we just avoid them. They seem to think they're going to learn something just standing around. They certainly don't make any money. It doesn't surprise me they're sending you around looking to drop some cash in a bank here; rumor's out there's some major Japanese funds looking for a home on the Street. But they shouldn't drop here—the Goldman partners are a tight group, you earn your way in. There really is a culture here, no bullshit. It's hard to see anybody spending their way in, much less your guys, who seem to specialize in being spooky outsiders."

The Japanese I interviewed were learning more than Bill gave them credit for, but they readily admitted to fears and frustrations in trying to gain firsthand experience at their host investment banks. Raised in a corporate culture where rewards are more for not failing than for outstanding performance, most simply looked forward to getting home without messing something up.

The most telling interviews, however, were with the Federal Reserve Bank and the Securities and Exchange Commission. I was surprised at their forthrightness. The Fed made plain that investment banking was simply not another American industry to be handed over to the competition from Japan, and that they viewed themselves as guardians of Wall Street's institutional brain trust. They were aware, they said, of Japanese interest in buying up a bank (I would immediately fear that Morikawa would figure I had spilled the beans here, too), and would take measures to protect U.S. interests. I was made to feel vaguely treasonous, as the regulators assured me that strict limits would be put on staff from Japan even in a Japanese-owned entity.

The report-back went very much as Morikawa had scripted. I laid in with quotes, figures, and schematics emphasizing the learning isolation of Japanese transfers and visitors to U.S. investment banks. I underscored the still widening gap in the speed, quantity, and sophistication of products and techniques between Tokyo and Wall Street. I conveyed the dark interest of the Fed and the SEC. Morikawa and Okada dealt their death blow, and it was met with respectful silence.

Then came the needed surprise. We had found a forty-man asset management company on Wall Street that had the specific knowledge and sophistication Koyo was seeking, but in much more digestible form. Morikawa and Okada had already had preliminary discussions with them, and they were open to a golden-handcuff arrangement where they would agree to stay and actively educate their new owners, for the right price. Their reputation and track record seemed sound, and the scale and type of business was not on the regulators' radar screen. Of course, there would be much work we would need to do to design the takeover and transition.

An elegant epilogue to the Koyo story unfolded just months after this presentation. It was announced to much fanfare that Koyo's archrival, Sumitomo Life, through its sister bank, had acquired a half-billion dollar stake in Goldman Sachs. Reviews in the *Wall Street Journal* and elsewhere soon emphasized the hollow victory. The Fed had stepped in and limited Japanese nationals to no more than ten persons working in New York at a time; education benefits were a strategic driver for the investment, Sumitomo executives admitted, and the regulators' stance was apparently unexpected. The press releases carefully pointed out that Goldman would conduct business as usual, with no joint products or efforts with their new investors. Rumors that there must be some secret codicil buried in the agreement that would create a future executive role for Sumitomo at Goldman proved to be false.

It soon became clear that Sumitomo had recognized the same needs and potential as Koyo and had unaccountably spent a fortune on the education of ten bankers a year. We were delighted to learn that BCG nemesis McKinsey had advised the Sumitomo deal and was taking some heat for locking Sumitomo in, without anchoring the key objectives first. Meanwhile, Koyo gained access to a much more intensive and inclusive training ground, at a fraction of the cost, and proceeded apace to bring new, jointly designed products to the Japanese and American markets.

The lesson for consulting firms would not be lost on the students of the field. According to what Koyo execs later learned from Sumitomo, McKinsey's tight integration with its client and poorly founded, broad assurances of relevant capabilities had blinded Sumitomo to McKinsey's lack of direct expertise in handling the complex of organizational and regulatory factors complicating the case. Even a mediocre specialist with Wall Street smarts might have averted the costly mistake. That BCG had blundered into a more appropriate solution for its own client did not make the press, but this was no disappointment to me; I merely wondered when we would all finally get caught out.

TOKYO AND NEW YORK, FALL 1987

Before I had too much time to think about it, Morikawa and Okada-san quickly expanded on my contacts with the BCG New York office to land me another transnational case and, more important, a prime opportunity to exercise some real consulting spycraft. Soon I would conclude that one of the greatest value-for-money returns in hiring consultants is in using them as industrial spies. "Competitive benchmarking" is the preferred term of art—assessing the level of one's competitive standing by sneaking a direct look into rivals' plans and performance. Depending on the consultant's disposition, the assignments entailed consulting at its best, the most fun, and the most dangerous, by far.

Ironically, it is at the more effete and intellectual strategy boutiques that competitive-intelligence gathering can be at its most refined and aggressively practiced. To seed real data into the more esoteric insights and lend scientific weight to such concept tools as experience and supply curves, price-value lines, and time-based advantage analyses, hard quantitative data must be secured or invented. The most prestigious consulting firms strive for both originality of analysis and authenticity of competitor data. Like the elite Skull and Bones club at Yale, which has made steady contributions to the ranks of CIA leadership, the strategy boutiques have produced some of the more ruthless and effective approaches to industrial espionage.

Many companies try to avoid consulting engagements of this kind, sensing that disastrous results might follow an express engagement designed to plumb their competitors' closest-held secrets. In fact, competitive benchmarking is one of the few areas of the consultant's craft where a client organization has literally written the book. A Xerox executive's text on the topic, Robert C. Camp's *Benchmarking: The Search for Industry Best Practices That Lead to Superior Performance*, is the industry standard, laying out a good systematic approach for gathering intelligence about competitors' current and future practices, and ways to continually adjust around them. But what can a client do when a competitor's product or market advantage is so great and well protected that it threatens to put them out of business or keep them out of a new one forever? Creative interpolation of what in the end amounts to publicly available information just will not do.

The happy client Morikawa and Okada turned me on to was a long-term Japanese engagement, Nitto Denko. Denko is a maker of tape and adhesive products, styling themselves as Japan's 3M. One of their major customers is Japan's largest disposable diaper maker, UniCharm. Our client Denko made the refastenable tapes that secure UniCharm's diapers, and also helped design diaper fabric coatings that would be optimally compatible with the tapes.

Any American parent knows the critical nature of this technology. After untaping and inspecting a diaper for damage and deciding things can wait, one hopes that the refastened tape will still stick and keep the diaper bolted tightly on even the most maneuverable baby. If it does not, the nightmare result is one end flapping open with the goods trawling wherever the baby can locomote. Make the tapes *too* sticky, though, and they tear the lightweight diaper fabric every time it is inspected, defeating the refastenable idea's whole purpose and tripling diaper changes and expenses.

An entire engineering science has developed to cope with this dilemma. Tape and diaper makers work closely together to ensure the finely tuned compatibility of the interface between diaper coating and adhesive surface. Every market-driven change in fabric and coating design creates a crisis in tape design, and potentially threatens one of a tape maker's mainstay businesses. The stakes are high: each year in the United States and Japan *billions* of dollars are spent on disposable diapers, with the worldwide potential still barely tapped.

The technologies involved are consequently fantastic. Procter &

Gamble and Kimberly Clark have developed diaper-making machines that are marvels of scale and ingenuity. Four stories tall, the size of a small house, each machine is a complex, finely tuned apparatus that can turn raw pulp and chemical components into diapers at a rate approaching two diapers a second. In hangarlike structures the size of airfields, dozens of machines in each major facility furiously clang about in a faint haze of trimmed paper and chemical powders. Entire research facilities are dedicated to the chemical absorbents and fabric layers of the diaper. Too absorbent and babies' skin dries out, becoming subject to rash and infection; not absorbent enough and the diapers just do not do their job.

P&G and Kimberly Clark are the giants of the industry, controlling 90 percent of most markets between them, with P&G leveraging its tremendous marketing and distribution power, and Kimberly enjoying durable cost advantages in internal paper supply. Uni-Charm dared to think it might challenge these giants on their home turf, and asked our client Denko to join them in a U.S.-based joint venture, based on their belief that American mothers would come to love the softer feeling, prettily patterned Japanese diaper.

Tape maker Denko figured that with our help they could hedge their bets and win whether UniCharm entered the U.S. market or not. By presenting them a detailed analysis of UniCharm's chances, we could help sharpen the issues for Denko's decision to join them. Even if they should decide against joining while UniCharm plunged ahead, Denko's gift of a multimillion dollar diaper study would go a long way to keep Denko as UniCharm's preferred supplier of refastenable tapes in Japan. Secretly, Denko also saw this as an opportunity to test the waters for supplying the U.S. giants from a new American facility of their own, and to see if their tapes could advantageously complement the next generation of U.S. diaper coatings and fabrics.

Our mission was accordingly broad and ambitious, with our hit list targeting:

- Details of the U.S. diaper manufacturing process, particularly its high-speed mass production techniques;

- Coating and fabric specifications for the next generation of disposable diapers, and their likely demands on refastenable tapes;

- Technology substitution threats (tapeless disposables);

- Supplier criteria and lessons learned;

- Distribution dynamics and marketing controls;

- Potential strategic entry points.

I was the lead consultant from Japan for this mission. The project would be based out of the New York office, where as the bearer of a mega-funded project I was accorded every courtesy: the chairman's Wang Building office, available for the summer while he vacationed, became mine; I got the office's best research associates as my full-time foot soldiers; and a promotion and/or transfer assignment to New York were plainly held out as the prizes for successful, trouble-free completion. As it was unclear to many in the office how the job would actually be done, I was welcome to own the project: the wheels were greased.

I suppose I had long been attracted to spying for a cause. My diverse appetites for ocean/space engineering, foreign languages, and law and policy had led me to interviews at MIT with the CIA and the Navy, and to flirt with an invitation to poke about in Japanese submarines to listen in on Soviet underwater activities in the Sea of Japan. In going to Japan on my own instead, I preserved my independence but found I still had a penchant for detective work, and through my early consulting years in Japan, under my new-found mentor's guidance, I developed a certain fluency in consulting's competitive-intelligence tools and techniques.

So while fully absent of the meaning such work might be ascribed in, say, science or politics, I knew where I wanted to start in the exercise of my diaper spycraft. After intensive review of everything ever published about diapers, we began first by chipping away at the real prizes, the diaper kings Proctor & Gamble and Kimberly Clark, and, for coatings, 3M, expecting that these efforts would only bear fruit toward the end of the case. The most persuasive first page of any presentation, most often, is a simple slide listing all the in-person interviews conducted, and I knew that getting these three companies on that page would make the case. A client's fascination about what their key competitors have to say about a strategic busi-ness, together with comments and context provided by target cus-tomers, suppliers, and distributors, can unlock huge, sustained fees. Successful, hours-long presentations can sometimes be completed without ever moving past a page-one interview list.

These companies had no interest, however, in being on my page one. P&G was very savvy about consultants and would not consider speaking to one without an industry referral they trusted. Kimberly Clark just said no. 3M laughed, and said we could phone them all we liked but it was their strict policy not to speak with consultants. But, with a large client budget at our disposal, we cracked them all.

The key to P&G was an informant we affectionately called "the Frog Man." Digging around at Fasson, a key U.S. supplier of refas-tenable tapes, we learned that the real expert in the field was now semiretired, but might be available for a fee. And so the rules of con-sulting spycraft were applied: "It happens we were just planning to be in that part of South Carolina, talking with some, um, paper sup-pliers. We certainly wouldn't want to waste your time; we'll share our full hourly fee, which is sure more than I make. We don't really know much about this industry; our client is thinking about going in to diapers. We don't really want to talk about tapes—we understand you'd be uncomfortable talking to us about that—but these diaper guys are a closed group and we're looking for ideas about how to approach them . . . perhaps we could meet for a drink . . . the Frog and Prince, tomorrow, for, uh, lunch? Sure, why not?"

Lacking any chance of a direct flight, I wound up overnight in Atlanta with "Josh," a New York research analyst newly deputized to my project. Despite our mad predawn race for the Carolina border, we were late for lunch. The obscurely located Frog and Prince appeared to be a dive of last resort, possibly abandoned—the cars strewn about might be alive or dead. Inside, downstairs, we broke the strange dimness fed by smoke and dirty daylight from the street-level windows. Josh, feisty of mind and motion, suddenly seemed conspicuously pale, thin, redheaded, and Jewish. For the first time I saw him subdued, and I deduced it was not the time to continue my conversation about Japanese space planes. Despite the surprisingly large crowd we were clearly on stage, and our jokes on the ride over about guns and the South seemed suddenly drained of any humor.

Unlike in the movies, the bartender could not direct us to our prey. I had my suspicions, though, about a large, apparently drunk man at the bar pawing at his female companion with one hand, clutching his drink with the other, all the while precariously negotiating his mass on the barstool. He was the only one, besides us, in a suit. This was the Frogman. Once he had us all over to a table and confirmed his payment, he was pleased to spend the rest of the day with us. He gave Josh and me a full detailing of Fasson's moves in refastenable tapes, and a list of names and issues to cover with P&G in Cincinnati. The Frogman sketched out what he knew about upcoming changes in P&G's supplier strategy, and suggested that we approach them as representing a company with an explicit interest in displacing Fasson. Of course we could use his name; he'd be mad at us if we did not . . . We were in.

Meanwhile pestering at Kimberly Clark and 3M had begun to produce the first signs of cracking. In our latest Kimberly rejection, mention was made of "a guy who quit who's now somewhere out on the West coast doing private label for Weyerhaeuser." Weyerhaeuser Paper, we soon learned, had developed a niche market in Washington and Oregon for generic disposable diapers. Using an elaborately developed partnership approach, which we knew in reality would be of only the remotest interest to Denko and UniCharm, we met with Weyerhaeuser division management with one purpose in mind: find out who the ex-Kimberly guy was, and get Weyerhaeuser to encourage him to be fully open with us.

Getting there, as they say, is half the fun. Josh got his clothes wrecked messing about with a gorgeous stewardess on the overnight nonstop to Seattle. I proposed we should stay at the posh Four Seasons, where they would know how to handle such things, and indeed they found him a whole wardrobe at seven in the morning. To be sure we could rendezvous with the ex-Kimberly target anywhere he might emerge and be ready to bolt back to Cincinnati or wherever need be on short notice, we rented a nicely able Porsche, with which we would later complete a high-velocity tour of the logged waste-lands. By now Josh was in love with this weird new profession, his university interests in acting and literature deeply and possibly for-ever submerged.

The Weyerhaeuser interviews were ponderous but productive, heavy on partnership potential and what we might like to sell to them by way of services in future. And they worked: a quick speaker-phone conference and we were directly on our way: "We wouldn't want to waste these consultants' time—Gary you should see them before they have to head back East."

"Gary" was the spy-consultant's wet dream. He had built two monster diaper machines, as close as he could get to the Kimberly Clark models, from memory and they were ours for a day to prod and poke, draw and photograph. Gary gave us a guided tour of each fea-ture that differed from Kimberly's machines, including both the lov-ing improvements he had made and detailed descriptions of Kimberly machine advantages he felt he could live without. He was careful to point out planned improvements on the Kimberly machines that might already be in the works. From start up to shut down, in every mode and at every speed, with different feed compo-nents and end products, we saw and recorded it all. Later we would see Kimberley rival P&G's machine line from behind glass, as mere industrial tourists, and fully realized what a gem we had found in Gary. We had better than anything we could have conceivably gotten from Kimberly Clark directly: detailed, annotated concept drawings and descriptions of Kimberly's disposable diaper line, all without ever having been there.

Now we were on a roll. Proctor & Gamble responded favorably to the Frogman's referral, and we set up interviews with the P&G supplier management division in Cincinnati. We were given a detailed description of their criteria for tape supply, and an excellent introduction to P&G's new supplier consolidation and management strategies, which next time we were in the office went straight into the general hopper for whenever anyone might need material for a supply management proposal. The supply guys felt predictably free to discuss marketing issues. In this craft we would often see that people are careful to keep their own secrets (incentives for particular supply contracts), but will freely discuss what other "rival" divisions at their own company try not to share with them. And so we got a good handle on what their marketing intelligence had to say about rival Kimberly's next generation of Huggies, and a friendly, later invaluable warning about their own commitments to developing a tapeless, pull-on disposable diaper.

Two more breakthroughs followed. Correctly assuming that our client was a Japanese tape and coating maker, P&G let on that they were quite keen to find a supply source for the cute, patterned tapes used on Japanese diapers (Disney cartoons and such), and a compatible bonding material for the new polyethylene diaper coating they anticipated sourcing from 3M. They bluntly suggested that if our client could make a coating like 3M was about to produce, and match it with Japanese-style tapes, we had a major core supply opportunity with the world's largest diaper maker, an opportunity worth hundreds of millions of dollars a year. Just the tapes alone could be a major opportunity.

At once we had the independent supply opportunity Denko desired, and a lead finally with 3M that might translate to new business for Denko, UniCharm, or both. Soon I was on the phone again with 3M to enjoy a graduation from friendly pest to competitive concern. I remarked that we had been speaking with P&G about 3M's new polyethylene coating, and that as representatives for tape makers interested in supplying P&G, we felt we needed to learn more: what was the new material to be made of; what thickness, color, texture, and breathing properties did it have; could we get a sample? Suddenly it appeared that 3M's business with P&G diapers might be at stake. After a quick verification with P&G, once on the line again our 3M informant, "Dr. Gray," clearly felt pressured to respond. Conveniently he seemed to have forgotten that we had introduced our client as a tape *and* coating maker ("but their main line is tapes and they're hardly in the coatings business the way you are, besides they're overseas . . .") and we were careful not to nudge him to think about what a good coatings laboratory might do with a sample.

In a brilliant if bizarre leap of insight and rationalization, our Dr. Gray saw his way out, perhaps hoping we would never follow through. "As I've told you many times, we don't even allow consultants to visit our facilities. But I'll tell you this, since it's public information and you probably know about it already. There's an international textile exposition in Geneva, Switzerland, next month. It's held every three years, and mainly it's all diapers: diaper machines, fabrics, coatings, absorbents, those things. We're going to have a booth there, and I'll be the one manning it most days. I certainly can't stop you from visiting the convention, and it's my job to talk to people who come to our booth. That's all I can say."

Soon we were back in New York making plans for Geneva. By now it was clear that we had the sexiest case going. The chairman's office was packed with different brands of diapers, diaper machine photos and drawings decorated the walls, and unreturned security passes and thank you notes from our client's competitors filled the bulletin board. The door was covered by a poster for the upcoming Textile Expo in Switzerland, stuck with a Post-It from Josh, "from the Frogman to Lake Geneva." On the whiteboard, the intellectual centerpiece (at least one is a must for any strategy boutique's presentation) of our efforts developed, a "value line" curve that showed how higher prices derive from increasing increments of quality, and how certain brands enjoy premium prices across the quality spectrum. Simple enough observations, but among the many grueling presentation-producing tasks ahead of us before Geneva was checking prices at hundreds of stores and among dozens of products to build the needed data base. Deciding what perceptions of improved quality, translated to how much willingness to pay more sucked up a surprising amount of our time and effort. Looking over the midnight Manhattan skyline while pondering whether improved chemical absorbents mattered more than a diaper's precision fit, I wondered once again how the world and I had gotten to such a strange place.

From Geneva it would be straight on to Tokyo, so we had to take stock of what we had, finalize and pack up the presentation materials, and take it all with us. We would recommend that Denko not join UniCharm in its initial U.S. venture: the scale advantages enjoyed by the big players, and their own moves to produce a Japaneselike product or whole new generation of products, could not justify major commitments. For UniCharm we did devise, however, a private label entry strategy via Weyerhaeuser, and, strengthened by the technical manual on U.S. diaper production that we built mainly from the Fasson Tape and virtual Kimberly Clark sessions, we gave them outstanding intelligence for improving and defending their home markets while establishing a small beachhead in the United States. UniCharm was astonished and ecstatic with the free results.

Denko was delighted to have avoided a mistake with UniCharm while at the same time gaining great face with them. The new business opportunities with P&G would prove critical to Denko's own international expansion strategies and kept intact further supply opportunities with UniCharm when they finally proved ready to move on to the United States themselves. Our Geneva visit, however, may have had the most profound impact.

"Come back later" was the distracted and somewhat worried

greeting I received upon finally meeting our 3M informan, Dr. Gray. For a few hours I wandered the many booths and displays at the cavernous Geneva Convention Center, and for the first time really appreciated the amazing scale of the disposable diaper industry. The minds and efforts dedicated to diaper dryness and convenience absorb a significant slice of human power and creativity, producing in the end just so much hard-to-degrade plastic and chemical waste. For six months my colleagues and I had given our all to be part of this economy; it was easy to forget that most of the world somehow coped without even knowing what a disposable diaper was.

The coast was finally clear at the 3M booth. With furtive glances entirely appropriate to the Cold War setting, Dr. Gray had me insert my hand into a flimsy, papery plastic glove fitted into an environmentally controlled box of some kind, and without a word began to change the settings from freezing to hot, numbing my hand, making it sweat, letting it cool. I found myself enjoying this strange ritual. I noticed that almost immediately after my hand had sweat, the moisture wicked off, leaving my hand comfortable and dry. I looked Dr. Gray in the eye. "This is it, isn't?" A bare nod. "This isn't just your new material for gloves and suits for electronic clean rooms, this is your new poly diaper coating." I pointed toward a stack of the gloves, and Dr. Gray resignedly replied, "We're giving them away to whoever wants one." Within minutes I was sealing the samples in a specimen envelope and carefully enclosed the spec sheet flyer from the booth. The FedEx package would beat me back to Tokyo and survive any plane crash or other disaster I might encounter.

The glove was the pièce de résistance of our spy gains. I was told that Denko and UniCharm agreed to a joint laboratory analysis of the sample, with first dibs to Denko to see if they could produce something of similar quality to satisfy P&G's needs and other potential markets. These companies had what 3M did not: the ability to study analogous coating materials and different types of diaper tapes in combination. Soon a softer, lighter, more effective refastenable disposable diaper hit the Japanese market, and might soon thereafter feature heavily in the plans of the world's largest diaper maker. Once again consultants dedicated to prostituting their minds had changed the world.

CONSULTING DEMONOLOGY, TRACT 3

CLIENT BEWARE: CONSULTANTS' SPYCRAFT CHARMS

1

Be open about representing a competitor. But defuse the sense of threat with harmless-seeming throwaways:

- Your company is a much larger organization than my client's."
- My client's new to the business, exploring what kind of a commitment to make."
- Our client is interested in partnerships with companys like yours."
- Actually, we're based in another country."
- Our client has only a few product lines that overlap with yours; this isn't really their main business."

2

Start competitor interviews with unlikely informants. Flatter them, and get their permission to use their names to open the doors that count.

3

Create decoy deliverables for informant discussions. While accurate and potentially valuable, well-crafted decoy deliverables are only watered down versions of the material given to the client, and serve mainly to get the competitor to talk and respond (sharing a survey about what customers want in a certain product is nearly irresistible, for example, and is almost certain to draw key responses about what a competitor believes it can deliver and why).

4

Look for disgruntled former employees. Be prepared to pay them for revealing information.

5

Go in an expert. Knowing exactly the one or two things you must learn from any interview, but appear casually ignorant, camouflaging the target items in a sea of questions of varying intensity.

6

Play to the competitor's sense of control. "Of course, you'll only tell me what you want me to know." Convey a casual preparedness to leave, and make good on it promptly if things start to go wrong.

7

Let your interviewees feel guilty about what they do not know or cannot share, and get them to suggest and clear the pathways to new and better informants.

8

Offer any venue, and if need be, the client's name. For key informants stubborn about granting an interview, offer to discuss matters by phone, outside work—over dinner or drinks, or at an industry convention. In extreme cases, with client approval, offer to reveal the client's name after completion of the study, or to share a copy of some version of the results, or both.

9

Avoid appearing overeager. Never suggest that the whole point of a visit to their site is just to see them: even if you have only one or two days available to see them, suggest that you are in town for a few weeks.

10

Recognize the opportunity to sell new work. Even if the conflict of interest cannot be finessed, the apparent eagerness to sell can greatly help disarm the wary informant.

CHAPTER 4

THE CLIENT-CONSULTANT MATRIX

TOKYO, WINTER 1987, AND BOSTON, SPRING 1988

UNDER INCREASING PRESSURE TO STRETCH ABILITIES AND MANPOWER, by the late 1980s virtually all the major consulting firms had begun to perfect the means to target client managers to do and sell the consultants' own work. Even the most boutique-style strategy firms like the Boston Consulting Group discovered that, while conveniently using some of their least experienced consulting staff, major on-site commitments allowed consultants to engage more of a client's management and workers in the task of doing and expanding consultants' case assignments.

Using the guise of "process consulting," firms began to emphasize program engagements that would involve an intimately interlocked matrix of consultants and specially assigned client staff. Once the most established firms like McKinsey would be considered cunning for singling out potential client sympathizers for individualized support and attention. But now a large portion of the client's organization would be cleverly enlisted in the task of execution and expansion. By tapping the resources and energies of both subordinates and clients alike, senior consultants learned to better shield themselves

61

from accusations of practice incompetence and the ever-present danger of burnout.

Business reengineering became the standard model for involving both clients and junior consultants in on-site engagements. Geared toward making a cumulative series of fixes in a client's business processes by de-bottlenecking choke points, isolating areas of high expense, and removing critical dependencies, business reengineering calls for a close study of daily activities that is best guided by clients themselves, in thoroughgoing reviews that well suit the more expendable time of the least experienced consultants. Newer firms like United Research, with no intellectual reputation to protect, would unabashedly build their entire business around such models of client interaction. Gemini Consulting would adapt, test, and expand these methods through the cascade of management motivation sessions, designed to trigger plain-vanilla reengineering work as follow-on engagements, as perfected on their Centurion project for Philips Electronics, which I would soon know all too well.

For the Boston Consulting Group, however, nothing less than a trademarked intellectual product would do, so to tap the client-leveraging economies of process consulting it evolved its own model, under the brand of "time-based competition." A book of the same theme was duly released to the popular business press, to entice new clients into BCG's more high-minded approach to reengineering. Under the principles of time-based competition, rather than focusing on dollar costs, clients would be encouraged to identify and isolate areas of high time consumption in their business processes, and then to rework these areas until overall process times could be substantially reduced. BCG persuasively documented cases showing that cutting total process times not only naturally reduced dollar costs along the way, but also put clients in an advantaged competitive position across the business value chain, allowing them to better and more quickly identify new opportunities, build productive capacity, negotiate with key suppliers, and capture new markets.

•   •   •

A transfer from BCG Tokyo to BCG Boston was put in the works for me to, among other things, learn just such client-leveraging techniques. Before I took up my Boston-based duties, my mentor, Yoshi Morikawa, set out to warn me of the differences I could expect.

"Lewis, congratulations on your acceptance at Boston headquarters. I'm not surprised they wanted you, after they saw your work with New York on the Denko diaper case."

We were at one of my least favorite noodle houses for lunch, a Tokyo *ramen-yasan* that served everything in broth seething at solar-hot temperatures. My Japanese acquaintances like to say that I have a *neko-jita*, or cat's tongue, an intolerance for drinking hot liquid, and indeed I have never been able to match the performance of my friends who can dispatch a hot noodle soup as if it were cold milk. Morikawa tended to take me here when he had a lot to say and he wanted my full attention.

I stared at the steaming pile of fried tempura shrimp atop my huge bowl of hot udon noodles, hoping that they might cool a bit before they completely melted into the still boiling broth. Morikawa had already happily slurped through most of his.

"Thanks. That was a fun assignment, and I'm sure it helped my transfer approval. I think they were impressed that you entrusted me with such a big-budget case, and that you got the client comfortable with our more, um, creative data-gathering methods."

"The spying you mean," Morikawa clarified, loudly inhaling a mass of piping noodles. "Well, they didn't really need to know too much. Everybody was happy with the results. Look, Lewis, I know Boston's going to make good use of you, and I even understand they're working up a role for you on an AT&T case, where there's some desperation to get some competitive client data on one of their new products."

I was immediately alert. I had heard that back in the States AT&T was signing on and apparently wanted to spook out the details of a still-in-the-works Northern Telecom product. It was a diagnostic package for bank telecommunications officers, designed to cope with breakdowns in the public phone networks that could imperil international transactions. This was a hot, very proprietary area in the telecom business, and I found myself thrilled but not a little scared at the prospect of trying to steal a look, literally, at Northern Telecom's planned approach.

"Hey, don't let that get cold," Morikawa scolded before I could respond.

"But I'm also supposed to warn you that they expect you to pay your dues on some of the heavy-duty on-site cases, you know, this time-based competition nonsense. I wouldn't really wish the work on anyone, Lewis, and I'm not a little worried that with your taste for the adventurous you might find it a bit tedious. I think it's good you get to headquarters and make some connections with the American staff, but I'm afraid you may not really see too much of them."

"I don't really know too much about time-based competition," I commented, warily suspending a single, blistering noodle from my chopsticks. I had heard really derisive descriptions of daily life on the new time-based competition studies and hoped for little or no part of this work. But on the other hand, I knew Morikawa was reluctant to let me go, and if I gave him the chance to justify my being held back in Tokyo he would no doubt take it. I was anxious to lend speed and authority to my BCG Asia career by logging time as a Boston staff member, and keen to both catch up with friends in the Boston area and to directly nurture my long-term prospects for a return to academia there. I did not brighten at the prospect of being dispatched to live at some client's factory far from our own office.

There was another factor I did not really feel I could bring up with Morikawa. A few months earlier, with much encouragement and congratulations all around, I had married the BCG Tokyo office receptionist. It had seemed the natural thing to do: we were dating a lot, I suddenly had money, and under ever-increasing time pressure for me and parental pressure for her, it seemed a logical way to stabilize things all around. I had only recently begun to realize the enormity of what this meant for our lives, and had engineered my transfer to Boston, with a surprising degree of support from the oth-erwise stuffy Dietmar Hoffstetter, with the idea of giving my new wife and I time to better acquaint ourselves with each other and introduc-ing her to America for the first time. That she hardly spoke English had seemed all the more reason for us to go. But now, confronting the idea of abandoning her somewhere in Boston while I effectively took up residence in some factory, I was suddenly not so sure this was a good idea at all.

"There's not too much to know," Morikawa droned on. "You fan out across a client's operations with maybe a half-dozen other con-sultants, hunker down with their staff, and pick apart the business. You find things to cut here and there, most of which I imagine were obvious to the client's own managers in the first place. Convenient for us, of course, because we get high hours on some of our best-billing-rate staff, with the client's own people doing much of the work. Perfectly logical, I can't argue against its business merits for us as a firm. But not too exciting. And I really do not want to see you stuck on these cases; they'll mark you as a bit of a dullard who can't find a more imaginative way to advance your ambitions."

Disconcertingly, Morikawa buried his head in the depths of his ramen bowl, finally bringing it over his face to noisily suck in the last drops. An appreciative display of good etiquette in Japan, it nonethe-less failed to jive with Morikawa's courtly British manner. Meanwhile a ring of condensed steam had formed on the table around my still mostly full bowl.

"I probably shouldn't go out of my way to take on travel-intensive cases," I ventured delicately, "given the marriage and all."

Morikawa-san paused and looked me carefully in the eye. "I don't want to tell you every time what cases to take on, Lewis; it's impor-tant that you learn to make your own choices, and develop your own path. If the trend in Boston is toward these longer-term, on-site assignments, then you may want to look at coming back to Tokyo sooner than later, given your circumstances and our needs here. Our clients are not much interested in these process-improvement engagements—they believe it was all invented here anyway. There will always be a market in Japan for competitive studies, market entry, and the more theoretical organization work."

I was not too sure that I liked either prospect. While I would soon come to agree that long-term, on-site engagements a lá time-based competition made for dull, confining, and client-exploitative work, the type of assignments I had done in Japan seemed to be bringing me closer and closer to some edge I wanted to keep away from. Each competitive data-gathering assignment seemed less scrupulous than the next. Every successive market-entry case seemed more geared toward simply flogging one set of clients as ideal partners for another. The theoretical cases were getting dangerously close to needing me to invent new theory, and I feared the working theories were already so thin on substance that it would be me who got caught out showing how bankrupt many of our conceptual frameworks had become. What I was afraid to admit to Morikawa and to myself was that I probably looked forward to some mental lazy time on a straightforward reengineering case, even at the expense of living on-site on an extended assignment. But neither could I reconcile this with my new obligations.

I swirled the now-melted noodles around in my bowl and made a last brave attempt to safely ingest its contents. Morikawa could see that I would not crack over the issue of the possibly duller casework in Boston and began to look impatient to go.

"I'm full," I declared. "I'll remember what you said about coming back sooner if things don't work out, thanks. But I'm sure it will be a good experience."

Neither Morikawa nor I knew it would be one of our last meals together as colleagues.

I learned that I would indeed be assigned to one of BCG's flagship time-based competition cases, at Harris Graphics in New Hampshire, shortly after I arrived in Boston. But first I would be asked to dispatch

AT&T's intelligence needs, and I was paired with "Mike Garrity," a recent Yale School of Organization and Management graduate, who would join me on both cases.

We took an immediate liking to each other. Mike was a large but graceful man, with one of the more enormous heads I have ever seen successfully balanced on a body. A person of wide-ranging interests and experiences, Mike could hold forth on anything from transocean sailing to national park management, the silicon chip industry, and the merits of public radio. He had a highly adaptable intelligence and capacity for hard work that made him a great teammate, and his devotion to his young family added a streak of conservative reliability that would both stabilize my work and provide a healthier, if ultimately ineffective, balance to my own faster-paced, morally and physically edgy life. I envied Mike his well-established relationship with his wife. In the course of our day-in, day-out work, the sad truth emerged that I was getting to know him better than I knew my own spouse.

For his part, Mike seemed to enjoy the stimulation of being around me as I worked. In my very denial of consulting's personal importance, my belief that any day I might leave consulting for some higher purpose or calling, I found myself wanting to be more of everything that a consultant is: smarter, faster, richer, and also more conniving and self-indulgent, more successfully lazy than even the most indifferent senior partner. Over time, I discovered that this incaution with client affairs, this recklessness with mind and body, was a phenomenon common to many successful consultants, that the risk-taking behaviors that make consultants attractive are rooted in some quiet but commonly held belief that consulting is not one's ultimate, lifetime profession.

Ironically, Mike and I each saw each other as something of a standard model of success in consulting. Mike would soon be broken free of the industry's grip, however, confirming my hazard-filled life as consulting's preferred norm. His visits to the edge with me no doubt accelerated his thinking on the matter.

The stakes with AT&T were high: staying on their approved consultants list meant upwards of $10 million a year in fees for a dozen or more consulting companies. Being responsible for losing AT&T as a client, or even a significant downgrading of the firm's share of AT&T's consulting needs, would be the fast path to career suicide, and this high-risk competitive-benchmarking case attracted few takers.

We began working up a dummy deliverable and a back-door referral chain to our key target informants at Northern Telecom. Although headquartered in Canada, most of Northern Telecom's manufacturing facilities are in the United States, and I started calling around the more obscure sites, introducing our client as a large, diversified communications technology company looking at getting into public network diagnostics. As we assumed, no one seemed to think we would be brazen enough to be representing AT&T.

Mike constructed a detailed survey for telecommunications managers in the New York area and structured an intensive series of interviews around their responses to the surveys. For fear of leaks, this was postured as a independent survey undertaken by our own firm, and to achieve some semblance of ethical conduct, we did not bill AT&T for the hours involved, but rather offered to later "sell" them the survey results.

The interviews were rich in substance and detail. Telecom managers at major investment houses command armies of hundreds of communications specialists, and they know their stuff. Several had already thought of asking for the kind of diagnostic access to the public switches that the telephone companies were considering— they didn't think of it as a product per se, but they were clearly willing to pay for the access. After washing out anything that AT&T might find uniquely useful, we prepared a "preliminary report" to be shared with Northern management if they would agree to interview with us.

By this time, we were well along a chain of referrals within Northern Telecom that could all be traced back to a helpful plant manager in Tennessee. It turned out that the key product strategists for Northern were practically across the street from our AT&T client in New Jersey.

Things did not start too well. Northern's point man for this product, "Bill Moberley," looked like a consultant himself, nattily groomed and dressed, relaxed and controlled, but with impatience and condescension somewhere under the surface that I knew I should not provoke. Bill began by methodically quizzing us on our whole referral chain, effectively forcing us to admit he was seeing us on a pretense. I put my hand on the emergency eject button—there are times when things can only get worse. I wrote a note to Mike on my clipboard: "Get ready to just leave."

"We don't really have to take any of your time at all. As you can see, many people in your organization have kindly made themselves remarkably available, and we really just wanted to share some of the results with you in person. Of course we wouldn't expect you to tell us anything you don't wish to share. But perhaps we just better leave now, and leave you with a summary document. We can send you more when our survey work is complete." Moberley just steadily held my eyes. God, had I been speaking in Japanese or something? Mike looked quite happy to get going. I started to get the summary sheet from my briefcase.

"How do we know you're not working for the folks across the street?" Yikes. I slid the summary across the table. I prayed to the god of Booz balls. The summary sheet was a sexy display of little balls filled in white, gray, or black to show different levels of customer interest for each network feature and attribute—a nice little Booz Allen invention ripped off by every major consultancy. *Please* take your eyes off of me and look at the summary, I willed at him.

"Of course you wouldn't know that we don't work for them. As we've made plain in all our interviews with Northern and *others*," I explained, meaning for Moberley to think AT&T was another interviewee, not our client, "we do represent a competitor, or more precisely a competitor in some businesses, but we do not have permission to share their name at this time. Perhaps when our survey work is complete . . ."

Yes! Eye contact was broken, and Bill seemed ready to take the bait.

"Wait here, please. I think I should discuss this with my boss."

I should have been nervous, but I had a good feeling about Moberley's interest in the survey summary, which he had taken with him. For good luck, I detached my security pass and slipped it in my briefcase, a trophy-collecting habit of mine from Tokyo. I had too many of these things, I reflected. Time to stop. Moberley returned with his boss and no security guards, always a good sign.

"Mr. Pinault, we're very interested to learn more about your survey," Bill's boss offered, "and if you're selling the full report later we'll buy it."

This certainly happens from time to time under the guise of "multiclient studies," but I chose not to push our luck. Bill's boss went on.

"I've asked Bill here to respond to whatever he thinks might be of interest to you; maybe you two could follow up together with some of these banks' telecom managers."

Bill the consulting-wise was suddenly Bill the nerd, intelligently passionate and forthcoming about Northern's new product, and briefly I wished we had been made to leave. Within minutes we realized that Northern was much further along than we or AT&T had thought. They had already completed much of their own survey and technical feasibility work, and were about to advance a fully featured product in several test markets. By working through our own survey summary, and getting Bill Moberley to elaborate on how Northern planned on coping with specific areas of customer interest, we built a complete map of Northern's planned capabilities and the stages in which they would be introduced. Whole new categories and subcategories had to be added to the sheet and, by the end of the session, it was so crammed with information that my greatest fear was that Bill would have second thoughts and ask for it back. He did not, and I knew we were walking out with a million-dollar presentation.

Mike was clearly nervous with the whole session, and I agreed with him that this was a stretch over the edge. At the final AT&T presentation meeting I carefully explained every detail of how we represented ourselves, as much for Mike's sake as for BCG's. Reactions ranged from "How could they be so stupid" and "Maybe they know and they're setting us up" to "My God, no one in this room is to talk to any more consultants." There was clearly some discomfort about the whole approach.

But when we got to the detailing of Northern's imminent offering, and the fine print at the bottom credited sources as our interviews and analysis and *Northern Telecom*, any faint-heartedness, real or pretended, was gone.

The focus shifted instead to the AT&T managers who had worked with us—"How could Northern be so far along and us not know about it or have something ready?" And so, as often happens, we wound up sacrificing our client friends and helpers on the project to the greater client-firm relationship. Not long afterward, the consultant vice president heading our case team was directly hired to become an AT&T vice president. In the end, AT&T declined to offer the product, leaving Northern to its devices in the public network diagnosis market. I would later wonder if Moberley or his boss might have known exactly what they were doing and hoped to preempt any annoying AT&T competitive intervention or market confusion by letting them know in advance that it would not be worth their while.

Within days of the final AT&T presentation, Mike Garrity and I joined a four-man team that had already been in place at Harris Graphics for several weeks, mapping out the basic business processes and tagging potential fix areas. Josh Zeldin from the New York office I already knew from Denko diapers. Josh was plucky as ever and raring to go, but soon deeply disappointed to find I was now married and that we would be mired in a factory for months to come. "Ed

Kemper" was the senior manager on the project. "Sean Connors," my new Boston office mate, and "Jim Wellington," a junior associate right out of college, filled out the team.

Sean would be in charge of day-to-day management on site. He was a contemporary of Mike's at Yale, but came of an entirely different background. A Brit and the wealthy son of a famous spy author, Sean burned with an alarming intensity and intelligence. He had been with BCG only a year, and all his working experience prior to Yale had been as a refugee camp manager in Thailand, but he was already a qualified case leader, something that normally came along after three or four years post-MBA.

"Right. This is a printing press company. Harris makes the presses that print magazines, and their biggest customer's key account is Donnelley, who prints *Time* here in the Northeast. Harris has attracted the attention of Heidelberg in Germany for a possible takeover, and Harris wants to make sure they get the highest valuation and selling price possible, that's why we're here. Actually, to be more precise, we're here because their orders are running late to customers. Last month, for the first time, a customer refused to take delivery of one of their multimillion dollar presses, because it was so late the customer decided he could get along without it. These are custom-built machines, made to fit the factory floor, so it had to be scrapped for parts. Harris couldn't hide this fiasco from Heidelberg, and they need to show assurances that these late orders are getting under control.

"Jim and Josh have been taking a look at quality control, which seems to be one of the major holdups. The one answer we could give them today to fix most of their problems would be to disallow QC from routinely sending back long-lead-time parts to their manufacturers for even minor rejections Harris's own in-house machine shop could repair."

"But we don't want to do that," Ed joined in, smiling, "at least not yet."

"There are plenty of things in need of help here," Sean said somewhat scornfully. "Ed and I are going to look in detail at the company's sales policies. It appears custom-orders get a bit out of control—at least we can make it seem they are. Mike, Lewis, I'd like you two to dig into the MRP system. I'm willing to bet there's a wealth of reporting that can be cut, after ample study, of course. Do you know MRP well?"

I had no idea what Sean was talking about. Fortunately, Mike did, and replied for both of us. "The management resources planning program? I'm pretty familiar with MRP version two. But there are so many custom report capabilities in any computer information system like this, I'm sure Lewis and I would need a lot of guidance."

"Well, you'll get it. We've got most of the management information systems group assigned to us for the duration."

"How long is the duration?" I couldn't resist asking.

"We aim to make this last about six months. By then the acquisition should be ripe, and we should have plenty of numbers to show improvement. Because the presses take about eighteen months to build, the timing for us is ideal, really. We can't get blamed for any further late orders while we're here because they were already started a year or more ago. If there are no late orders, and there's a chance of that if we get them to drop orders at risk now, then we can take credit directly for getting things under control. If things don't work out or somehow get worse, it will happen long after we're gone, and probably under new management."

We laughed and admired the flawlessness of Sean's logic. I looked nervously toward the door to our conference room, fearful that a member of the client team might walk in.

"Lewis, I want you to get started on one of the most important tasks, when you're not helping Mike with MRP. We need to get some measurements in place, fast. Pick the things to measure and the standards to measure them with. I want things that can be readily tracked, and that are almost certain to show improvements, but improvements that we will be able to take credit for. I'll get you a bunch of clients to help you run down the data every week, and you should start talking to people now to get all their ideas on this."

"In fact," Ed observed, "if we can write up a large number of MRP computer reports now to aid the tracking, we can add that to the list of things that we cut down later, so that becomes another improvement right there."

This was greeted with more laughter, though I would shortly learn that Ed was entirely serious.

Josh took me aside after our meeting broke up.

"Boy, am I glad to see you. I knew you'd get over here from Tokyo! This assignment is already getting so dull, we need you around here to liven things up a bit. I can't take much more of quality-control statistics. Would you mind if I joined you for some of the measurements interviews, if it's okay with Sean?"

I assured Josh that I welcomed the chance to work with him again, and set off to be sure Mike knew that I had no idea what to do about MRP.

"Oh, I kind of guessed that, no problem. That's just Sean's way of trying to intimidate. He knows from Yale that I know MRP, and he's trying to make it look as though it's something everybody already knows. Sean even makes Ed nervous, I wouldn't worry about it."

"That's a relief."

"Well, it doesn't mean we're done exactly, either. We will need to get information systems people to cooperate and do a lot of this for us, and I'm sure they've got other ideas about what to do with their time. But let me handle that. This is a lot easier than your brand of industrial espionage. I'd be more worried about your task. No one is really going to want to share new data and measurements. Basically you're going to be asking them to hand you the tools to measure how badly they do now, so you can force them to work harder in future."

I gave Mike a look of glum acknowledgment.

"And you need to get them to do the reporting, too! Good luck! My suggestion would be, start working on something really trivial, with the potential for dressing it up later."

I thanked Mike and thought of the yawning chasm of the six months ahead. How am I going to fill my time without going crazy?

I wondered. The answer emerged: by being there as little as possible.

At first we dutifully plugged away at our assigned tasks. Mike persuaded the systems managers to shut down MRP and start the system essentially from scratch, with none of the dozens of custom-designed reports that had become largely obsolete. Parts orders alone, sorted by vendor, due date, received date, QC status, and so on, nearly filled a room with several years' unread printouts. But if the system could run this way, without custom reports, the systems managers would have reason to fear for their jobs, and so we soon had their full cooperation in looking at new ways to analyze and report the state of the business.

My job was to help them on this task, finding things to measure and report. One day Josh and I sat dazed through one of the daily manufacturing meetings, which seemed dedicated to an unending review of late parts from vendors across the country.

"The cylinder heads from Houston are still at the top of the list; we should get Brad to call them again," "Wilbur," the assistant manufacturing manager, announced.

"List?" I asked hopefully. "Do you keep a list of these late parts?"

"Sure, I have to. It's impossible to keep 'em straight. Gives a place to put down phone numbers, order numbers, and whatever, too."

Josh looked at me and asked Wilbur, "You don't have an MRP report for this?"

"I think maybe there was, but it's hundreds of pages to carry 'round, wrong stuff drops out week to week. This here list," Wilbur said as he unfolded a single sheet from his denim work jacket, "does a fine job of telling me how deep the doo-doo is."

"Wilbur, do you keep your lists?" I asked, feeling my first excitement in days.

"Oh, I got stacks of 'em in my desk. If you can read my writing, you're welcome to 'em, but don't you lose anything."

Wilbur's lists became our treasure trove. We assembled a five-year record of late parts deliveries and, with the help of a small army of systems and manufacturing people, traced each part to its eventual home in a machine, and in turn traced the machines' delivery dates.

With some intensive detective work, we assembled a giant map showing which parts from which vendors had been critical to the late delivery of a given press machine and by how many days. Some of this information was no surprise to Harris managers, like the cylinder assemblies from Houston, but others were, identifying specific needs for longer order lead times, and in some cases, more time-reliable vendors producing higher quality parts.

Josh was impressed.

"We actually did something."

"Well, yes, I guess that's the idea," I replied smiling. "But adjusting the order lead times and negotiating new vendors will take time, and in fact I'm afraid it will temporarily inflate the backlog problems."

Josh looked briefly concerned but then brightened.

"Okay, but why don't we do this. Put in all the new order lead times into the MRP system now, and generate a new report for measurement. We could call it just the short parts list."

"I get it. When all the new order lead times go in, the list is going to be huge, instantly making tons of stuff late. But presumably, most of it can be cleaned up or accelerated in the next couple of months, or even weeks."

"We start with a nice fat list and whittle it down. It's a measure!"

Ed and Sean were immediately taken with the idea, and Mike got the MRP staff to load it all through the system over a long weekend. Enlisting a further army of staff specially dedicated to negotiating the difficulty of improving against the new lead times, we soon had a visibly busy workforce fully engaged, and every appearance of the sincere and serious effort that was expected of Harris by its soon-to-be parent, Heidelberg.

The success of this work in the first two months left us with four long months of getting paid to massage things along. Senior management had little interest in taking on new initiatives until the takeover was complete, and we became the de facto day-to-day executive management of the factory. I had rarely been more bored.

We soon took to driving back to Boston each day. We had agreed as a team early on to arrive before and depart after our clients, and though this was difficult in the mornings, with departure from Boston no later than 6 A.M., the evenings were much easier, with our managing to almost always leave by six in the evening. Dave and Josh, Ed and Sean, and Mike and I paired up in three rental cars, and we took to dashing out to the cars each night, first to race each other home, and then to see who would be the first to arrive in Boston by 7 P.M., no mean feat when none of us so far, even at well over the speed limit, had made it before 7:15 P.M.

Mike, a good conversationalist on the morning drive, became manic in the evenings, making a convincing appearance of using sheer will beamed from his massive head to move cars out of our oncoming pathway. Josh always seemed to be having fun with his drive, but both Ed and Sean seemed seriously possessed whenever we caught a glimpse of them, usually passing us. We learned that they had their own competition going each day, to see who would finish with the best time.

Soon we organized weekly prizes for our nightly escapes, which kept escalating through the final months and weeks of the engagement. Whiskey and cigars became Red Sox tickets and restaurant gift certificates, then high-tech goodies and strip club nights. At work, we talked of little else and developed elaborate rules for assuring our departure together at the same time. Ed was the first to upgrade his car, and we soon each had vehicles that just managed to stay on the side of client respectability.

In the last weeks it became clear that the assignment had gone well enough to help ensure acquisition, and that Heidelberg wanted a BCG team to stay on to follow through. Ed delivered the bad news.

"At least four of us are going to have to stay on. Myself, I don't have any choice about it, I have to stay, but I got agreement that I can go down to half time. I need at least three others, and I'd like to have all of you, so I'm afraid you should all get set for another two months."

I immediately began to scheme how I could get out of this, as I suspect the others did as well. But Ed already had a solution.

"This Friday's our last day till after the acquisition. We'll get a break of about two weeks. Here's my proposal. We're down to 7:03, that's Sean's best time. On Friday, let's make the prize a real prize. Mike or Josh, if your car wins, you're off the assignment, and the other guys are on. But if my car with Sean in it wins, you're all on, except Sean. Whoever finishes last is on the case again for sure. We all have to agree, and it has to stay secret."

The look on Mike's face was worrisome, but I agreed, like all the others, to do it this way. It seemed a fitting end to our increasingly crazed existence at Harris, and somehow gave terrible purpose to our nightly rampages of speed.

Over the weekend, Mike pored over a set of U.S. Geological Survey maps of New Hampshire, convinced he might find yet another shortcut, and after much debate we reserved a mammoth Toyota Landcruiser for Friday, counting on the usual jam out of town to give us an advantage. We badgered Josh into telling us that he had already rented an MR2, the Toyota sports car with a Porsche engine, and that he would keep it at home as a surprise until Friday. We had no luck trying to find out what Ed would drive, though we tried calling rental agencies in the hopes of canceling his reservation. We tried to scout out routes during the week, but usually wound up confounded by darkness.

That last Friday as we dashed out the door, our worst fears were confirmed. Ed had procured an all-black, late-model Ferrari from one of his banking buddies from the Harvard Business School. I did manage to take a little satisfaction in seeing that Ed gave our Landcruiser a curious, and perhaps worried, look.

We were off. Mike took us immediately down the road opposite the one we usually used, and I was relieved not to have to deal with watching the others' cars. We would use two portions of road we hadn't yet tried and were prepared for pretty much anything, with a tool kit and bolt cutters in the back. I navigated, and, clutching the USGS map as we violently collided with every bump on this first back road, I tried to assure Mike that life was still worth living, even should there be two more months to go at Harris.

"Don't be so sure," Mike intoned darkly, in an unconvincing attempt at humor.

By our calculations, we should cut ten minutes from our total time on the new route, even assuming a relative crawl through the two private pathways, one farm road, and one unaided stream crossing we planned. We hoped to enter I–95 off the shoulder, north and further away from Boston than our usual highway entry, but with luck a good deal sooner than we had ever hit the highway from Harris before. From there, it would be a straight run for speed, but we were counting on Friday's heavy traffic and Boston area jams to keep Josh's and Ed's sports cars in check.

The pathways were horrifyingly narrow, and we took down two small trees. We sensed we had put a substantial dent in the front, and though it was only starting to get dark I could see that one headlight now pointed at the ground just to the front and right of the Landcruiser. We pushed on. At the farm road, we could see in our rearview mirrors that someone seemed pretty upset, shouting and waving at us. We honked, laughed, and screamed, right up to the stream crossing. The stream was about 30 feet across here, and it was now dark enough that we couldn't tell how deep. We stopped to get out and inspect.

"Look, it's not even to my knees," Mike observed.

"Your knees don't count, you titan. But still I guess we could try. You can swim, can't you?"

Suddenly we heard the sound of another car racing down the road.

"It's a pickup! It's that mad farmer!"

"I bet he's got a gun!"

We rushed into the Landcruiser, and Mike promptly plunged us into the stream. The Landcruiser gamely made surprising progress across the stream. The embankment at the other side was less cooperative, however, and would not let us climb out.

We heard honking.

"Keep going!" I yelled. "That way, go down with the river toward the highway!"

Mike did as instructed, and within a minute or two we found a gentler embankment close to the road and made our way up and out, no sign of the pickup behind us. Tears of laughter in my eyes, I guided Mike back to the highway. We figured we had maybe a five minute advantage now.

As we neared the highway we were relieved to see an already building backup of traffic. We paralleled on the shoulder for a while, and eventually we were delighted to see Josh in his red MR2 stuck in the lane with no shoulder, with no possible passing room. We pulled up alongside to jeer, shouting across one row of cars.

"No, no, please, don't leave us, we can't stand it," Josh and Dave chorused, "No more Harris, please! Ed's already at least twenty cars ahead!"

"What if we put them in our car?" I asked Mike

"Well, Ed might get all anal about the rules, but who cares. I know I'm not going on this case again no matter what, and Ed said whoever's last stays for sure. Let's get them in!"

Dave was more worried about abandoning the car than Josh, even though the MR2 was in Josh's name. In the end, Dave agreed to stay with the car, admitting he would rather stick with Ed on this first case anyway, that he was afraid to make him mad. Josh was eager to join us, however, and piled in, delightedly thumbing his nose at Ed as we slowly cruised by him on the shoulder, never to give up the lead before Boston. Though deeply displeased, Ed would ultimately let all three of us off the hook, sensing, quite rightly, that he should have a fresh crew for the final, redundant round at Harris, and not an ornery gang of process mutineers.

CONSULTING DEMONOLOGY, TRACT 4

CONSULTING SORCERY FOR CO-OPTING CLIENT TEAMMATES

1

Assume complete solutions may lie with the client. There are only three honest and productive benefits that a consultant can bring to bear on a client's needs: 1) the objectivity to see beyond internal strains and politics, 2) a single-mindedness of focus and a sheer force of manpower that clients cannot spare other tasks and employees to achieve, and 3) a perspective of insight from work in other functions and industries that may allow a successful translation of best practices among clients. Many cases today, of course, are sold using stratagems and deceptions that bring none of these benefits to bear, and clients can also make fraudulent use of consultants in a way that has little to do with these benefits. But of these three benefits it is the first two that most commonly motivate clients to buy consulting engagements. The third, an outside perspective informed by experience elsewhere, may in fact be the most valuable of all consulting benefits, but it is objective focus and temporary manpower that drives most sales. In such cases, the answer lies within: the client is not buying an external solution, but is rather, often unknowingly, inviting the consultant to come in and find the solution among their own people. This presents easy and efficient opportunities for consultants to achieve high billings strongly leveraged by client knowledge.

2

Design systems to capture fullest credit for the client's own work and insights. Managing the expectations of key client informants and sympathetic co-executors of the work is critical to creating a sense of "rewards received" that need not seek beyond the consultant for validation. The consultant's client friends will ideally be happy with a thank-you from the consultant. More likely, however, they will seek recognition for their efforts from the people who pay them, potentially endangering the senior client's perception of the consultant's value. To defend against this, consultants should design systems early in the engagement to set up readily accomplished measures and standards against which the consultant alone will be perceived to have uniquely overachieved.

3

Befriend and help key client informants. The more knowledgeable client employees are often already equipped to think in consulting terms about possible solutions and simply lack the voice, power, or motivation to articulate their vision. For this very reason potential key informants can be disposed to resent and distrust consultants and can even work against them to hide ready solutions or sabotage consultant-proposed alternatives. Cases that allow these kinds of behaviors to take hold can be among the most dangerous and destructive for consultant and client alike. Far preferable is an early befriending of as many potential informants as possible, and a focused lavishing of positive attention on key client informants who offer critical insights or may already harbor near-complete solutions.

4

Cultivate client executors of the work. Befriended client informants usually enjoy the attentions of a consulting team, and indeed may fantasize about being consultants themselves. In the course of an engagement they may be receiving more and better recognition for the value and potential of their work than they have ever experienced. Given that demands on consultants increasingly stretch capabilities well beyond personal and practice-area expertise, it is a wise investment to enlist sympathetic clients wherever possible in the direct execution of the work. For the working client, it may fun, an opportunity to play consultant; for the consultant, it can a vital means to overcoming shortfalls in manpower and experience, and to extending the reach of the consulting firm further into the client's organization to scout for future sales.

5

Be prepared to abandon key client informants. There is little reward for consultants who simply advance the client informant as the fully credited key to a desirable solution. Seeing that they had what they most wanted right under their nose, an enlightened client may thank the consultant for helping to find it, but many clients will react with embarrassment and frustration at the high fees spent. In either case any further perceived needs for consulting services may end then and there. Specific risks also attach to becoming closely identified with a given informant: the fact that he had the answer, but did not come forward with it, may be seen as reason for internal censure, and the consultant may suffer by association. Generally, it is safer for the consultant to gently ease away from the client informant, and adopt and disguise the informant's work as one's own, if possible by amplifying it to dimensions that suggest no one person could have it produced alone.

CHAPTER 5

THE HIERARCHY OF FEAR

BOSTON, SUMMER 1989

ONE OF THE CONSULTANT'S WORST FEARS IS BEING CAUGHT AT THE CENTER of a failing engagement. Normally, foundering cases are quickly made right. Client and consultant alike can usually be counted on to keep things afloat, or at least mount a salvage operation together to avoid a complete break-up and loss of all the hopes and energies invested. But as demands for faster results and more sweeping coverage build, consulting firms often find themselves navigating in darkness with inexperienced helmsmen, plowing ever deeper, more dangerous waters. Whole assignments, I would learn, could vanish without a trace, their surviving crew left with nothing to fight but the sharing of the blame.

In what would be my final days with BCG in Boston I would barely survive my first major wreck; worse yet, it did little to teach me how to avoid them in future.

Mike Garrity joined me for lunch in the main conference room at BCG Boston. It was a beautiful summer day, and the blue waters of the harbor set off the perfect, noble skyline of careful Colonial-era brickwork and restrained modern masterpieces.

"I heard Ed was in here just the other day with Clarkson," Mike managed through a monster bite of pastrami and swiss.

"That's right. Missed half our recruiting list to McKinsey. They still pay more, and we're starting to lose our reputation for less travel, I think. I don't think the view here really makes news like that any better."

I was enjoying my sandwiches. The deli downstairs had begun producing king-sized works of art. Unable to decide between chicken tikka with cucumber, and tuna with bacon, grapes, and avocado, I simply got both. Just returned from a few weeks in Japan, and surprised to find things were slow back here in Boston, I was happy to indulge in the one kind of food that just could not be found in the right greedy quantities in Tokyo.

"Tell me about Japan," Mike asked, foraging through a full-sized bag of Cape Cod potato chips, reduced to kid-sized in his gargantuan hands.

"Oh, it was entirely surreal. We're on this case for the Pentagon, right? The Defense Advanced Research Projects Agency, DARPA. They have this scheme to bring back the American television industry through high definition TV manufacture, so they can get a more reliable supply of heads-up radar displays for fighter jets and tanks. It's amazingly far-sighted, really smacks of industrial policy."

"I got the impression the Pentagon doesn't care where components are made, as long as they're the best quality and come from our allies and all that. They won't buy American unless it's really the best in the Free World."

"Well, that's kind of the point. DARPA is tapping into fears that the United States is about to completely lose another industry to Japan and Europe, namely televisions, by promoting this big U.S.-based effort. But they're not ruling out foreign participation by any means, in fact they seem to be pushing for it."

"So that's why you were in Japan."

"Right. Sony has this Mexican cathode ray tube plant across the border and some supporting facilities and suppliers in Texas. Basically, they're making the case that they are already an American supplier, and that they should have a role in this new U.S. plan to prop up the industry in the States."

"I'm surprised the isolationist types aren't screaming bloody murder."

"Doesn't matter, apparently. The Pentagon wants the best. So they cut this deal with Sony. If Sony would open up its key plants and show just how advanced they really are, then DARPA would support their entry into the program."

"Amazing. U.S. funds to support an already dominant foreign competitor."

"Well, the Pentagon isn't the Commerce Department."

"And so they got you to handle the show, of course. Our number one spy, and you speak Japanese, too. I'd love to see your notebooks."

"Oh, it was fantastic. The factory managers had never let any outsider in before, much less one with a camera and million questions. Zenith and these guys programmed me really well; this was supposed to be their booby prize for letting Sony in. Thing is, I saw things at Sony they'd never be able to use before the next generation of sets come out. And the HDTV work at NHK studios is awesome, perfect screens and images you just hang on the wall."

"So where are you headed with this?"

"Congressional testimony! We have this proposal for a billion-dollar, government-subsidized, Advanced Television City project. With it, a blend of U.S. and Japanese manufacturers, on U.S. soil, make all the cutting-edge stuff for consumers and the military both. In about ten years, it's fully independent, world-class competitive. Without it, well, the Pentagon does its shopping in the Far East, and our consumer practices group goes to the Tokyo electronics shows to see what will hit the American market in a few years."

"Wow. Really sexy. You'll make qualified case leader in no time. Any sign BCG Tokyo wants you back?"

"Yeah, they're talking about another six months, maybe a year here. They seem encouraged about what I'm picking up. Maybe one more assignment, but I don't know what. What's in the works?"

"What's in the works you may not like. You really having both those sandwiches?"

I nodded. Mike had commented toward the end of the Harris case about my growing poundage, but this had not really entered into the orbit of my concerns yet.

"What's up?"

"Well, I had a few fun weeks, too, I took Susie and the kids sailing, and mostly I was involved in this last recruiting drive."

"That's nice," I offered a little hollowly. I decided it was time to share something with Mike.

"You probably noticed I don't talk much about my wife these days."

"Now that you mention it, Susie was asking after her. We didn't really want to say anything, though, thought it might be some kind of Japanese thing, you know, no discussion of home life."

"No, not really. It's more like no home life. She's still back in Japan now, with her parents. I don't think she even really wanted to stay, necessarily, or she wanted me to stop her from staying or something. Here in Boston we've hardly been spending any time together, and she's had a lot of trouble making friends. Her only friends, really, are from her English class. I met them once. They're from all over the world, and their English is really primitive—to listen to them, I think they're just holding each other back and reinforcing their mistakes. Her vocabulary seems to be shrinking, not growing. At home, I should be talking to her in English, but I'm hardly there, and when I am, I'm way too exhausted to try anything but Japanese, because that's what works."

Mike absorbed this without comment.

"Keep talking," he instructed, taking one of my sandwich halves for himself.

"Anyway, she dropped all her other classes; she couldn't keep up.

She tried out a couple of jobs, and that was no good. What she does do, and with increasing sophistication, is shop. Sometimes, I think everything is fine. When she talks to her mother on the phone—also not cheap—she gets advised to put up with it, men earn the money, leave me alone. She takes her pleasure in buying stuff, and of course I buy her stuff because I see that makes her happy, but our debts are really building up."

"Happens to a lot people," Mike munched.

"I wonder. At least they're not flying back and forth to Tokyo all the time. When we went back to Japan for this HDTV trip, it was supposed to be a big family get-together, reaffirming it was all worthwhile and everything. Of course, I got so busy I virtually didn't show up, and wound up in a hotel by myself most nights. Thing is, nobody seemed to care, like this was just fine, Lewis the walking paycheck."

"So what happens now?"

"That's just it. Nothing. Or it's up to me. Or something—everyone seems to think I'll get less busy, things will calm down, and everything will be all right. Or maybe everyone just plans to figure a way to enjoy things this way. I feel like I could have rampant affairs and no one would blink. I'm afraid to tell them we might be up against a bunch of client site–based work. How do you and Susie handle it?"

"Mostly, we talk about my quitting. But I don't think I have to worry, because I can probably count on getting fired."

I absorbed this with some shock. These are taboo topics among consultants, a sure-fire way to trigger rumors that become facts. Managers avoid budgeting for consultants they believe are at any risk for leaving a case midstream, and their resulting lower billability lights up the admin systems like a Christmas tree. Mike was a bright, solid, likable worker and retained incredible calmness in all situations—I could not see the cracks.

"I didn't have any hint," I finally commented honestly.

"Well, we have our home situations, too; unfortunately that's where a lot of the stress gets released, which is a real waste given how little time we have together. My time's coming up, you know. I'm a straight MBA type, not some unique foreign character like you. I'm just meat and potatoes, and I have to have the hours and cases for qualified case leader by a certain time, or else. Mostly, I think it might be a good thing. We keep talking about rafting down the Grand Canyon, or sailing to Hawai'i.

"But who knows, maybe I'll clock all the hours I need, get some really interesting cases, and stick it out for a while. Now George Cranston has sold Shell Oil and Nick Fong is the manager," Mike announced, ending our brief reverie about nonmarried married life.

"Nick Fong," I knew, could be bad news. "George Cranston" moved in very high circles in BCG, as head of the new High Technology practice group. I did not expect that he would put much time into a done deal, particularly something as low-tech as oil.

"Cranston's a great guy and everything," Mike continued, "but he won't be around much, I think, and that leaves Nick."

"Uh-oh."

Nick tended toward supervisor qualities in his work. A former brand manager at Proctor & Gamble, he had an easygoing way that readily charmed clients. Unfortunately, Nick's expertise never seemed to stretch beyond the impressionistic to the analytic. For meat and substance, for quantitative analyses and original frameworks for creative problem-solving, he was known to rely heavily on other members of his team and was reputed to be hell to work for.

"Yeah, uh-oh. This is an eight-month project, an operations analysis case. I don't think anyone here at the office has done anything like it before. Nick is going to come looking for you, like he did for me, because with Harris behind us we're now considered operations experts."

"What about the case?"

"It's mind-boggling. Shell has just bought rights to a unique Venezuelan crude oil. From what I've been able to learn in the past week, every crude is uniquely suited for producing specific products out of the hydrocracker where its refined. Some are better for gasoline, some for diesel and motor oil, some for petroleum wax. So they've got this crude, and an old refinery in Houston. They think they know that this stuff is best for heavy duty motor oil and high-grade waxes. So they want a bottom-to-top analysis, as far as Nick has been able to explain to me: what the hydrocracker in Houston can really handle, in what proportions, and what the potential markets are for the end product."

"They want to optimize the hydrocracker for both the crude and final consumption. Umm. Not Nick's kind of thing."

"Well, he thinks it's ours. If I were you, much as I'd miss you, I would get back to Japan now. Any openings there I should know about?"

Despite our misgivings, Mike and I were both soon locked into the Shell case, slated for eight months of mostly living out of hotels in Houston. At first, even Nick seemed to balk at this kind of commitment, and in his eagerness to put off the on-site commitment time, he had sold Shell on a heavy weighting of general market investigation. His strategy, however, made me extremely uneasy.

"Lewis, we know that this crude can be cracked for heavy duty motor oil, gasoline, and wax, right? We can worry about the wax markets later, that should easy. But I've convinced the client that HDMO and the gasoline might bear a closer examination, a look at branding potential and influence in local markets."

"This is a branding study?" I asked, openly skeptical.

"Haven't you ever wondered how four different gasoline stations at the corners of a big intersection can have different prices for the same grades of gas? What makes them change their prices, who leads and who follows, by how much, and why? How do the prices for subsidiary products like HDMO and antifreeze follow the shifts in gas prices?"

"I don't know."

"Right. Neither does Shell, not at a deep level anyway. I really want to drill down on this issue. I want us to link the crude prices down through the distribution chain for a bunch of major grades and players, and link them to selling behavior at the pumps. With enough station data, we should be able to show where the behavior is logical, and where cost advantages in crude, processing, and distribution lead to price advantages at the pump. Where they don't, where the prices are either sustained at inflated levels or undercut the cost advantages, we can show the influence of branding. Shell has a powerful brand name, and I want to show them exactly how powerful it is, and how much incremental benefit they really might enjoy from this new crude source.

I was staggered. The amount of data involved would be overwhelming. Even if it could be gathered, from hundreds or thousands of clusters of gasoline stations around the country, each cluster would have to be analyzed for its price-changing patterns, and the computing power required would be more than I had ever handled. I struggled to picture how the data would be displayed against the differing crude sources and distribution chain costs.

Defeated, I felt I had to show Nick I was overwhelmed. "Nick, don't get me wrong, but this could wind up looking ridiculous, particularly in my hands. I don't even see what we would show them, exactly." I could tell Nick heard the insubordination rising in my tone.

I could see anger flare. "Lewis, you shouldn't be afraid of ambitious data tasks. We all have to do them sometime. I've already spoken to Ed, and Hoffstetter and Morikawa in Tokyo, about your working on this case, and they're agreed that you need to dig in and show you can hack it at the quantitative level. I'll help you get through this, don't worry. But you've got to do this one, and there's no other billing prospects coming up. You can't just be idle."

Inside, I was fuming. This was quantity work, not quantitative, and a move by Nick that appeared to me nothing more than a desperate attempt to show that his own skills, limited to brand knowledge, could be deployed on operations cases. I knew he needed to show a breadth of case skills to secure his own bid for officership. But he was correct that there was an expectation that I would make it through more than one rite of passage on plain-vanilla U.S. cases, and I needed a more prominent success than Harris behind me. I could only hope he knew what he was doing.

"I understand all that, Nick, thanks. And I have no doubt you'll supply the necessary air cover. But what kind of output are we talking about," I pressed.

As desperate as I was growing to leave this meeting, I had to have some better idea of what we were supposed to be doing. Shell employed large teams of planners and Ph.D. economists to follow the kinds of things he was discussing, and while I admired him for his gall in getting this part of the casework sold, I simply could not envisage a product worth paying for.

"We could do something like this." On a piece of blank paper, Nick began to sketch a graph in pencil. His strokes seemed uncertain, retracing the same things over and over as if waiting for the next idea to come along. I sensed he really hated doing this kind of thing.

"We could have two axes, like this. On one, we have the price differentials at the stands, positive for leading and brand-advantaged, negative for trailing. Down here, we have crude costs, adjusted across the distribution chain. We connect up the dots, showing where there are patterns."

On its surface, I knew this could work, it would be a nice message to show. Certain crude oil advantages might be shown to translate to brand advantages, or a lack of them. It might raise expectations about this new crude source, suggesting how much to invest in its processing and the marketing of its downstream products. But the room for error seemed huge, and the statistical requirements for accuracy would involve tens of thousands of data points and hundreds of triple-checked analyses. I was out of my realm, and so, I knew, was Nick.

"Anyway, something like that. You can't always expect someone to spoon-feed you like this, Lewis," he remarked, passing me the single, sloppily marked up paper. "Not every case is about client personalities and high-visibility intelligence coups. I'm sure Mike will help you out on the data; his computer skills are very strong."

Afraid of what might lie ahead, but more afraid of how it would look if I refused the case, I plunged ahead. Mike had his own concerns about making manager in Boston, and had no recourse of friends in Tokyo to count on. So we put our heads down and began assembling one of the largest pricing models ever constructed in BCG's history. Even with a direct download of much of Shell's own database, the key entry alone took weeks. Long into the night we would take turns reciting data to each other as one of us read and one of us typed: "Montgomery Amoco twenty-four, zip oh-one-nine-five eight, eighty-seven's sixty five point two five, and eighty-nine's sixty-eight point five . . ."

Visits to stations to discuss pricing strategies and subsidiary products were occasional highlights of the work, but eventually it boiled down to corralling the data and making up the graphs. From the graphs we soon worked up a thick presentation, the heart of which was fifty slides of pure data display. Certain trends seemed clear in the data, but they varied substantially by location and product. We hoped to discuss the presentation package in detail with Shell to see if they could help us further isolate the patterns.

Nick glazed over when he saw the draft. Claiming to be busy on another case, he had not spent much time with us.

"Lewis, you realize you're going to have to present this. It's impressive stuff, I'm sure they'll like it, but it would be a good experience for you to present it, and you and Mike are the only ones who could hope to explain it."

"It's not really meant for formal presentation. I thought we should go through it with the working group first."

"Well, we'll have plenty of time with the working group later. "Ron Hixon," our client, wants to see what he's spending his money on. You've got plenty there to keep them busy, don't worry. George's going to be there, too, and we'll want to discuss the next phase of the work."

And so we made our way to Houston with an excess baggage load of presentation copies and dozens of computer diskettes chock full of pricing data. Strangely, the presentation began with Nick, the case manager, explaining what we were doing to George, the case officer. The description did not make me comfortable.

"Before we dig into the hydrocracker and the direct potential for its downstream products, I've let Lewis run with some ideas on the influence of branding and price strategies on exploiting the potential of unique crude sources. He's put a lot of work into this, and I thought he should share it with the group today."

George nodded neutrally, and Ron Hixon looked absolutely eager to hear more.

"We know that Corporate Planning's been busy supplying you with lots of data. Hope you had fun with it," Hixon joked to the dozen or so upstream markets executives in the room.

I smiled nervously. The preliminaries did not take long, and soon we were on the first data-graph slide. I glibly went through the construction and concept of the framework, which I still did not buy after these many weeks, and began to go through the possible trends detailed on the next few slides.

"Hold on there please," Hixon interrupted. "Could you go over how this data is set up again?"

I began to describe the layout of the axes and data points in detail. I had the sudden image of me standing naked with Nick's original scrawled graph on the overhead.

"You know, I appreciate the effort and everything," Hixon went on, winking to his subordinates, "but this just doesn't make sense. There are too many disconnects in the chain, too many other influences along the way. What we sell and trade product for goes through too many changes before it hits local distribution for it to be meaningful. At the other end, on your top axis, the local pricing is subject to too many shifts in different companies' policies and local decisions. You don't show the actual volumes purchased anyway, so it's hard to say what kind of affect this is having at all."

I was scared, but also weirdly relieved. So I was right, after all, this was just a mess; Nick had no clue what he was talking about. It was embarrassing to be up there delivering it, but now Nick would get his. Or so I thought.

George addressed me directly before I could begin to supply any answer.

"Lewis, do you mean to say there's a connection here between buying behavior and crude costs? Surely that's too long a stretch of any data chain? What were you hoping to show here?"

"Um, well, Nick . . ." I began, unaccustomed to being called on the carpet before any consulting officer, much less in front of a client.

Nick jumped in immediately.

"Lewis, I had no idea this is where you were going with this. I thought you were going to suggest brand *strategies* for the new crude's possible products, not give us an historical survey of Shell's database," Nick declared, leading a few of the Shell executives to chuckle. "I thought the data was just for the appendix."

I was speechless. There was no Mike here to corroborate; Nick had suggested he stay in Boston so as not to not incur unnecessary travel costs. I was sure the look on my face communicated "But Nick, this was your fucking idea," and the look on his face brazenly dared me to make the accusation.

"Look, why don't we just go on," Hixon suggested, clearly embarrassed for me. "I'm sure there's something in the data we can all dig out later, but let's leave this framework behind and just make some progress."

My heart fell through my stomach. This *was* the presentation, there was no more, and Nick knew it. But he just sat there silently, looking severely disappointed for me. George apparently felt sorry for Nick and was beginning to give me a threatening look.

"Well, this is pretty much it," I replied lamely, flipping forward a few dozen slides to what I thought were maybe the most interesting trends. "I still think we might extract a few ideas for product positioning for HDMO."

The heavy duty motor oil manager actually looked interested, and was about to speak up, but seeing Hixon's skeptical look, George overrode any further discussion, and dressed me down then and there.

"Lewis, this is just irresponsible. You've taken weeks with this data and not shared it with any of us, including Nick. We're all here to help you, but you can't just show up and ask us to buy your theories if you don't really know what you're talking about. I'm going to ask you to sit down now. Shut off the overhead. Nick, why don't you review where we're at overall and go over the next steps."

I sat down as instructed, utterly humiliated, and wishing the black death upon Nick. In later postmortem, Nick would claim he had only sketched out an idea of the kind of thing that might be useful to analyze, and that he expected me to come up with my own framework and test it rigorously to my own satisfaction. If I thought it less than perfect, it was my responsibility to go to Nick, or if necessary, George or someone else, for validation and reassurance. That I felt Nick had been avoiding me carried little or no weight.

For the next six months, I stayed on the Shell case, condemned to outlining the petroleum wax refinery's capacities for handling the new crude. It was a literal purgatory, crawling across rusted, hot gratings in the blazing south Texan sun, hoping that the boiling crude and venting fire streams would not consume me in their greed for more fuel. The assignment would weigh heavily against both Mike and me for many months to come and even influence a discussion years later at a BCG partners meeting in Europe, where my proposed rehiring as partner for the Boston Consulting Group's new office in Singapore would be bruited.

On the occasions I got home to Boston—where, somewhat to my surprise, my wife had taken up residence again—my sense of defeat was palpable, and frightening to us both. We began to retreat to a pattern where my main worth seemed to be only in supporting our comfortable but lonely lifestyle, augmented by frequent and expensive trips to Japan. The most we really shared was a sense that it was time to find a respectable path back to Tokyo, whatever the cost.

HOW CONSULTANTS DIVINE A FRACTURING ENGAGEMENT

1

Overreaching. Most engagements that are likely to go bad begin with overreaching commitments to clients, involving more time, manpower, and expertise than the consulting firm can really provide. That this happens with some frequency is not something that consulting companies mind clients knowing, since it can raise anxieties sufficiently for clients to spend much more than needed on an assignment, just to ensure that a lack of capacity does not ruin the client's investment in the help. Ironically, the ever-larger commitments that result, in the attempt to provide the broadest possible coverage ensuring against failure, encourage specialized sales forces, which greatly increases the danger of overreaching. The senior partners and marketing executives tasked exclusively to sell these large cases are typically so far removed from the conduct of the work that they are much more likely to oversell than undersell.

2

Ignoring inner danger signals. Most consultants develop an important inner sense of what can and cannot be accomplished on an assignment, of whether personal and professional resources will be overstretched, of how pleasant or horrible a given engagement may become. This is an inner voice that deserves heeding. Based on experience, consultants learn the limits of their own physical and mental capabilities, and the strengths and weaknesses of their supporting team. A consultant also learns to sense when a client may be asking too much out of fear or ignorance, or is instead consciously exploiting the consultant, fully aware that limits may be dangerously crossed.

3

Misplaced trust. Another sign of potential case catastrophe is early evidence of abused trust, whether shown by consulting colleagues or clients involved in the day-to-day running of the engagement. Awash in their own stress and anxiety about the case, other members of the case team will often signal to both their clients and colleagues, subtly and subconsciously, that they are not to be relied upon. Late deliverables, missed appointments, and irregular responses to requests and instructions are all indicators that under major stress, things are more than likely to come apart. Forced control of these smaller issues is no guarantee of better outcome for the bigger stakes, either: resources and energy may instead simply be channeled into micro-compliance, creating even higher risks for major outputs and objectives. Reliable consultants try to spell out explicit expectations for the things that matter, and either readjust commitments, or create and use progress checkpoints that can better ensure the desired outcomes.

4

Inordinate faith in weight of data. Cases that begin to show obsession with large quantities of data also run a high danger of fractured expectations. Clients, of course, usually take little comfort from large amassing of data, unless the key objective is to explicitly exhaust data and information to ensure the validity of a particular point of view. Most often, consultants know that clients are looking for reassurance and understanding, a bigger picture that somehow incorporates all the facts and data, whatever the quantity or state of completeness of the research may be. The ideal study in almost all instances suggests a call to action, with a strategy for the long term, but complete with immediate next steps as well. A mound of data is only likely to create a higher sense of urgency for finding such a strategy and course of action.

5

Alienation from the client's business. Consultants are presumed to love business, the creation of advantages for making a better profit. The expectation by clients and consulting firms alike is that the particular line of business that the client happens to be in should not matter. The reality however is often the reverse. Consultants almost never make more money when their clients do, even when the additional income is a result of their work. Consultants instead take a natural interest in the nature of the business itself, strongly identifying with the client's customers, products, and corporate culture. Unraveling the problems of a cosmetics company, a software firm, or an airline will have different appeal for different consultants than helping along an automaker, cigarette manufacturer, or logging company. Consultants who fight to get on cases involving businesses that they like, or at least do not hate, go a long way toward good client-consultant relations and successful completion. Chances are high that an unattractive case will have at least one other alienated consultant assigned to it and may involve clients with destructively low self-esteem. Avoiding the resonating effects of shared disillusionment by staying off the case is best for consultant and client alike; a growing sense of alienation during a case should call for a deeper examination of what might be attractive about the company and the work, or suggest an early exit.

6

Missing scheduled meetings and deliverables. A simple, clear, but often ignored sign that a case is going south is recurrent misses of scheduled meetings and outputs. They are a sign that the case was poorly designed and structured, has reached unmanageable proportions, or is creating dysfunctional behaviors in the case team. Signaling the need to pause and reevaluate the dimensions and ambitions of the assignment, too often they are met simply with admonitions to work harder and faster.

7

Poorly structured outputs. Despite high-stakes pressures, seemingly intractable problems beyond in-hand expertise, and often impossible deadlines, consulting case teams do normally produce satisfying solutions of some kind, be they small but critical insights revealing how the larger issues may be worked out, or broader clarifications that suggest a complete answer to the client's needs. With much of their whole being tied up in such results, consultants take immense pride in such outcomes, and almost always find a few spare hours to dress up the documentation of the results. Even modest conclusions are usually well presented, perhaps in the belief that the client deserves at least that much for their money. Too often accepted as the inevitable result of mere haste, poorly produced or illogically structured presentation material and reports are in fact more often a sign of low confidence and little pride in the work, as well as confusion about direction and outcomes.

8

Constant checking of the original proposal. Even at their best, consulting proposals are typically wishful expressions of hoped-for outcomes, lent some structure by who is assigned to what tasks, at what billing rate, and for how long. Though usually highly critical to the initial sale, once signed, the proposal becomes a contract for billing purposes, but normally serves little purpose beyond acquainting new members of the case team with basic presumptions and providing boilerplate for future proposals. Later frequent referral to the original proposal, by either client or consultant, at best signifies an anal-retentive literal-mindedness or a loss of direction and confidence. At worst, and in all probability, it marks defense strategies for an anticipated mortal confrontation.

9

Secret meetings. Clients are typically more clued in about the significance of secret, private, and unscheduled meetings than are consultants. Consulting and case team hierarchies are designed to be open and fluid, obviating the need for private lines of communication. When client or consultant team leaders, who are supposed to be at the nexus of all concerns to the engagement, find that the buying client is holed up unexpectedly with the case officer, or client team members with their boss, or their own consulting subordinates with each other, this is an omen that things may not be on course.

10

Not getting paid. Amazingly, this final, fatal signal is one that is too often missed. A client can skip or withhold a payment, and the consultant will simply believe it is a mistake of accounting. Contacting the day-to-day liaison from the client team and being reassured that it will be checked into, the consultant allows the delay then to be forgotten, ignored, or wished away. What is likely happening, however, is that a higher level authorization for payment is being withheld, unknown to the client liaison, until some specific element of perceived failure of performance is addressed. The senior-most client is unhappy, and needs to see more: once satisfied, payment will be quickly made; dissatisfied, and delay can unfold into nonpayment and total loss of the client relationship. Clients should not assume this signal is understood!

CHAPTER 6

BIG-TIME CONSULTING

FROM BOSTON TO LONDON, SUMMER 1990

THERE IS A WIDE-OPEN RANCH LAND NESTLED AMONGST THE ROCKIES, A place where great wealth and architectural indulgence make a kind of home from otherwise magnificent isolation. It is a place where, in a few short hours, I learned more of the changing textures of the consulting industry than I would by any other means or experience. There, I also first glimpsed a life portending much of what lay ahead for me and the industry as a whole.

I arrived in Big Sky country in a state of mild disbelief. By this time in 1990 in some respects, I had lived a relatively short and simple consulting life, and the new job I sought seemed a straightforward enough hire. After four years with the Boston Consulting Group, in Tokyo and Boston, I had all but given up on consulting, and my Japanese wife had all but given up on me. The blame-sharing and finger pointing that followed my ignominious presentation to Shell had worn out my hospitality at Boston headquarters, and my return offer for work at BCG Tokyo was unexciting, aimed more at closing the internal company culture gap than developing clients of my own.

101

Instead, I left BCG for a respectable client corporate planning job
with a General Electric–Japanese joint venture, in the hopes I would
get a more attractive assignment back in Tokyo. In less than six
months I found myself way out of my depth, unable to cope with the
intrigues of veteran bureaucrats from the joint venture's parent companies. My summons to Wyoming was the final leg in joining one of
BCG's competitors, the MAC Group, who apparently happened to
need a manager for their new Tokyo office.

As a consultant, one's life and work are uniquely exposed to one's
colleagues, a fact that makes for relatively simple cross-hiring from
one firm to another. The long hours, frenetic travel, and routine over-
commitments and deceptions assure a high level of stress. The big
money and big egos involved are also almost sure, from time to time,
to yield some crazy responses to that stress, and reveal either a well-
polished surface of promising grace, brilliance, and stamina or
glimpses of a fear-soaked, punished inner self, desperate, stupid, and
dangerously frayed. A few phone calls can usually turn up a handful
of stories of client engagements won and lost, recoveries good and
bad from mistakes major and minor, and personal sacrifices made or
avoided in good or useless causes.

Asking former colleagues and clients "Would you like him on
your team today?" is a quick and almost always accurate way to
assess an experienced consultant's fitness for a new firm, if you can
trust your informants. Following a few intensive interviews to assess
any possible indoctrinated culture clashes and to determine interest
and capabilities for the work at hand, a cross-hiring can be quickly
decided.

So what was I doing here, I wondered. MAC and the Boston
Consulting Group were close, incestuously close in the parts I hailed
from. BCG Tokyo's founder, Jim Abegglen, had left to form his own
company in Tokyo, Asia Advisory Services, and had set up an alliance
with MAC. Lots of ex-BCGers worked for him, and at least in theory
he still worked with the Boston Consulting Group on some of his
writing and case leads. I had friends at MAC and AAS, and they had

plenty of friends at BCG. I had known Abegglen, and he certainly had access to my history at BCG. I had no doubts that it had been thoroughly sussed out.

MAC and BCG were also culturally very similar. Originally the Management Analysis Corporation, MAC picked up "Group" in identification with BCG. They were both Boston/Cambridge based, drew heavily from the resources of the Harvard Business School, and excelled as boutiques specializing in niche consulting applications. They tended to favor smart, upstart solutions over the stodgy formulas of industry stalwarts Arthur D. Little and McKinsey, but nicely trimmed their brashness for well-mannered presentation in the boardroom. I was confident that my relative comfort with BCG's bright-but-gentlemanly style would serve me well at MAC.

The case-content interviews also seemed to have gone fine. They had not been particularly challenging, and mainly allowed me to explain problem-solving approaches by using examples of my own selection, from my own experiences. Variations of "what if the client had done this" are usually more fun than taxing in these situations.

I felt like it was just time to get on with it. I looked forward to finally moving back to Tokyo and was confident that working with Abegglen, my AAS friends, and the MAC Group would restore me to greater freedoms and self-respect. I was still ambivalent about consulting as a career and had toyed with a return to school instead, but reasoned that I had not yet had enough of the money and experience I craved in Japan. I was excited at the prospect of being closer to the top than the bottom of the consulting hierarchy, and, having had a sobering stint in client-land that distinctly lacked glamour, I was prepared for more and better indulgences.

I was afraid these were the issues "Alan Johnston" wanted to probe, that somehow he sensed that I did not want a return to consulting badly enough. I was on my way to Johnston's Wyoming home, for reasons no one would specify. I went with some resentment, believing that, having already discussed salary and all the other niceties in detail, I had the job already and Johnston represented a waste of time at best, and at worst, a threat to my new job.

Ostensibly, I was to see Alan because he was slated to be MAC's representative officer in Asia. But in my one telephone conversation with him this did not seem to be the case. I was staying with Mike and Susie Garrity in Hawai'i, the last leg of my journey to Japan, when we first spoke.

"Lewis, this is Alan Johnston from MAC calling. How is it there in Hawai'i? Have I got you in the right time zone?"

"Absolutely," I replied, "It's really nice here, pretty much always is." It was early morning, and from the phone in the kitchen I could see that Rob's kids had discovered that my pile of luggage made for an excellent king-of-the-hill battleground. Rob's exit from consulting and BCG, and subsequent sailing to Hawai'i to make a new home, seemed to me just then one of the noblest and most enviable things imaginable. Unlike me, he had come out of BCG with his marriage fully intact. He had not made qualified case leader on his specified time line, but the company had offered him another six months to *really* bust his nuts and try again. Sanely, Mike had made his way here and was gently trying to persuade me to join him in consulting to a new boating venture.

"In fact, if I stay much longer, I may not leave," I added to Johnston, surprised to hear the edge in my own voice.

"Well, I'm sorry we've kept you suspended there for a little bit. You know, I've heard great things about you, I can't imagine anyone better suited for our needs in Japan. Morikawa over at BCG thinks you're the greatest."

I let that hang. Was I being paranoid, I wondered, or was that a subtle message? At this point I did not know whether Morikawa would count me as friend or enemy. He was sympathetic to my exit. In fact, he and other BCG Tokyo officers felt I was getting a raw deal and had dutifully tried to introduce me to BCG clients, which had ultimately led to my assignment with the General Electric joint venture. But no one had really suspected that I would hook up with a competitor, and I knew feelings were getting bitter between BCG and

Abegglen. Moreover, and probably worst of all, everyone back in the office there felt protective of my now twice rerouted wife, their former receptionist.

"Thing is, there's a lot going on here now," Alan went on, "There are some things we should discuss."

"Are you going to be in Japan?"

"No, I'm still based in London. Right now, I'm on vacation with my family in Wyoming. Normally I'd ask you to see me when I'm back in London in a few weeks, but I think you should come see me here now. This breaks one of my strongest rules as far as my family goes, so I would have to ask you to help me keep things sharp and brief, leave when I tell you." I would later discover that Alan had a rather amazing set of rules as regards his family.

"Um, of course. This isn't something we could discuss by phone? It is kind of going back in the wrong direction, and it *is* your vacation."

"No, this really isn't a phone thing. Look, my secretary will get you all set with tickets and everything. I don't want to send you the wrong signal. Obviously, we're very interested in you. I think it would be good if we got you set up on our voicemail system now; it might help to get you in the loop and catch you up on some things. My secretary will call you from London later today."

With that, Alan hung up, and Mike wandered into the kitchen.

"What's up? Ready to change your mind yet?"

"I'm not sure I have one to change. Look, I'm sorry about this, but looks like I'm supposed to go visit this grand pooh-bah's vacation home in Wyoming for some kind of final anointing before I can go to Japan. Do you mind if I leave most of my luggage here?"

"'Course not. The kids will take good care of it. You must really mean something to those MAC people. Maybe they think you're worth even more than they thought, want you to head Asia from Cambridge or something."

"Nice fantasy, but it's exactly what I don't need. I started a life in Japan and I'd like to see things through."

"You might be surprised. Anyway, remember what I said. And if they have something more important in mind for you, remember to ask for lots more money and come back and buy us a nice dinner. And if they look like they're going to change their minds, go and have fun with it, pee on his dog or something, make a scene. I'm still wishing I had done something like that when I left BCG."

"Fine, but if I pee on anyone's dog, you're buying."

Wyoming and Honolulu do not share a lot of air traffic, and I wound up renting a van in Boise, Idaho, which arrived dusty and sulfurous at Alan's ranch after a journey of a couple of hundred miles, much of it by Yellowstone National Park. Any other time I would have enjoyed the geology, but I was too worried about arriving late.

Alan greeted me in his newly graveled driveway. "What do you know about the history of consulting?" Tall, spare, and very much younger than I had expected, he had a gentle appearance that immediately disarmed his directness. He had much the appeal of the young Jerry Brown, and indeed I would learn they shared certain mystic fascinations. We headed inside.

"You mean, generally? Um, probably a fair amount, I guess. Out in Tokyo everyone kind of makes a big deal of their roots. Everybody's offices are jammed together in one city, managing the whole country, if not all of Asia, from there. The consulting firms arrived about the same time in Japan, and the firms all look alike to most Japanese clients. So anything that can distinguish among the firms gets a lot of emphasis, and history can count a lot. But I recall we're pressed for time."

"No, I mean yes, we are, but I'm interested." Alan settled us with coffee at the kitchen table. "I'd like to get your perspective on a few things, get your sense of MAC's competitive positioning and how it got there. Just try to be concise; don't be surprised if I cut you off here or there."

I had hardly caught my breath or had time to soak in my surroundings. Alan's ranch looked oddly like a suburban development. It was beautifully constructed, rich in stone and wood, bright and cheery. But, surprisingly close by, there were apparently identical structures, some still being built. Surrounding these replicants seemed to be endless open scrub, nothing one would actually "ranch" on, cut through by a new road. Designed as a ski refuge, I concluded, but it was high summer now, and I sympathized with Alan's two young sons, who looked very bored; his wife was nowhere in sight. It seemed like it could be a very lonely place.

"Well, um, in the beginning, then. In the beginning, there was ADL. MIT, where I graduated, kind of gave it birth about a hundred years ago. Arthur D. Little was an MIT student too bored or too smart, I guess, to graduate, and he really set up what would become the first general consultancy, building from a chemical analysis business. He had some important insights, finding a niche in bridging high-academic smarts and the needs of good old general industry."

"Ever been over there?"

"Sure. They used to actually be on campus; now they're not far from MAC's Cambridge offices. Looks like MIT must have in the 1950s, very clean and scrubbed, no posters, guys in short sleeves and pocket protectors. Not my scene, but they helped create the 'deeply experienced' and 'expertly knowledgeable' aura that they and McKinsey still seem to try to generate. 'Knowledge at Work' and all that."

"They were first—so why aren't they biggest now?"

"Well, there's business, and then there's government. McKinsey picked up on ADL's strengths just about before the World War Two, I guess, and began to emphasize much more of the organizational skills and issues that became so important to the war effort. After the war McKinsey applied these systems to the private business sector, and they really took off. ADL became dependent on the more reliable, but slower growing, government contracts business. They didn't even get to own that niche for very long; Booz Allen and Hamilton stepped in later to take a large chunk of it."

"For a long while, though, it was just ADL and McKinsey."

"That's right, at least until Bruce Henderson came along. I spent some time talking with him at BCG's twenty-fifth anniversary party last year. Mostly we talked about *Scientific American* articles, how he used to pluck them for ideas for business applications. He, like Abegglen just before he teamed up with him, had worked with ADL and I think McKinsey and decided that there could be a more idea-driven, research-intensive approach to consulting. He formed the research arm of what I believe became the Bank of Boston, and then took that independent in forming the Boston Consulting Group in the early 1960s.

"Henderson and BCG got great mileage out of producing a bunch of intellectual products, you know, neatly summarizing strategic situations and options: the portfolio matrix, the experience curve, the two-by-two matrix. It was revolutionary stuff. Clients loved these things, they could use them themselves, but by the time they figured them out, Bruce would come up with something new."

"Imitators rose up, of course."

"Yes, BCG spawning quite a few of them. Bain was a BCG vice president before he started Bain and Company. A.T. Kearney, with its operations emphasis, more closely followed the button-downed McKinsey type approach. Specialists like the MAC Group, of course, began to find their niche."

One of Alan's kids brought over a drawing for our inspection. I realized I must be the only visitor he had ever seen here, and I was probably quite a disappointment on the entertainment front.

"What's happening now, Lewis? What do you see changing?"

"Well, in Tokyo we see the international expansion of all these firms, of course."

"What about the accounting firms?"

"Oh. They're kind of interesting in Tokyo. All of the Big Eight firms, Price-Waterhouse, Ernst and Young, they've got a strong presence going. The Japanese think we're the same kind of firm, and it's helping them, not us. We can't do the tax accounting and auditing, but they can sure give advice. And they've been in Tokyo decades longer than us; they've built up a lot of trust. The Japanese companies are still pretty tight with their secrets, and they'd rather give them up to people they know. Arthur Andersen is getting surprising mileage out of their technology businesses, too."

"Tell me about that," Alan instructed, an added intensity in his eyes.

"Well, they had the same start as the other accountancies, but they've been very aggressive in deploying computers and software solutions, not just their own stuff for the books, but business systems generally, stuff for order handling, materials control, the whole lot. They seem to take a lot of off-the-shelf product from different vendors and package it all up, put their seal of approval on it. They install and train, too. Now they're calling themselves more of a technology solutions company, and that's attracted them some general consulting business too, though at BCG they never seemed a threat."

"Ever had a proposal run up against Andersen?"

"No, I don't think we did, at least I didn't."

"Suppose you had had one: How would you distinguish BCG? How would you fight it? Suppose it was in Europe, say. And let me flip that around. Suppose you're Andersen, writing against BCG, and the client has both strategy and technology needs."

I could sense Alan was on to something now, but this was new territory for me.

"Well, if I knew the only other serious contender was the Boston Consulting Group, I'd be afraid to segregate the strategy piece out from the work. I wouldn't want to tempt the client to split the strategy to them and the systems to us. So I'd find ways of revealing strategy needs in every parcel of the technology work. In fact, I might low-ball the technology price by picking out only the system elements that might have strategic impact. I might have a summary paragraph on strategy up front, but I'd embed as much detail as I could into the technology and systems approach part, make them seamless.

"I'd bang hard on how essential it was to do the technology work, and how much cheaper it might be to integrate knowledge of the systems into the strategy from the beginning, rather than discovering that the strategy and the technology didn't work out later. I'd try to illustrate with a bunch of examples, you know, systems as strategy or something, Federal Express's one central hub logistics, that kind of thing. I'd pound all the savings elements, of course, two for the price of one, and training. We'd do the training, sensitive to the client's strategy needs, something like that. We'll be around more, 'cause we have to, to get everything running, we won't just drop the presentation and run. I don't know, I'm still reaching. There's no getting around experience in strategy."

"I think you maybe just did," Alan said with a brief smile. "What do you know about United Research?"

"Not much, we never ran into them at BCG. All I really remember is that their headquarters is in Morristown, New Jersey, which just sounds embarrassing to me, and they do factory floor cost reduction, like A.T. Kearney but more gimmicky. They have an eight-hundred number or something. Not strategy consultants."

"Ever hear of C.K. Prahalad, or a company called Change Management Initiative, CMI?"

"Prahalad, I think. He was in Japan, doing some research. Isn't he a business school professor?"

"That's right, at Michigan. Do you think BCG would ever sell to an outside buyer?"

"Wow, maybe, but it doesn't seem likely. The European and Japanese partners would create a stink, for one thing. They don't get a full cut in the company, something to do with the Bank of Boston's lingering influence on the company's shares. Culturally, the company seems very big on its independence. You know ADL tried an IPO, made a huge mess of it, withdrew to being privately held again. That kind of thing makes BCG cringe."

"So if you wanted a strategy house, what would you do? Suppose you were Andersen, and like you said, you could do all those things in combination, but it would be hard without the strategy reputation."

I had a glimmer of where this might be headed. Oh, this might be good, I thought, very good indeed. I began to wish Mike could hear this conversation.

"Well, I might look at the MAC Group, since you put the idea in my head. It's smaller, and very focused on financial modeling and analysis, and still viewed a bit as the toy of the Harvard Business School professors who created it to be their research arm. But you also have a great strategy cache, a reputation for smarts, innovation in thinking, a polite ability to question every assumption, all that BCG has. Being even more of a boutique makes you more BCG than BCG. You're bite-sized, the firm could probably be pried loose without too much complication, very limited—sorry, not to be insulting—international expansion."

"Go on," Alan added quietly.

"Thing is, why hasn't it happened yet? Maybe like BCG there are a lot of stubborn partners who wouldn't be ready to work with or for something else. Not to pry, but there was a rumor, you mentioned United Research."

"They tried to buy us, and we fought and they lost. I would prefer that stayed a rumor, by the way. Look, Lewis, let's get some more coffee."

By now Alan's boys were getting antsy, and I joined them in their repeatedly aired curiosity about when Mom was getting back. They seemed to have finished their drawings. Without having even met her, I found myself unaccountably annoyed at Alan's wife for not being here to take care of them. Of course, I had no doubt ruined whatever plans they had for the day. We spent a couple of minutes suggesting new things for the kids to draw.

"My wife will be back before long, and that's when you should go. I'm sorry about all the questions and hypotheticals, but I'm going to confirm your offer, and before I do I want you to know what you're joining. Ideally, I'd like to know that you've accepted before you leave, because I have to tell you, I'm uncomfortable sharing some of the details with you."

In other words, if I do not accept, you will have to kill me, I could not help thinking melodramatically to myself. "If MAC is in motion, you've got my professional assurance that whatever you helped me deduce here, stays with me. And I'd like to think that won't be an issue, because I'm sure there must be an attractive solution here."

"Right. Look, United Research and MAC *are* going to get together, but only because we will have a joint parent that can regulate the pace. It will be a merger of the two firms, not a takeover, with time to draw best practices from both."

I nodded encouragingly.

"The parent is European, the French software services firm Cap Gemini Sogeti, number one in Europe in their field. They'll want active involvement—Cap Gemini already has its own Andersen-like consultancy."

"So, we'll have strategy, systems, *and* operations. We could do really huge cases."

"We can do *only* huge cases. The way this thing works, with the assignments absorbing the full staffing of five, ten, or twenty thousand people, is through engagements in the tens of millions of dollars. We all still find this a little incredible, but we now have those kind of cases lined up."

"In Japan?"

"No, that's an issue. It makes *you* an issue. We at MAC acquired Asia Advisory Services, and our new partners will live with that. Some of our new assignments, on global deployments, will catch up with Japan and Asia, and I know we'll be glad for the infrastructure. But the expectations for someone of your seniority will be different than any you've experienced so far.

"What I mean to say is, Lewis, I'm not sure you should head for Japan right away. We could do it, but then you'd be one of Abegglen's boys, an acquisition buried in an acquisition. All the excitement's about to happen in Europe, where there are a lot of fresh cases to be sold under the Cap Gemini blanket. The United States will stay status quo for a while, two firms. I'd like to get you on the front lines of one of the big cases, maybe for a year, first. You'd learn more about how MAC is different from BCG, and you'd learn day by day with us how the Cap Gemini and UR integration will pan out. I still plan to go to Japan myself; it's been my dream for years. But we could go together as a working team."

Money. It was now time to take up Rob's advice on money.

"You know, Alan, I had sort of worked out a package with MAC based on different assumptions."

"Oh, I think we can help you out. In fact, if we position your assignment in Europe, in London with me, as strategic and temporary, I think we can get you a full expat package—which you shouldn't expect for Japan, by the way."

"That's great, that would be really good." It's terrific! I fairly wanted to scream. On foreign assignments subpartners rarely got to spend their money on much more than essentials. The high life in London could make it very pleasant to wait for Tokyo.

I tried to focus. Okay Mike, here's your dinner if this works: "But Alan, you know in my last transfer I lost out on more than just the living package, I got cut down on the bonus. I imagine there will be some retention awards for managers to stay on after the merger, but I won't be there to be retained, I'll be new. I'd kind of feel like I was losing out, just when I should be excited."

"Funny, I just got an voicemail on this before you came over. Look I can't give you a total guarantee, but there is a deal in the works for the managers. The partners got settled weeks ago, of course. I don't know if there will be a pool finally approved for the managers or not, but I promise if it is approved, you'll be cut in like the others. I'll put it in your file and the voicemail I'm going to send soon as you leave. Right now the pool for managers is at $150,000, vested over three years."

This was a *lot* for a mid-level consultant in the early 1990s, and would certainly justify a dinner for Mike. My last semiannual bonus had been $14,000. I was eager to leave before Alan began to change his mind about things.

"Well, that really addresses the one basic issue for me, finding acceptance as a manager like any other. The time in London, and the time with you, with the compensation you've just outlined, more than addresses all that. I'm happy to be joining something as big and exciting as you outlined. I'll want to learn a lot more, of course, but it sounds like the delayed move to Japan makes for a better move there. I want in."

We shook hands. "You've got it. We probably have a couple of minutes left, Lewis, tell me something about yourself I don't know from the others." Uh-oh, I thought, the dreaded motivation questions are coming. Time to head this off and show a healthy interest in money.

"Well, you *do* know a lot. But with everyone else I talk about why consulting is such a strong fit for me, not so much the motivations. Truth is, I've lived in Japan as a poor entry-level salary man in a big Japanese company, and then had a reasonably nice setup there under BCG. But my commitments will grow, and Tokyo is really fun place to live really well, which basically means expensively. Some day I might like to do some teaching and writing, maybe in some kind of sabbatical arrangement with consulting. Just getting to that point could take an awful lot of, well, money. BCG's last offer for me in Tokyo was exciting but much thinner on the pay and almost zero on the promotion prospects. This last client job had a lot of non-money security, but I got hemmed in fast for trying to push my own ideas."

Alan nodded approvingly. "You may find we're a lot alike. I like you, Lewis."

I *felt* liked. I would find Alan to always have a winning sincerity, an ability to be open from which he could draw tremendous energies.

Now I wanted to get out. Gratefully, I heard the sound of car tires crunching gravel. "Lewis, one day ask me to tell you about my days at divinity school. They have more to do with my consulting than my Smith Barney banking experiences."

I had heard that Alan had built his MAC career on the back of the small miracle of quitting Smith Barney, and then bringing Smith Barney into the MAC client fold with him. Nonetheless I found the divinity school clue more intriguing.

"I want to hear all about it."

I was really charged up. A new, unforeseen career in one of the most profound blendings in the industry, being close to the hub of one of the largest linkages ever attempted, and getting paid well for it, seemed nothing short of marvelous, especially when six months earlier I had thought I had left consulting for good. Images of Mayfair flats, the best of London's pubs and clubs, museums and bookstores started to pulse between my upper and lower brain stem.

In the next instant my brain was in fight-or-flight mode.

"Janet, this is Lewis. I told you about him. He's just leaving."

Was I ever! Janet Johnston in one piercing look made me feel like the most evil of intruders and violators. Flight mode. I hoped, vainly, that she would not figure in my newly imagined consulting life.

CONSULTING DEMONOLOGY, TRACT 6

CLIENT BE DAMNED: HOW CONSULTING COMPANIES BEDEVIL EACH OTHER

1

Out-acquire competitors. Consulting industry growth continues to accelerate in a way that defies homegrown staff development and training. At one time, a handful of aggressive firms would acquire key competitors' senior staff or, on occasion, smaller firms, with the aim of picking up their long-term clients. Now, growth by acquisition has become so critical, and demand for consulting services so overwhelming, that virtually all leading firms lean heavily on acquisition for their expansion. In the process, they usually could not care less about the clients served by the staff they poach. The acquiring firm already has its own, no doubt better paying, clients beating down their doors. Ideally, these firms prefer to strip out lower-fee consultants from their acquiree's lower-paying clients, and then mark up the newly acquired consultants' billing fees for use against larger game. The new client pays a high premium, while the old client is left stranded or in search of new, no doubt higher-cost assistance.

2

Go under budget. Finding what appears to be a priority client for a key competitor, and getting in a low bid for services before the competitor can react, is an increasingly common tactic for disabling competing firms' price structures. If the competitor should win with an even lower bid, they will be stretched to meet the tasks committed and will be in a constant struggle with their client to see how much of their best-quality consultants' time they can withhold. If the intervening firm wins instead, fair pricing for a first phase of work can be introduced, with much higher pricing reserved for later phases.

3

Steal client staff. United Research led the charge in the use of more mature, but lower-paid, general industry MBAs to staff up large assignments and flummox the pricing strategies of the traditional consulting houses. Other firms have quickly discovered not only the cost advantages of these arrangements, but also that the industry expertise acquired can readily be used on assignments with the newly hired staff's old employer's competitors. Now, the more audacious firms engage new clients on otherwise unattractive assignments for the explicit purpose of discovering and working with potential new recruits. The victimized client stands to not only lose their key staff, but to see them deployed, albeit indirectly, in the service of their competitors, circumventing contractual non-compete clauses forbidding direct employment.

4

Use caged gurus as offensive weapons. With the growth of interest in consulting, and as senior consultants are increasingly stretched for time and become all but inaccessible to the average client, clients and would-be clients have turned with considerable appetite to the works in print by leading consulting gurus. The expanding number of books offering consulting advice and the increased readership of journals like the *Harvard Business Review* and the McKinsey's and Booz Allen's strategy magazine reflect this trend and challenge consulting companies to keep up client perceptions of intellectual leadership in print. For all the major firms there is now a general expectation that if the wisdom offered by the firm is so great, there must be some guru in the company who is reasonably well published. Savvy firms now employ such gurus, typically business school professors with time on their hands and not billed-out engagement consultants, to do nothing but keep up appearances. They focus on churning out a steady stream of material to the press, feeding on case reports and client documentation from consultants in the field, and are rolled out for the occasional sales call or board-level presentation. This forces other consulting firms, which do not have these pet improvisers at their disposal, to make expensive use of their stretched senior resources to take time to get things in print, producing thin treatises with lots of graphic fillers that are more likely to be embarrassing than revealing.

5

Propose everything. In the hope that competitors will stretch themselves as thin as possible to keep up, some consulting firms have taken to proposing, or better still, appearing to propose, every new opportunity. Traditionally, proposal writing has been something of an industry art form, involving detailed preliminary analyses and hypothesis development and careful alignment of staff resources in anticipation of a possible acceptance. Since proposals are free to the client, proposal-writing economics are singularly unattractive to the firms creating them. Consequently, for all but the most demanding, high-priority clients, proposal outputs going into the new century tend to be thin on thinking and content, featuring more recycled product and less actual commitment of the most suitable resources.

CHAPTER 7

BUSINESS PROP WASH

LONDON, WINTER 1990

I<small>T TOOK ME SOME TIME TO GET SETTLED IN</small> L<small>ONDON</small>. H<small>OUSEHOLD</small> goods shipped from Boston and my GE job site in Virginia to storage in London and my in-laws in Tokyo, while I took up residence in a serviced apartment, and my wife, probably wisely, stayed clear of the havoc. I was given immediate work on a standard bank reengineering case, a not particularly demanding review of a savings and loan operation that had gone too quickly into free checking accounts and debit cards. Alan and Tokyo were out of sight and mind, and I contented myself with weeks of utterly mindless bank process diagramming by day, and whiskey and cigars by night, waiting to see what would happen next. What happened next was change management.

"Change management" is now general consulting jargon for products and processes aimed at helping companies manage change. By the time I was ensconced in Gemini London in the early 1990s, it had become the hallmark of Michigan Business School professor C.K. Prahalad, the central icon of his Change Management Initiative company, or CMI. Change Management's absorption into the consulting argot, and its considerable continued attraction for clients, attest to its impressive evangelical power in justifying headcount reductions in profitable and unprofitable companies alike, and in nimbly keeping large workforces cowed, ever on edge and in fear of further, unfathomable random acts springing from the weird matrix of management, consultants, and investment analysts.

For consulting firms, change management offers a secure way to continuously field large numbers of consultants through the greatest pyramid scheme in the industry. A typical change management engagement will involve extensive internal interviews with key managers, some external competitive homework, an emotionally bludgeoning three- or four-day off-site revival-style meeting of forty or fifty top managers, and a commitment by those managers to carry on the flame through similar meetings with their own top fifty reports, creating a cascade of trauma and strong-armed commitment that does not end until the last and lowest worker has got the touch of that old-time religion. Throughout, consultants stoke the flames, facilitating and often leading the sessions, creating a dozen or more follow-up projects from each one, each often requiring further consulting supervision.

The continuity of the exercise rests with the consultants alone: few managers would agree to sustain the week-in, week-out pace of travel to far-flung operations in order to camp out away from family and endure sessions designed to provide no relief from the pressure to dwell on one's inadequacies and failures. To be sure that the one channel of venting and relief approved by the facilitators, namely nothing but even harder work to achieve the impossible, is fully embraced, the sessions are purposely designed to offer no private time, no exercise, no non-business discussions, ensuring that the only way to blow off steam is to redirect it into the company engines. Typically the consultants come to know the global health and capabilities of the client better than any client executive, enabling them to move beyond being mere facilitators to indispensable leaders of new business projects, ever extending the net of consulting engagement fees.

The simplest and perhaps most cynical use of change management are engagements sold to help clients cope with changes inflicted by the consulting company itself. Such engagements are typically poorly defined add-ons, bought as an insurance or transition policy that the client hopes might encourage consultant accountability rather than a consult-and-run finish. For the consulting firm, such add-ons ensure extra billing hours, a potential absorber of overruns, and a paid excuse to hang out and look for more work to sell.

Some firms sell change management as a kind of communications pool, a hub or focus for multiple angles of attack. Gemini pioneered this use in rationalizing simultaneous sales of services from each of its newly merged consulting arms. In a kickoff $35 million sale for the overhaul of Mobil France, the newly formed Gemini brought all its newly acquired entities to bear: United Research for reengineering, Cap Gemini Sogeti for computer systems, and the MAC Group for financial modeling and strategy. These three were the "blades" of the business propeller model, with change management becoming the fourth and central activity, the coordinating hub of the propeller that would confidently thrust Mobil's business to waters unknown. For Gemini, it became a means of absorbing the coordination costs of its own merger, while delivering a package of work for which Mobil would arguably have paid much more in separate sourcing.

The success of the Mobil sale greased the skids for Gemini's multimillion dollar acquisition of C.K. Prahalad's six-man Change Management Initiative. Gemini was willing to pay a high premium for a defined process or product that could unite and help justify multipronged engagements bringing every division of the company to bear. Other consultancies would soon follow suit, offering change management as a sales wedge to create extensive reengineering engagements.

But Prahalad would bring change management to entirely new heights under Gemini, making it a self-sustainable product in its own right. With a $20 million one-shot sale to Philips Electronics, building solely from Gemini's use of Prahalad and his methods, CMI became a welcome and unique member of the Gemini family.

The nature of CMI's products are deceptively simple. In the early 1990s C.K. Prahalad authored a seminal pair of *Harvard Business Review* articles, capturing the coveted McKinsey Prize for excellence in consulting writing. The first focused on what C.K. termed "strategic intent," the second "core competence"; both are now common coinage in the consulting industry. More impressive than any ideas presented in these articles, however, was Prahalad's proposed use of these concepts in consulting practice.

Strategic intent, Prahalad's first article explained, was what got us to the moon. Eschewing the tactical domain of the business planning cycle, rejecting the calculated comfort of the probably doable, President Kennedy had charged his nation with the visionary task of getting a man to the moon and safely returned to earth, in less than a decade. Requiring a scale and focus of commitment unprecedented in peacetime and the use of unknown and uninvented processes and technologies, the president's challenge was at once cleanly focused, all-embracing, and highly energizing. On its face, it was also impossible, at least in the time stipulated, requiring resources and capabilities beyond any that could be rationally anticipated.

It was such an overarching goal, Prahalad maintained, that led to the success of corporate mobilization campaigns in Japan. Drawing on a series of interviews there, Prahalad modeled a variety of less than rational, obsessive campaigns that had successfully focused the energies of Japanese companies on their Western competitors. Maru-C, shorthand for "Encircle Caterpillar," was one such campaign employed by Komatsu's earth-moving equipment division that particularly fascinated Prahalad. With posters and sloganeering built around Maru-C, with every company project and action hinging on its contribution to defeating Caterpillar, Komatsu had achieved the kind of energetic focus Prahalad was convinced was critically lacking in Western business organizations. Tracing the success of a variety of Japanese companies to such focused campaigns, Prahalad built in his article a persuasive case for beyond-the-quarterly-profit, emotionally charged mass mobilizations of corporate vision, focus, and effort.

The well-received strategic intent article was shortly followed by another, the "core competence of the corporation." Again drawing on Japanese interviews and examples, Professor Prahalad outlined a new vision of the company portfolio, one emphasizing not excellence in a given product or service, but rather a superiority rooted in a coalescence of highly integrated and specific expertise. Honda was not a car company that also made motorbikes and lawnmowers and outboard motors, Prahalad argued, but rather Honda was more simply an engine company: an engine company drawing on its competencies in ceramics, combustion, fuel systems, and so on to make unbeatable engines of the highest quality and lowest cost; from there, it was natural and straightforward for them to succeed in any business where engine technology was strongly featured.

Engines, Prahalad argued, were Honda's core competence. Prahalad defined a core competence as 1) a complex mix of knowledge and technologies that would not be easily replicated by competitors, 2) a harmonious blending of skills that could be leveraged to great competitive advantage, that would bring 3) unique perceived benefits to a company's customers. Though met with slightly less enthusiasm than his strategic intent piece, which seemed to immediately resonate in business spheres across America and Europe, core competence was nonetheless suggestive of some yet unrealized key to successful organization. It soon found imitators, most notably in the Boston Consulting Group's core capabilities approach, shamelessly offered in the same *Harvard Business Review* shortly afterward.

But C.K. Prahalad was content to outline his theories in the business press, leaving them in half-finished form to tantalize clients and torment consulting firms unable to make good capital of them. Prahalad had found the means to unleash their power in his own CMI practice, and with the reach and manpower of the newly agglomerated, mammoth Gemini behind him, he began to ruthlessly unleash their full powers.

• • •

Christmas 1990 in London I learned that Professor Prahalad had just concluded the first "Centurion" session with Philips Electronics top management in Eindhoven, Holland. Based on Prahalad's success there, Philips CEO Jan Timmer was prepared to propagate the process to the entirety of the global Philips organization, and was ready to enlist Gemini behind Prahalad to get it done, at a starting cost of $20 million for the first year of what was envisaged to be a five-year project. Gemini's acquisition of Prahalad's Change Management Initiative was quickly consummated on the back of this agreement, and Prahalad was given carte blanche with the likes of mid-to-senior level consultants like me, to make sure the Centurion gold mine produced.

Alan summoned me to his office to brief me on Centurion.

"Twenty million," he intoned without preamble. I had not even made it to the chair across his boat-sized, antique partner's desk before he began his recap of the Philips opportunity, and his enthusiasm was infectious. But though I did not want to douse the hungry flame that clearly sensed a forest of opportunity in Philips, I had to wonder. Philips Electronics was one of the world's largest companies, a hundred-year-old bastion of engineering excellence, and it was very, very sick. Its bloated two dozen divisions and 300,000 employees scattered worldwide were still, quaintly, ruled from Holland, and the general feeling was that now that the Japanese electronic giants had wiped out RCA, Zenith, and any other American company foolish enough to stand in their path, Philips, with its heavy commitment to the vulnerable consumer electronics industry, would surely be next. The financial papers were a-buzz with plans to split up and sell off the company's key divisions.

But I wanted to believe. I did some quick math. Unless Alan had reinvented the basic logic of consulting sales, the twenty million dollars he anticipated would break down to day-by-day charges, based on individual consultant's rates. Even using virtually all of the most senior Gemini officers, at the highest billing rates, and at an unheard-of full capacity, I could barely get to ten million. I decided I needed to be convinced.

"Is this on some kind of success-contingency basis, Alan? I mean, twenty officers at two thousand dollars a day, even assuming they had nothing better to do, doesn't even get us halfway there. How are we sure Philips is going to be around long enough to pay us all this money? And, not to be *completely* discouraging, I'm probably the best electronics industry guy you have, and that's not saying much. Philips would exhaust my knowledge in a week, maybe a day."

"Lewis, it's not like you to be a doubting Thomas," Alan chided in his most disarming manner. Alan carefully nurtured his minister's son, Harvard Divinity School, nice-guy image, brilliantly balanced by his "Hey, I'm a divinity school *drop-out*, I've seen the light of the shining silver dollar," unabashed appreciation of money and all it could buy. If you were going to fall, Alan was the man to show you the way. I would have loved to have seen his application essay for transfer from Divinity to the Harvard Business School.

"This isn't about electronics," Alan continued, "this is really C.K. Prahalad's catch and his terrain. This is a process consulting sale."

"Process, versus content, you mean?"

"Exactly," Alan replied, ignoring my implicit cynicism. "We are going to facilitate a process of corporate transformation, of revitalization. C.K. will gather Philips' top management in small clumps, starting with the top one hundred. He calls this program Centurion. He'll challenge them, embarrass them, exhort them to do better. I've seen him work these; it's a bit like a pep rally, but it lasts three or four days and basically exhausts people into emotional submission."

"We're going to do pep rallies?"

"And get paid handsomely for it. Here's how it works. Before a session, Gemini consultants will do background interviews with the Philips managers, identifying all the hot issues, plus some external competitive analysis. In the sessions, Prahalad, and eventually, as the sessions cascade and expand down the Philips organization, a whole cadre of Gemini officers, work the issues and fully expose and examine Philips' poor competitive position. Before each session ends, we agree and budget a set of follow-on 'projects' to help turn Philips around, projects which in turn will be overseen and advised by more junior Gemini staff. Eventually, the cascades are designed to include every one of Philips' employees."

I sounded a low, appreciative whistle. "So the United Research guys can handle the projects."

"Right, and Abegglen leads the charge for Asia."

This was very neat indeed. Alan, of course, hailed from the MAC Group, and had helped secure its top ranking as an elite strategy boutique in financial analysis. United Research had a much less polished, but very respectable, reputation for its success in factory-floor cost-cutting operations. MAC had been flirting with both Prahalad, the Michigan business school guru, and with Abegglen, whom they saw as an icon of business consulting in Japan. Now, under Gemini, all could be combined on the Philips project in a way that would justify the new consulting company's immense merger and acquisition costs, and make Alan an unquestioned, and rich, hero.

We began to sketch out the details, specifically how Alan and I would manage the acquisition of Abegglen's Tokyo office and use it to leverage Gemini's expansion into Asia through Philips. What Alan left unsaid was that this new Philips Centurion project would destroy any remnants of a home life: week-in, week-out three-or four-day sessions, for years, was untried territory for even the most masochistic consultant. My wife had taken to staying with her parents anyhow, I reflected glumly, and I did not relish becoming merely an increasingly sizable, remote paycheck, however much that might be appreciated.

I sensed correctly that this would be the turning point of my consulting life. The Centurion project would save Philips Electronics: however much I saw it as smoke and mirrors, as one of the high priests of its black arts I had to acknowledge the life-saving publicity and confidence it generated for its bankers and investors. Seven years and another bad marriage later, I would be an established Financial Institutions Consulting Partner with Coopers & Lybrand Hong Kong, largely on the back of my success with Philips. Only then would I begin to meaningfully question the hollow values and destructive schemes I had embraced as a way of life.

Centurion was a brilliant moniker for the exercise, but it is unclear to me whether this was CEO Timmer's coinage, as claimed, or Prahalad's own. We at Gemini were under strict orders not to discuss Centurion with the outside world, and in all matters public, including a *Business Week* cover story on the program, Timmer was given sole credit for the initiative, and consulting involvement would be given only glancing mention if at all. Presumably, Timmer had to mention the consulting expenditures to the close-watching investment analysts and bankers, who at the time continually threatened to force Philips' total restructuring and possible disbandment. Facing an opportunity to increase its revenue base by a third or more, Gemini was content to perpetuate the myth of internal creation and ownership, which in the end would prove essential to creating belief among Philips' financial backers that the company could survive on its own without outside help.

In the days of Caesar's empire, Centurion referred to the top one hundred elite of the Roman Legion, and to groups of one hundred within the Legion. For Philips it conveyed the essence of the cascade process, taking the top group of managers and instilling a feeling of elite leadership and responsibility in both them and in every group to follow below them. Centurion conveyed a sense of centennial commitment, purpose, and importance as the company completed its first hundred years of operations. Throughout the world Philips remained largely a company run by white Dutch men, and there was no little pride of connection, for the program's first participants, with the glorious legionnaires of their own Roman past. Centurion bespoke tight organization, and well foreshadowed the all-sacrificing, militaristic demands that would soon follow from the program.

At $80,000 to $100,000 per weekend session, and with hundreds of potential sessions awaiting among Philips' Asia Pacific operations, Centurion was seen as the key to bankrolling this expansion.

"Lewis, how much do you know now about C.K. Prahalad?" Alan called me into his office again the night before I was to leave for Christmas break. The prior week's discussion of the sale of the case and how it would impact Tokyo was sufficient, I had hoped, for me not to have to worry about it until well after the holidays.

"Still not much, just what you mentioned the other day—twenty million and all that," I replied. I knew something of what was up with the CMI acquisition from Alan, of course, but I also knew from the junior consultants who had worked with Prahalad there that his work seemed to inevitably involve weekends, hellish hours, and a lot of client bruising, with no product to show for one's efforts. Alan knew one of my brain lobes was operating on Mediterranean time already, and that he thus had a good chance, I feared, of securing my commitment to pretty much anything just so that I could get out the door. I tried to calm down.

"That's right, *Harvard Business Review*, strategic intent and core competence. You know, you did a great job with Nationwide Anglia. You got a lot of compliments on your interview style from the clients, and you learned from them just what we needed to sell the follow-on systems case. And everybody liked your presentation." I nodded in appreciation. We were in the large office the London partners shared, the one that got the most use during the day, and tended to empty out first each night. We were now alone, Alan affecting his best hard-working-American-among-the-cushy-minded-Brits pose, leaning over his desk buried in presentation materials, sales forecasts, and an impressive array of message slips. The fine cufflinks and colorful striped Thomas Pink shirt somewhat defeated the impression; Alan was more likely getting ready for a fine night out than an evening of paperwork.

"We're on to something very exciting with Prahalad and strategic intent and core competence—we're calling it SICC now. It's a prod-uct, not just theory. With our help, C.K. is going to be the biggest the thing to hit consulting in a long time. This is more important than anything else Gemini's going to do next year. The future's not really in the United Research stuff and brown paper, you know that." United Research's use of room-lining rolls of brown poster sheets, to capture cartoon illustrations of client business processes, obtained widespread fame and never-failing sniggers within the old MAC Group cadre. "We've outgrown the MAC Group approach," Alan continued. "Or more importantly our clients have. The key now is scale, and that's what this new work with C.K. is all about. He's got Philips and DEC computers, and pretty soon we think he'll have AT&T and two or three other Fortune 100 clients, for some really big work. Prahalad is after nothing less than a remaking of the Western work ethic, and he's willing to drag us along the way. The consultants who work with him are going to have golden careers at Gemini, and I want you in among the first."

Alan had a personal stake in this, I knew, and I did not realisti-cally see a Gemini career of any kind, golden or otherwise, without him. The vise would tighten quickly, I reckoned, and I had maybe one chance to try to find an out. "This sounds like a long-term com-mitment, Alan. What if we really get mired in it here, and Philips isn't ready to translate the exercise to Asia? Wouldn't you still want me out in Japan?"

"That's just it, we'll probably need you back in Japan sooner than any of us thought. Philips has huge operations there and throughout Asia, and we'll need consultants who have been through the Cen-turion experience at Philips headquarters to lead the work in Asia. Honestly speaking, I wasn't sure we could justify your projected costs as manager in Tokyo, but now we should have the base for that and more."

Ah, rank and money, and a thoughtfully disguised threat. Alan and I had not discussed my Tokyo package yet. I knew it could range from a minor adjustment above my current arrangements, to a full panoply of apartment, major salary boost, transfer allowances, promotion, and early bonus. I politely ignored the fact that this was the third or fourth time Alan had tried to sell me on the latest and greatest new thing in Gemini, from telemarketing to spin selling. It was time to start listening and bargaining.

"Um, what does this involve exactly? You're not mentioning the interviewing and presentation stuff by accident, are you?"

Alan looked pleased—he'd probably be on time for a dinner date with his wife, I figured. "This is exactly the thing, Lewis. I have a mission within a mission for you. You see, C.K. doesn't really know us yet, other than that we've just given him a pile of money. Way he sees it of course, he's just given us a whole lot bigger pile, and he expects to call the shots.

"On its face, I don't expect you to like this assignment. C.K. basically just wants his consultants to play backstop, to do some homework to come up with some competitor dirt to put the scare into the client, and to suss out some of the hot issues on the inside through preliminary interviews. I'm pretty sure he doesn't want us too near the client. You'll find C.K.'s got an ample ego, and he'll always want to be in front of the client, cheering them on, beating them up, consoling them, pushing them. He sees us as low-cost providers of input to the sessions, not necessarily leaders of the sessions themselves, at least not till way down the road. I want you to help change that."

"Me," I answered wonderingly. Bad enough to head out into the hinterlands with an unknown partner and process, but to do so with a secret agenda seemed fairly self-destructive.

"Prahalad's pretty disposed to like you. He knows you went to great schools, worked for BCG, and can speak and read Japanese. You've got a reputation for sensitivity. I've made you out to be one of the best hot consultants we've got. You and I are going to dog him throughout this thing, and we're going to get all the air time we can in every session we can. We're going to introduce how to do small group work; we're going to facilitate the small groups; we're going to present the competitive data; we're going to spin out the follow-on projects right there in the sessions. C.K.'s going to be positioned as the professor he is, a lecturer on a new theory vital to Philips' survival. Soon there's going to be more sessions than he can cover even as a brief keynote speaker, and in the end we'll be doing the whole lot, over and over again."

And so my enlistment was completed, as was the final slide to the destruction of my first marriage. My wife, once again in Japan, could not get a later flight to the Spanish resort where we were supposed to rendezvous. Rather than idle around waiting for me, she remained in Japan, and in a stupid huff, I left for my now curtailed, solo "vacation," loaded with strategic intent and core competence articles and material. I had little concentration to give them, but as I pored over the material I became increasingly insecure about these articles' ability to sustain a three- or four-day intensive session. They seemed like a theoretically interesting way of analyzing past organizational behaviors, but did little to suggest what one should do about presently stressed organizations. I began to believe all this would best be left with Prahalad, and saw little we might be able to add to the equation.

When I first met Professor Prahalad he seemed inclined to agree that I might have little to add, but he had brilliantly clear views of what to do with strategic intent and core competence. "This is all about audience control. This is not a rational process; it's all intuitive and fundamentally emotional. You work with the Japanese, Lewis, you know that they mobilize tremendous energies with sheer psychic bonding. That's our business here: we're going to take these guys on a journey, and only we know the course. It's an emotional roller coaster, and only we can anticipate the ups and downs, and only we can keep them on the rails."

This was not the discourse I had expected, and Prahalad was not quite the business theorist I had pictured. It was four in the morning, and we were sharing cigars in the Eindhoven spaceship, the new fully sealed and insulated Philips Management Training Centre. We had just finished our first day's session, and I was just as stunned, tired, and confused as the Philips participants. Prahalad seemed full of

manic energy: we were to start again in three hours and he showed no
hint of planning to sleep. His accent and bearing betrayed little hint
of his upbringing, schooling, and early working years in India as a
Union Carbide plant manager. No silly man, no Peter Sellers cut-up
of the Indian fool, Prahalad was instead, I would come to learn, the
American's American, a man who saw U.S. corporations as the leading edge of Western civilization, and who felt that nothing less than
a mobilization to war would preserve the West from the dominance
of Asian automatons. To defeat the Asians, he argued, we had to
beat them at their own game, ending an era of self-indulgence and
beginning an era of absolute devotion to company success. Sweat
glistening on his ample form, the whites of his possessed-looking
eyes clear behind his severe horn-rimmed glasses, he was the sort
who could will you to share his beliefs, a man who would not give
up the cause. For some time, he would suspect my loyalties: was I a
Japanese sympathizer? Or had I learned their secrets to better able
Western companies to defeat the Japanese?

"Strategic intent is the first step. You saw today that I always
make this an inspirational presentation, something that is all about
people reaching beyond themselves, planning for what can't be
planned, daring to commit to a brighter, shining future. After forty-
five minutes or so of this, which is just enough time for them to catch
the excitement and not have their attention wander too much, or
worse yet, have them distracted by the realities and limitations at
hand, we send them out into small groups of eight to ten people. I
never take questions during this session; we don't want to be disturbed by a single sourpuss. This is all about building up, up, and up.
We're going up the roller coaster emotionally; we're not even necessarily connected to Philips anymore. Half of them are fantasizing
about being in the Apollo program and going to the moon."

Prahalad took the napkin from under my whiskey and refilled the
glass to the brim. Participants were not allowed liquor, except in their
rooms by themselves if they could spare the time from sleep to drink.
He began to sketch the upward curve of a roller-coaster track. "So

they're all riled up, their emotions are high. In the small groups we ask them to come up with a strategic intent for Philips. It's fun! Most of them spend most of the time trying to come up with a catchy slogan. You know, "We light the world," "Short-circuit Sony," that kind of thing. Then they come back and present a summary of their thinking. We don't say anything. We tell them they've made a good first try, and tell them to go back after dinner and try again, to get more specific to Philips. They start feeling disgruntled, a little unsure of their footing. They stay up late, they see us wandering the halls checking up on them, afraid we'll report the ones who go to bed first."

Prahalad began to draw a downward curve over the top of the emotional roller coaster.

"So tomorrow we'll start to help them out and sustain the charge they got from your first session?"

"No, no! Tomorrow we kill them! They don't know what they're in for! Tomorrow you start off with your lecture on the competitive homework you gathered. I want you to emphasize everywhere they're behind or slipping, European and Asian market share, the telecommunications and computer fiascoes, the works. I'll ask some questions, serious and neutral, like I'm hearing it for the first time. It should make them nervous. Then we let them present their strategic intent proposals. They'll be weak; I purposely didn't give them much help.

"After the presentations, I hammer them. I take your data, point up some weaknesses, then pull out my own data, confidential stuff from the top management meeting, which they won't have seen. It makes their situation look much, much worse. I'm going to humiliate you a bit, too, by the way, making a point that you've been too kind to them in your analysis. You'll be grateful for it later; it will draw them to you in the small group work, give you some control we'll need you to have later."

No doubt I looked as worried as I felt, but Prahalad seemed to take this as a healthy sign.

"I'll go over their strategic intent proposals and begin to really ridicule them. I'll start to take questions and comments from the floor and make them wish they never spoke up—I'll be as cruel and humiliating in my responses as I can. They'll hate me, but I'll make them hate themselves more."

Prahalad was grinning in a worrying sort of way. I would come to believe that this part of the cycle was his favorite, a setting of the challenge, with a dash of unadulterated sadism, just for fun.

"We'll have two slide projectors. You collect the strategic intent proposals after each is given and bring them to me. I'll display each side by side with the data that shows the depth of the trouble they're in. They should be hurting and confused, and right then I'm going to send them back to small groups to try again. I'll go away, and you make the rounds to help them out, but you should seem just about as lost as them."

"You want them to come up with something more realistic?"

"Exactly, but too realistic, back to where they were." The roller coaster sketch showed the tracks down to the level where they started off. "They come back, I tell them they still don't get it. By dinner, I tell them we have to have a full working session, through the night if need be, to arrive at strategic intents that have enough reach to get past the scariest of their problems, but with some hope of actually getting accomplished." The roller coaster now plunged below the starting point.

"The quality of what we see the next morning should be pretty good. They'll be tired, and probably a little aggressive, ready to show off what they've got. This is where we change channels, catch them off guard. We tell them we like their goals, but see they lack the ammunition to achieve them. I introduce the core competence material. We hope for an epiphany: they see organizing around Philips' core competences as a means of achieving the strategic intents. We get them excited about identifying what Philips' core competences are. They'll be good at this: it's a complex company with too many divisions; they could come up with some really good stuff. The strategic intent material will be crap, unusable at the broad corporate level, but the core competences could get really interesting. You and I will need to have some side meeting time to cull the ones we think might go somewhere, so after the presentations they'll go back into small groups on their own."

Prahalad sketched the roller coaster on the rise again. It was two hours to go to the next day and I felt like I'd lived through it already. Where was the energy for this supposed to come from? Knowing we were saving the Western world? My cigar refused to relight, no doubt, I reflected, because Prahalad's manic brain had probably burned all the room's oxygen. The money, I decided, wouldn't be enough, and I began to make a mental checklist of my Tokyo demands for Alan. The downtown apartment just added a room.

"Here's the good part. We give them back strategic intent, but tell them to focus on their own divisions and departments, no less ambitious but scaled back to things they know and can do things about. We tell them to couple these to local core competences. This is the great key: the right core competences will cut across divisions, no budgets will be ready made for them. We'll encourage them, force them, to come up with specific projects, with budget needs specified. The project names we'll lift right from the strategic intent slogans. The core competences will justify new budgets outside the present structure. Since the organization won't be flexible enough to change around these projects, we'll become the material that lets them flex."

"In other words, we get the budget to facilitate these new projects."

"Exactly! There's a lot to do. We need the core competences, the new strategic intents, the project budgets and proposals, time to prioritize them, and off-line, choose the best ones. We've got to get it all documented, photocopy every hand-drawn transparency, put it all in a big binder, copies to everybody, give them some heft back for their time. You'll do that while they sleep."

"So then I'll be working on these projects with them after the session's over?"

"Sure! But you also have to sell every one of the participants on doing the same thing with their own groups reporting to them. Dozens of sessions! You'll need to get help. But eventually, Philips' entire business activity will be supplanted by the projects we facilitate out of them. It will be a new organization." Prahalad drew a another downward turn on the second roller-coaster peak. "Not everybody's project gets picked, of course. Some more people are going to get left out, get cut. But they'll finish on the roller coaster above where they started, and it will be your job, and the other Gemini folks', to keep them at that level."

So this was a consulting guru, I thought, someone who could perfect a McKinsey Prize–winning theory and bring it into practice in a wholly unexpected way, making money hand over fist all while perpetuating the true faith. However exhausting the whole scheme might be, it seemed really neat and well packaged.

Sometimes, of course, the Centurion march would find people out of step. At one of the first sessions for which I did the lead facilitation, I found myself unleashing powerful and largely uncontrollable emotions. In the main group sessions, with sixty or more Philips managers packing the seats in the central training atrium, I never knew when an angry outburst or tearful confession might surface. One small group representative reporting on his session, for example, had decided that the design engineers needed to be more consumer-minded, to think more like salesmen. A red-faced engineer immediately stood up.

"I worked hard all through school and most of my life to be a design engineer, a Philips design engineer. I make the best products, and I believe people will buy because they will know they have the best. Now, you want me to find some other way to sell what I make. Time I should be spending on the design you want me to worry about guessing what people can be tricked into buying. You want me to be a salesman. But if I wanted to be a salesman, I would work in a shoe store. I would sell shoes. I am a Philips design engineer; I am not a shoe salesman."

The moment was beyond my control. There were uncomfortable

snickers, angry assents, gestures of embarrassed sympathy. I was sure he was about to cry, but instead the engineer just sat down heavily, defeated, spent in having had his say. There was sporadic applause, and an opening to recapture momentum. "None of us, I think, want to be shoe salesmen, and I guess that's what we're here to avoid," I ventured. Others picked up the theme, and we got general agreement that engineers catering more to consumers was just bad medicine that would have to go down. But "I am not a shoe salesman" became a sort of underground rallying cry for the disaffected of the Centurion program, for its Philips legionnaires and Gemini consultant-facilitators alike.

In time, over a period of nearly two years, I became a Centurion veteran, facilitating sessions not only in Europe, but with my move back to Asia, in Japan, Australia, Taiwan, Hong Kong, Singapore, and India. The humiliation cycle worked well wherever the management was largely non-Asian, as in Australia, but had little deep effect among most of the Asian participants. In one particularly ironic session that Prahalad led, and for which I translated, in Japan, the rehashing of the ideas Prahalad had originally tapped from Japanese companies served little purpose but to make the Japanese participants seem to envy their fellow citizens who worked for "real" Japanese companies, instead of confusing foreign interlopers like Philips.

The Centurion sessions in Asia did make for excellent project output, however, and the Gemini consultants were quickly co-opted into a process that allowed greater creative freedoms and independence to take hold, across division and country boundaries. In one particularly successful cascade we helped facilitate the multicountry and multidivision production and sale of television sets, with tubes manufactured in China, components made in Japan and Singapore, assembly in Taiwan, and sales in Hong Kong. It was an unqualified, seamless success, involving few tears and attempts at humiliation, and a lot of emphasis on cross-fertilization and organization around core competences. In another, we helped involve Japanese designers in creating a "European" look for sales of Philips consumer electron-ics in their home markets.

We began to downplay the more sadistic and destructive aspects of the emotional roller coaster and substituted emphasis on "making meetings work" in the small groups in place of the continued ham-mering on Philips' inadequacies in the context of strategic intent. There is not a single strategic intent phrase, concept, or slogan that I can recall making it past a given Centurion session. But the "making meetings work" skills came to have lasting value: we began teaching separate skills sessions in advance of the sessions, drawing on client facilitators to help us create better buy-in for projects and to better cope with the sheer numbers involved. We emphasized the impor-tance of sharing and regulating the speaking space in the small group sessions, drawing out the silent types and firmly containing the would-be dominators, by getting every idea down on flip charts, with no attention to merit or priority, and allowing no repetition of ideas. We trained the facilitators to stand aside from the process, neither contributing nor interfering with the content of the subject matter at hand, except in the most clear and controlled circumstances. We taught constructive rephrasing, how to use wording that invited solutions, rather than personal attacks. In the end, we emerged with a highly consultative process that cut across all the company's tradi-tional boundaries, owing in large measure to our inability to sustain the emotional energy demanded by Prahalad's explicitly manipula-tive cycle of control and dominance.

Beyond the bounds of Philips and Centurion, however, the beast had been unleashed. The old United Research arm of Gemini, which had still to make it out to Asia, found in Centurion a replicable for-mula, the very essence of the kind of approach on which they thrived. For them this would be business reengineering par excel-lence, a way to get the unwieldy emotions of too-human workers into the charts and graphs for brown-sheet poster-boarding.

Change management would become an able disguise for the worst of the reengineering process, becoming a ready means of asserting control in otherwise futile situations, a way to mask dicta-torial, dehumanizing decisions and programs in the practice of a dark emotional psychology, and at its worst a sinister mechanism for surfacing the unfaithful under peer pressure stress. To me it began to shed stark light on the freedoms lost when entering the corporate workplace, the very antithesis of democracy, where workers are held in thrall, away from family, and stripped of any sense of personal self or privacy, where total commitment is the absolute norm.

This was at the crux of a transition that would take me away from Gemini. Even in the more creatively productive sessions we ran in Asia, it became clear that as consultants we functioned less through our business skills and more as implicit surrogate leaders and enforcers of both corporate continuity and authority. To the board and shareholders we became more representative of ongoing reality, more trustworthy, than its own employees: we seemed less likely to quit, and could be held on a tighter leash to speak the true voice of the shareholders. I began to see this kind of change management as the wave of the future, and began to sorely miss the more glory-filled wining and dining that went with strategic advising.

I had entertained the idea of going the C.K. Prahalad route, to turn to academic writing and produce from it a cult and a product that could sustain the billings and interest of the largest companies and consulting firms alike. I knew I presented well and could momentarily attach and communicate a sense of great importance to almost any material whatsoever. Perhaps I lacked Prahalad's sense of mission, the belief that any company or set of companies could actually be worth demeaning people en masse. But mostly I knew I could not go the route because I wanted a better, more honest, and perhaps more com-fortable if not wholly glorious life and profession.

My would-be sanctimony has not put a dent in change manage-ment, however. In a variety of forms, Prahalad's original strategic intent–core competence system has now taken firm hold among the world's top corporations, enabling unflinching, massive firings even in the midst of robust performance and profits, with megamergers readily justified on the basis of achieving some version of an over-arching strategic intent or combining and organizing around key core competencies.

All in all, I might rather be a shoe salesman.

STRATEGIC INTENT AND CORE COMPETENCE, OR THE INCANTATION OF YOUR CHOICE: PROCESS FACILITATION TECHNIQUES FOR THE CASCADING OF BILLINGS

1

Process consultants will first instigate actions that tap into the repressed emotions of corporate servitude. There is tremendous latent energy coursing through any large company, in the form of repressed emotions and hidden frustrations. Organizing a process that lets the raw energy surface, by creating a seemingly risk-free group environment, and then encouraging a belief that until-then impossible goals might be reached through sheer willpower, can release the tide. Getting clients' managers to dare to believe that their own version of their company's strategic intent might become the all-purpose rallying cry of the firm's next great achievements is a key facilitation objective.

2

Facilitators then seek to demean and degrade the client's managers, after giving them a glimpse of hope. Having exposed the innermost concerns and hopes of the client's core workforce, facilitators are prepared to humiliate them with an expert view of their real competitive position, and their unpreparedness to cope with coming changes. Contrasting the naïveté of their strategic intent dreams with the competitive realities looming in from all sides justifies sending participants back to rethink the whole thing.

3

The process consultant seeks to make the client's managers grateful to work twice as hard, in a narrowly confined and strictly controlled manner. Introducing some tool that client managers can hang on to, for example the license to cut across current division and budgetary lines in search of core competences, that redirects humiliation into positive channels, instills a belief that at least more limited goals might be achieved. Creating the budget and measurements to further instill a sense of pride and responsibility ensures all-hours striving and account-ability.

4

Consultants become an integral part of the emotional cycle, and an essential element of outcome policing. Each manager is cajoled to agree to go through the whole process again with each of his or her own reports, ensuring a continued facilitator role for the consultants involved. Creating measurements and reporting structures that require consulting supervision and output emphasizes the importance of cross-disciplinary projects that will require outside mediation.

5

Consultants gear to measurements and output that can protect the human resources buyer and give something for industry analysts to follow. The client's human resources department or its power equivalent is vigorously pursued for intimate involvement in the process, to ensure manager availability and enforced participation. Ensuring that the results of the facilitation process give the human resource types successful out-comes allows advertising both internally and to outside stock analysts.

6

Facilitators create a cascade cycle that can involve increasingly low-paid consultants in easy-to-manage forums. Especially with large orga-nizations, it will become impossible for top management to follow every facilitated session. As the process cascades down to the reports of the reports of the reports, making use of junior consultants in more readily managed forums like town meetings gives essential leverage. For this to work, consultants are careful to lock in a fixed per-session cost for all meetings first. Before top management finds the time to look into these lower-level sessions, the process facilitators seek to cycle back to the top to "refresh the energies" of the whole process.

7

The consultants then create a canned team of their own undemanding traveling consultant facilitators. Cultivating a core group of consultant-facilitators prepared to make do without any semblance of a normal life, and encouraging them to perfect a cookie-cutter approach to psycholog-ical manipulation, sustains the process. The cynicism they will need for the process will draw its energies from the very meaninglessness of their own lives. Moving them quickly from one engagement to the next, leveraging local client capacity wherever possible, becomes key to the process' potentially never-ending viability.

8

Consultants then replicate and translate best practices to other clients. Discovering what most excites the fears and concerns of one client can often be readily translated to others. Facilitators routinely use industry data and headcount cuts at one client to underscore the dangers to another. Letting the client know that they were there to both cut and heal at the firms involved is seen to generate further credibility and sales.

9

Facilitators connect the process to a greater system of transformational beliefs and ideology. Be it capitalism over socialism, America over the Japanese or Chinese, or the money-fearing over the impracticalists, connecting both the practitioners and the receivers of the facilitated process to a broader set of beliefs encourages translation of the exercise to other firms, justifying referrals, data sharing, and positive publicity wherever possible.

10

Finally, the process consultants intersperse the process facilitation with periodic bloodlettings, particularly when performance seems to actually be on the upswing. In a successful process the release of energies and their subsequent manipulation may coincide with markedly improved performance, creating a sense of comfort that the facilitative process might be sustained without consulting intervention. It is then time to ensure, from the consultants' point of view, that the client sees the merit of doing more with less, with the less being fewer employees, not consultants. Encouraging a new series of headcount reductions to entrench the successes earned is seen as a means to hold out against the future, etc. Your consultant will be there to help cope with the resulting strife.

CHAPTER 8

THE CLOCK-FACE SALES INTERVIEW

PARIS, SPRING 1991

"Lewis, you're a newcomer to both sides. How close do you think the old MAC team and United Research can get?" Alan Johnston and I were stuck in Paris traffic on the way from De Gaulle to Cap Gemini's sumptuous Paris headquarters. We were here for one of the first joint working sessions of MAC and United Research managers, him as senior American partner in Europe, me for training and a briefing on Gemini's upcoming Asia expansion. The Asia briefing interested me—it felt like I was visiting the seat of the French Empire to help plan its latest colonial strategy. And certainly anything in Paris was a welcome break, particularly from the increasingly intense Centurion sessions at Philips in Eindhoven. But I had not really been thinking much about the dynamics of the merger: I was a stranger to the past of both companies, or at least to the ultrarational United Research. I had friends at MAC, and found their cultural assumptions ran closely parallel to those I first learned at BCG. In Asia, however, my move back there being less than a year away, I anticipated being far from the cultural influences of either.

From his first mention of my joining a universe larger than MAC alone, however, it was clear Alan wanted to be delicate with me in relaying the details of the Gemini merger. At first, I assumed this was just natural reluctance to share information about a transaction still in progress. But I would soon see that Alan was looking for an ally, a fellow BCG-MAC heritage strategist who might see beneath the theory, and take an interest the merits of deconstructing the consulting sales process itself. I would come to understand that Alan was one of the chief advocates of directly teaming with MAC's new stepsister, United Research, specifically to draw from it critical lessons about controlling the sales process itself.

At the Boston Consulting Group, with few exceptions, the cultural belief continues to run strong that based on brilliance of insight and excellence of execution, the firm's reputation for good work will create its own sales opportunities. Occasionally BCG might join in competing against other firms' proposals, when there is news of a good opportunity suitable to BCG's thinking-in-writing style, but the notion of any kind of cold call is alien and repugnant. The MAC Group, as a smaller, more focused cousin of its Boston neighbor, very much shared this cultural bias as it built a growing practice from its specialized skills in financial analysis, under the tutelage of Harvard Business School professors.

United Research grew from a novel approach to creating and nurturing a consulting practice, one diametrically opposite to the BCG school of thought. A group of investors from outside the industry had decided to make their own firm, beginning with an intensive study of consulting clients' met and unmet needs, and examination of clients' strongest preferences and dissatisfactions based on their consulting experiences. The creators of United Research found that guaranteed results, a stick-it-out commitment to bread-and-butter implementation, and an ability to constantly see the consultants at work featured strongly at the top of their potential clients' wish list. Somewhat surprisingly, strategic brilliance and fine business school pedigrees surfaced as either unimportant or undesirable characteristics among the types of consultants that clients seemed to enjoy working with.

United Research neatly bypassed concerns like the nature of consultants' offices or whether a consultant had her own secretary: the yardstick was simply whether the client would care or not. Most offices and secretaries were simply dropped. The investor group unabashedly borrowed the most effective techniques from both the best consulting firms and other service industries, primarily business reengineering methods then just under development, and telemarketing services that at the time were just moving beyond general consumer target markets. They created a generalized model of consulting firms' own value chain, and scrutinizing it for characteristic weaknesses, found tremendous inefficiencies in both the consulting sales process, scale of assignments, and client retention efforts.

The creation of United Research synthesized these findings into a wholly original, immediately successful consulting marvel, filling a wide-open niche and sustaining growth rates among the highest in the industry, right up to its absorption into Gemini. Its economics were astonishing. If clients want to see consultants at work, and they do not care about their offices, why give consultants offices at all? The company's founders reasoned: just leave them at the client site, five days a week, and let the client absorb the overhead. And if the intellectual thoroughbreds of consulting would get too bored with those kind of hang-out-at-the-client's type assignments, well, clients seem to like just having regular guys as their consultants anyway, not ego-driven prima donnas. So, the ruthlessly practical investors decided they would recruit from general industry, not the premier business schools: the ideal profile became someone with ten years' general industry experience following a second-tier MBA. Lower cost, stable, and grateful for any kind of a change, these recruits were readily attracted to the promise of better money and working among people much like themselves.

Ensuring that lack of consulting experience would be no obstacle, these recruits were styled as implementation officers, consultants who would be handed tightly scripted instructions as to what to do on a virtually daily basis. They would form the bulwark of the com-

pany, and deliver the longest duration pieces of the work, on implementation assignments typically eighteen months in length. They
were to be ever-present, highly visible, and easy to get along with.
Importantly, they would impress clients as being always busy with
the client's work, following their own detailed implementation
schedules.

Ensuring that the implementation consultants had something to
do fell to the business analysts. These were key professionals most
like traditional strategy consultants, many being recruited from the
manager ranks of the leading firms, including McKinsey and BCG.
Their job would be the most critical and stressful. In the United
Research standard model they would inherit the sale of six to eight
weeks' diagnostic work, in which ostensibly they were to better
understand the problems the client wanted addressed, assessing their
severity and, if possible, recommending immediate solutions. In reality, their assignment was strictly expansionary. Business analysts
were to identify evidence of the clients' worst fears, the "red spots"
that drew the attention, irritation, and worry of client management,
and then amplify the urgency and importance of addressing them.

Simultaneously, it was the business analysts' task to be sure that
the red spots identified were ones that lent themselves to both
lengthy solutions and readily measurable progress: cutting wastage
in a complex but evidently sloppy manufacturing process or trim-
ming weight from an aircraft prototype never designed for lightness
or cutting lead times in a notoriously casual assembly process would
be ideal candidates for long assignments with handy benchmarks, if
they could be tied to management worries; a new market reporting
system or brand management strategy would not lend itself as easily
to measurably reducing key client anxieties.

The United Research business analyst's work thus became key to
selling in a large implementation team over a year or more of work. It
also enabled UR's trademark guarantee of success. The guarantees
would not normally be contractually tied to a client's actual red spot,
but rather to something that the business analyst was confident could

be fixed and measured in a way that directly reflected UR's successful intervention. The red spot, for example, might be chronically late deliveries and inventory tie ups on the factory floor of a custom printing press manufacturer like Harris Graphics. The savvy business analyst would not suggest a promise of sharply reduced late deliveries and inventory problems, but rather a measurable reduction in parts-order lead times that might—or might not—alleviate those problems.

Completing United Research's division of labor were the marketing executives, the front-end identifiers of the potential client's red spots. Looking from the outside in at the consulting industry, UR's designers concluded that the best people to sell consulting would be salesmen, not consultants. Consulting sales involved too many failed attempts, and too many wasted, brainy proposals involving great expenditures of time and effort, for the United Research investors' tastes. Instead they would enlist only proven sales professionals, people who had strong track records in making large and complex sales of everything from telecommunications systems to company pension plans.

Limited to a truly unthinkable role for those accustomed to the schmoozy world of CEO strategy advising, the UR marketing executives would be devoted solely to the initial sales call. In most cases they would meet their client contacts no more than once or twice before moving on to other prospects, and in their first meetings they would follow the tightest script among all United Research consultants: the clock-face sales interview.

In a clock-face sales interview, the marketing executive promises to take but one hour of the interviewee's time. Every five-minute segment of the hour is meticulously planned, tied to a rhythm and purpose proven to yield the exact mix of trust, concern, revelation, and identification of benefits required to secure the purchase of the business analysis team's time. The MEs, as they like to be called, are drilled in their training using pie charts that divvy up the five-minute segments as different color pie wedges on the face of a clock. In an actual interview they are likely to use a clipboard with wristwatch attached, tracing their progress against the carefully paced goals of the hour. Deviation is fail-ure. If the client cannot be maneuvered into the programmed discus-sion, then the chance that they will be able and willing to ultimately authorize the multimillion dollar spend required is too low to expend further effort; it is simply time for the ME to move on.

The marketing executive would hit three or four client prospects on a given day, every day, often covering as many cities as days in a given week. Bolstered by this impressive coverage, the statistical probability of one or two conversions a month, per ME, was good.

It is the key to this full coverage that the traditionalists in Gemini found most galling: telemarketing. United Research's designers did not want their top-flight sales executives wasting their time phoning up prospects cold or sitting in offices researching and dreaming up sales proposals. To get them in the field, and keep them there, they hired a professional telemarketing team to blanket American industry. There are probably an average of a one thousand potential gateways to consulting sales at each of the Fortune 1000 companies, a tidy one mil-lion sales prospects. If 1 percent of them agreed to some face time with an ME, and 1 percent of those converted, United Research would fare better than any firm in consulting history. The telemarketers shame-lessly and systematically called the secretaries of every potential buyer they could surface, representing themselves as the MEs. The market-ing executives could then go on to clock-face interview for two or three months without a blip, cold-bloodedly sticking to the planned regime, confident that the one-in-a-hundred beat would continue to signal the good health of the company's vital signs.

United Research's multistaged approach to the sales and execu-tion process was uniquely successful in rocketing the company to success. The generously fueled, bulky telemarketing and ME stages did the heavy lifting, bringing the business analysts to a low tempo-rary orbit, from which they could fire the implementation team into the desirable highest orbits of long duration and low maintenance. The parts of the system seemed infinitely reusable, if to the general-ist consultant they also seemed weird in their distinctness.

Consultants like me, of course, had been trained to pile into a big single-stage rocket with everybody on the team, and grandly blast off together, swiftly passing orbit to a glorious landing on the moon or Mars, launching all together in the monster ship again when the time came to make our way back to the mother planet. This was the satisfying sequence in the science fiction movies before Apollo, when spaceships looked like spaceships, all of one smooth piece, standing ever ready on their fins for another adventure. All the complicated bits and pieces of multistage launchers, translunar injections, bugs and rovers and a trail of discarded space debris from earth to the moon and back emerged much later, from cold analysis of the economics and success probabilities. UR had learned the lessons of Apollo, and built a multicomponent system ideal for the relative safety of long-duration earth orbit missions.

This system was most antithetical to consulting orthodoxy in its doing away with the normal hierarchy. Consultants were almost universally recruited at the bottom of an organizational pyramid, which they were duly expected to climb, in an up or out fashion. Everyone could look forward to sharing a place at the top as partner, if you could continue to hold on and make your way up without getting jostled off. The sharing of this goal, the golden *benben* atop the pyramid's peak, created common focus and understanding. By knowing one's place and that of one's colleagues at any point on the pyramid, a predictable order and system of respect followed. Job descriptions, pay scales, and appropriate degrees of client interaction were all clearly marked on the way up.

In my naïve sense of the merger that had brought MAC and United Research together, I had believed that the two organizations would coexist, held at arm's length. Alan's ideas were to take us elsewhere.

"I thought the idea was to hand off leads and assignments from one company to the other, you know, so the client got the most appropriate solution and all that. And the Cap Gemini computer science types are there to play catch, pick up the big juicy Anderson-style engagements. We double or triple everybody's prospects, and leave it to the CMI guys to experiment with blending lessons from all three, maybe using MAC partners in the facilitation sessions and UR and Cap Gemini teams for project implementation. That's starting to happen at Philips now—pretty neat stuff I understand."

Alan nodded approvingly at my assessment: I had absorbed the party line well. His head rested against the Paris taxi's back seat, eyes closed. I would grow accustomed to Alan's carrying on conversations while catnapping in odd places, and find it important to realize that he could be listening quite carefully indeed. He was fully feline in his ability to relax anywhere, jump to frenzied alertness when needed, and dope out on sleep again at will.

"How much do you know about MAC's history with UR?" he intoned from some middle distance of sleep and alertness.

My curious shrug invited a lesson but went unnoticed.

"Not much, really," I quickly added. "Just a hint you mentioned back in Wyoming."

"It's actually a pretty long history. They'd wanted to acquire us for a long time. We resisted, or at least most of the partnership group did. I was in London starting MAC's first overseas office. I was the guy with the passport," Alan smiled to himself in recollection, "and I missed most of the first ruckus with UR.

"See, UR was already getting huge, growing fast, still totally backed by their first deep-pocket investors. They hit their stride quickly with big cases, guaranteed results, split roles for sales and execution. But they started to get a bit worried they might be missing out on something with the marketing executives. What if they really did need someone to sound out on strategy? What might be falling between the cracks of the clock-face and the manic diagnostics of the business analysts? Their cases work great on the factory floor, but what about organization work or market entry or joint ventures? They saw a chance to add some polish and glitter, as well as some strategy meat for broader case possibilities, with the MAC Group."

Alan paused and said nothing. Was he going back to sleep, I wondered? Was I supposed to say something? Two minutes later, as if it had been two seconds, Alan continued along.

"Basically, they wanted to acquire the partners at MAC and make them MEs, and feed the junior consultants to their implementation teams. It was a pretty brutal approach, not nicely done. Of course, they were offering a hell of a lot of money, got my attention out in London anyway. The whole thing was rejected. UR tried a bit of muscle, calling everybody, their families, everything, but it didn't work, and we forgot about them.

"So meanwhile here's Cap Gemini Sogeti, Europe's biggest computer services giant, on the prowl for a promising consulting investment to add to their software specialists and code writers. Of course, they find United Research; its growth curves are all over the business press. Well, the UR folks are nothing if not planners and schemers, and in their mind they never let MAC go. They tell Cap Gemini, 'Fine, you guys acquire us. We know you would offer nothing but the right price. But the deal is, you have to acquire the MAC Group, too, and in the end, we get to be in charge.'"

This is not, I decide, the party line. I am beginning to wish I was the one catnapping, and could just pretend to be asleep. Alan is looking at me now. The traffic's moving nicely, but I had not noticed. "Of course, you would have found this out eventually—you seem to make friends with everybody. And as a new partner it would be your responsibility to start sorting this out anyway."

Alan was not usually so blatant. It was not long before that he had implied that I would not make manager if I didn't take the Philips Centurion plunge with C.K. Prahalad and the CMI crew, and now he was talking partner. I could get used to this process, I reflected. But I wondered what enticements came after partnership when the next duty-honor-company request came along.

"I can't imagine you're just sitting still on this," I offered, carefully ignoring the partnership stakes.

"I'm not, no, but I could use some help and ideas. You know, we lost some good people when the merger came down, some of the best brains at MAC. It's important this joint training session works well. We've still got 'Alain DePuis' he's amazing. He's the centerpiece of the MAC side in this session, but I think he sees it as more of a crusade to bludgeon the UR folks with how great and smart we are. Alain's a real card; you should get to know him. But he's been manic about creating a kind of bible of MAC learnings and techniques, a glamour piece that's more meant to show Cap Gemini that MAC is its brighter child. Secretly, I think he's still hoping for a higher cut on the deal, or at least a bigger share of this year's bonus pool for the MAC veterans."

We had finally come off the freeway and now hit a more serious slow down, though Gemini's offices were not far away. A vegetable truck barricade and a swarm of desultory looking workers and farmers with oddly ridiculous-looking signs apparently accounted for our delay. A placard featuring a scrawny Michelin tire man standing in a barren farm patch caught my eye. It was really nicely done, and I had an embarrassing impulse to get out of the car and try to buy it. I repressed a welling discomfort, a queasy awareness of how very skewed my notion of reality had become.

"I want you to give the UR guys a chance, Lewis. Unfortunately they're not going to discuss their best stuff here, and you may have to put up with a lot of their brown-paper fanaticisms. They have a lot to offer for rationalizing our sales processes, though, and they like to keep it to themselves. If we want to routinely win more cases like Philips and Mobil we should really try to rethink what we're doing, with the help of their experience. Be friendly. They're going to be strongly attracted to you as a potential business analyst, but for our purposes in Asia I think you might best spend some time with them as a marketing executive."

"I guess that could be interesting," I managed, thinking that I just plain liked talking too much to inflict the UR clock-face techniques on myself. The clock-face pie charts were a source of much humor among the MAC rank and file, and not a few partners would guffaw at the sight of them.

"Really, I want to talk to you about learning their sales process and adapting it, improving it, tailoring it more to strategy needs for triggering cases like Philips. By next year there will be no separate recruiting. New faces will just be joining Gemini Consulting, not MAC or Asia Advisory Services, not CMI or United Research. There's going to be a lot of pressure for partners to go the route of marketing executives, and we need some of our own strategies to cope."

We approached the Gemini Paris headquarters. I had been by here once before, and found myself again thrilled to see it. In a neat leafy ring of a dozen period buildings surrounding a central fountain just off the Arc de Triomphe, Cap Gemini's graciously curved, five-story structure hugs the finely stoned pavement with its elite neighbors, notable among them the Japanese embassy. Alan was the senior officer slated to shortly run Asia, but I was the most senior consultant in the now bulging Gemini workforce that had actually worked as a consultant anywhere in Asia. With news of my recent successes behind me, including my anointing as one of the few consultants Professor Prahalad would approve to facilitate Philips sessions without him, I could surmise from a pleasant visit last time that I would be treated well.

Our Asia expansion meeting was brief but surreal. Set in the beautiful main conference room, around a massive honey oak conference table facing views of the Seine and the Eiffel Tower on one side and an ornate walk-in fireplace on the other, our meeting of a measly five, representing the whole of Gemini's experience and apparent interest in Asia, barely gave life and presence to the room. Alan was here to pitch to two of Cap Gemini's board members. Anton Milliard, an info systems sales executive who had just completed a large insurance company job in Japan, was there to show that the Cap boys could field their own man in Asia, too. There was no convenient way to place and view the flip chart Alan was intent on using, so we huddled around it in one echoey corner of the giant room.

The first item on Alan's agenda, I was startled to see, was acquisition of Jim Abegglen's six-man outfit in Tokyo, Asia Advisory Services. Back in Big Sky country Alan had given me the impression that this was a long-ago done deal. AAS, through its strong BCG origins, was my first tie to Gemini. Abegglen had left as founding partner of BCG Tokyo and led the friendly spin off of AAS about the time I was first recruited by Morikawa, and as the only other non-Japanese in service I had been called on for a few bridging functions between the firms, mainly to talk about how BCG would support Abegglen's new book on Japan's role in the Asia economy. Abegglen's strong pull with Western clients in Japan and his core team of hard-working BCG veterans, not to mention his nicely located little office space, were crucial to Gemini's making a running start of it in Japan.

It quickly emerged that though some money had changed hands while MAC was still technically MAC alone, Cap Gemini did not necessarily feel bound to follow through on the ambitious little plans of its new MAC Group acquiree. This deal was Alan's baby: building a consulting practice in Asia had become one of his fondest dreams after building up MAC's first overseas presence in London. I would discover that the seminarian in Alan was much drawn to the real and imagined aesthetics of Asia, and that he was determined to rediscover some of the mystic territories of his college-day travels; later Alan confided that he had threatened to quit if the MAC partnership did not let him take on the AAS deal. I was astonished Alan had not prepared me for this meeting, and I feared for my future in Asia being dismissed with a casual Gaelic shrug. Later I learned that Alan was afraid United Research would learn about this loose end and snuff the deal before Alan could jam it through at headquarters.

"Lewis has worked with Dr. Abegglen before; he knows their team. Lewis, what are your thoughts?"

This was my cue to be authoritative, and I knew it would be a stretch. I had never worked directly with anyone at AAS, though on a late night out in Roppongi I had thrown up on one guy's shoes. Jim Abegglen in my view was a relic of Occupation-era Japan, a bombing-survey marine who had joined the hordes exploiting the good times of a war well won. He had managed to parlay a doctorate in sociology, brutally pronounced but effective and colorful fluency in Japanese, and a brief stint with Arthur D. Little, into becoming BCG's beach-head in Asia, and an icon of expert advice on Japan, way back in 1966. By now, though, Western clients who regarded Japan as a jour-ney to the exotic Orient, requiring trustworthy white guides, had begun to fade from the scene.

"Yes, Dr. Abegglen is an invaluable asset. As excited as I am to be part of the breakthroughs at Gemini, it was Dr. Abegglen who first attracted me to joining this new team. He has an extraordinary depth and breadth of client contacts, and it always seemed to me that all he lacked was the manpower, the analytic horsepower, to field large teams in response to client needs. He was like the brains without the body. Frankly, I'm surprised and pleased we captured his commit-ment. I know McKinsey and others were expressing strong interest."

"Thanks, Lewis, that's right. Let's look at Dr. Abegglen's client list." Of course what I had trotted out was fiction. I was very wary of Abegglen. He could get a meeting with any Western executive in Japan, but in part this was because he was easy with his advice, and the occasional research assignments he won came cheap. For all his rough edges, he seemed basically too polite to ask for a big budget for his work. I could never see him selling or managing a large case, cer-tainly not the kind Gemini envisaged: $30,000 sure, $300,000 with extraordinary luck, but never $30 million. When he did have work, I knew Abegglen to be very hard on his consultants, florid anger quickly exploding if things did not go right; it would be difficult to get any manpower to stick close to him. As for McKinsey, it had just seemed like the right thing to say, a magic name and a bit of compet-itive spice to help give Abegglen some needed allure.

I was glad I had had my say, because the client list was more of a stretch than I could have handled. Several old prospects I knew to be dead were still on the list, but as sold cases, not prospects. A short-term retainer of $15,000 a month for Ferragamo (Abegglen reportedly liked going out on their yacht) had magically been projected to $200,000 a year for the indefinite future, effectively showing that Abegglen's office space would always pay for itself. Kodak, a solid regular client of Abegglen's, but one with whom he had no current prospect or engagement, miraculously had a $100,000 sketched in. The picture that emerged was that of an easy $500,000-a-year business on the back of some friendly advice, suggesting that with some leverage and implementation work this could readily be pumped to ten times or more in value.

"Of course these figures are still rough; we have to make adjustments for the transition, and a few costs for promoting Dr. Abegglen in the marketplace as chairman of Gemini Japan." Alan quickly flipped past the inked-in figures to a map of Asia. The financial projections chart would be trashed within minutes of the meeting's close.

The Gemini managers had looked a bit bored and skeptical in the AAS review, but seemed resigned to giving Alan what he wanted. They were more alert to his next proposed round of acquisitions. In Hong Kong and Singapore, Alan explained, there were strong prospects for acquisition, including some of the leading market research outfits, like the local branches of the Economic Intelligence Unit, the *Economist* magazine's money-spinner, and PacRim Consulting, the Asia business conference specialists. The appeal of these outfits, and the Gemini managers seemed to agree, was that they produced hard products, reports and conference deals, that could nicely anchor a growing advisory business.

I did not get the feeling, however, that we were headed toward approval for an expansion into Asia anytime soon. It seemed Alan would be lucky to get what he had spent on Abegglen written off, and that we should start learning how to pitch like UR marketing executives. But then Alan pulled out a surprise card.

"The final thing I'd like to discuss is Philips Centurion in Asia. As you know, Lewis and I and about twenty of the partner-manager group from the old MAC have been facilitating these revitalization sessions for the transformation of Philips' worldwide business. So far, most of the sessions have been at Philips' training center in Holland, with C.K. Prahalad as the key facilitator. In the past few weeks we've begun to hold sessions independently of C.K., both at the Centre and now at other sites, usually hotels near Philips' work sites. Almost all have been in Europe, a few now in the States."

"How many of these sessions will there be?" one of the board members asked, clearly refreshed to discuss something a bit grander than sub-million dollar operations on the other side of the world.

"We cannot say for sure, because as the process evolves, cascading from groups of top managers down to the workers on the factory floor, both the type of session and the degree of our involvement begin to change. But we've done some estimates, and assuming that we are running sessions free of C.K. and his CMI cohorts and get good use of managers and up-and-coming partners like Lewis, there might be between three and five hundred sessions a year, for five years, based on their needs, the logistics coordination, and our availability."

"And what do you, that is to say, we, make on these sessions?"

"Well, now that we are out of the Centre and starting to run our own shows, we've worked up a pricing model that averages about $80,000 per session. The exciting part is that individual facilitator billing times are not built into the model. As long as the local Philips manager signs off on a given session's success—and they know all hell will break loose and headquarters will come swooping in if they declare a failure—it's $80,000 before expenses whether you, me, or Lewis does the session. I figure with two consultants per session, after fees for time, we'll make $50,000 clear per each one. This is like having a $20 million a year growth fund at our disposal."

The Cap Gemini men looked at each other nervously and laughed. The quiet one, who apparently managed little English, spoke up for the first time, and announced with a grin: "This is why we bought consultants."

"It seems a little too good to be true. Now tell us what can go wrong."

"There are some risks. We may be in danger particularly of being overwhelmed by our own success. What if the cascade moves faster than we can handle? Already there are a lot of Philips managers who don't want to be left out of the first wave; they want to go down in Centurion history as being among the first to get projects budgeted. The clever ones know this is a good way to get money from head-quarters for new projects, and the cross-disciplinary aspects of the work are being seen by some as an excuse to build new empires beyond their own divisions. So we need trained facilitators in a hurry.

"There's an exhaustion factor. As Lewis and I can attest, this takes a lot out of the partner or manager who's facilitating. And, as good as the money is, these are the people we want to keep sharp, to sell and manage the next round of Philips-size cases."

"What about United Research? There are so many of them?" Yikes, I thought, how did Alan let them get that idea? The UR staff I had met were more suited to football coaching than sensitivity training.

"We thought about that." We did? "And that might work in some situations in the States. But after Europe, Philips is mainly an Asian operation. In fact the majority of the sessions, if we do really well, may ultimately be held there. And unlike here in Europe, where, for-tunately for people like me, English is spoken widely, in Asia it takes someone like Lewis to make these things work."

Click, I could hear the pieces of the puzzle snapping into place.

"What stops Philips from hiring other consultants?" Both board members were beginning to feel the problem more clearly and acutely, and Alan was ready to help them along.

"In theory, our agreement with Philips' Human Resources is that no other consultants will be engaged for Centurion work. But already we see some strains on the system. In Australia, for example, where the country manager has always been a fan of BCG, he's scheduled us to do the first day of the top session, and then designated everything below it as 'follow-on projects,' which are not strictly in the ambit of our contract. HR put up some fuss, but Australia replied that we were already late in doing preliminary interviews, they had no one to contact on the ground, and they had no confidence we would stick with the exercise."

Click, click. This was beautiful to watch: Alan was about to have them explicitly state the needs we had come to discuss.

"So what we really have to have are people on the ground, people of our own, facilitators and project coaches that Philips can draw on anywhere."

An excited conversation in French burst out between the two board members, with Anton joining in vigorously.

"We might see other benefits, too! With the right infrastructure in place, we could sell other large assignments that even McKinsey and BCG are afraid to staff in Asia. We wouldn't have the costs of flying expensive partners in and out. And they could make excellent prospectors for our own work, selling in computer solutions in Asia."

The loudest and final click, with the board as buyer of the Asia growth plan stating both explicit needs and benefits.

"Well, Alan, at least we should start with Japan. Looks like Japan pays for itself with Dr. Abegglen anyway, and we can start working with PacRim and some of the others, maybe Lewis could facilitate some sessions together with them, help us make the right buying decisions. We think Anton should be involved, too, we're sure you'll like him."

Seldom had I seen the orchestration of such a complete victory. Alan had finessed his pet project in Japan, deflecting hard questions about the numbers with a buzz of excitement about Philips. He had staked out all of Asia as his own domain under Centurion, and laid out a plan whereby Philips money would build Gemini's infrastructure there. Most impressive to me, he had kept the profits from simply refilling our new parent's coffers, and somehow kept the whole scheme from United Research. In fact, by demarcating Centurion as MAC territory, and making Centurion the bulwark of Gemini's Asia expansion, Alan had basically blockaded UR from getting anywhere near Asia.

It also confirmed my suspicion that the relentless Centurion machine would not easily let me go. The long weekends locked in the Eindhoven spaceship of a training center with adrenaline-saturated, emotionally brutalized managers were beginning to tell on my energy reserves. The buffet, from which all meals at the Centre were served, had begun to feature in my nightmares: to this day the sight of a hard roll with sliced ham and cheese can make me spit. Now was a moment to seize on the good life: Alan and I agreed to meet Anton at the Maison du Caviar later that evening.

First, though, it was off to the hotel where the joint training program was to start. Alan went off to contend with the visiting UR partners: they were headed for a struggle session on why MAC consultants did not need personal offices. I joined up with one of my best friends from the London office, the stalwart "Brett Norman." Brett had amazing common sense, for a Cambridge University graduate, and a no-nonsense style that suited his bulky and unkempt appearance. A constant smoker who never seemed to leave the habitat of his trench coat, even indoors, he called to mind a more generous Humphrey Bogart, with the advantage of a plummy British accent. Fluent in French, and with a taste for the best of what Paris might offer, I knew from our last visit that I should stick by him.

We were late getting into the session. Brett had actually driven here from London, a process whose mysteries earned him no little respect in my eyes. He had been busy negotiating parking.

"That's five dollars for the kitty!" The speaker at the front shouted the moment we entered. "That's what we do whenever someone is late. We keep 'em for basketball tickets," he explained to his audience smugly. He was looking at us expectantly. God, I thought, he really wants five dollars.

"I only have francs and sterling," Brett remarked commandingly in his best public school bully accent, striding toward the speaker, "and I dare say this crowd might never get to see one of your basketball games. But here's enough for a few drinks tonight." To cheers all around, Brett noisily piled a hoard of currency, coins, and pocket lint on the table and walked calmly away. As he headed for the seats I had found us in the rear, his back already to the presenter, Brett remarked more quietly, "That should cover my friend here, too," to a number of chuckles.

And so we made our first UR enemy. It would not be the last. I had tried to settle in quietly during Brett's spectacle. We were among some thirty or forty mid-level types from MAC's European operations, maybe half of whom I had seen before. Encircling the room was a continuous sheet of UR's infamous brown paper, a meter thick, of the kind you find in roll dispensers for hand-drying in public restrooms. Drawn and pasted all over it was what at first glance looked to be the work of disturbed children whose only toys were office supplies. Hideously complicated networking arrows connected a variety of icons, creating a kind of stretched-out bird's nest that sprouted pictures of desks, telephones, offices, trucks, and warehouses. The handwriting of evidently dozens of different people was scrawled throughout, tiny but painfully precise. Like a blueprint for a Rube Goldberg contraption, it seemed to make a dizzying kind of sense—at least everything seemed to connect up somewhere, with no clear beginning or end, making a kind of Möbius strip of organizational dementia.

We would soon learn that the "brown paper" held pride of place in United Research's impressive arsenal of implementation makework. "Skip," our coach from UR, explained that nothing was more effective in his experience in engaging the client workforce and impressing upon them that what they did on a daily basis was in fact more complicated than mere mortals could fathom. When at the end of a given engagement a client was shown a cleaned up, streamlined process on a few neat charts, in a room dressed up with brown paper chaos like this one, they received nothing but accolades and expressions of marvel. And best of all, making it kept dozens of consultants busy for months.

The questions were hesitant. Skip read this, I believe, as an appropriate degree of awe.

"So, what you're saying is, you make things look complicated on purpose."

"Exactly. Sometimes, we don't really have to streamline or change things much at all. When we're stuck, we just remove a bunch of the detail, and try to tie it to reality by suggesting that some reports and documents just get dropped out of the process we're mapping."

"How is this different from business reengineering?"

"Well, this is reengineering, we just don't get into the theory much. I read Mike Hammer"—"Congratulations," Brett muttered—"but I don't think the whole team needs to be hampered by theory."

"Um, why do you think this works so well," I managed to ask, mindful that we'd all been drilled to be polite and receptive if we wanted to earn our free weekend in Paris.

Skip seemed to brighten at the sound of my American accent. "If you ask me, the secret is these cartoons." Things got uncomfortably quiet, but Skip did not seem to notice. "See, everybody just loves these things; clients come up and ask if they can draw and paste on their own. It's one thing to talk about telecommunications problems, but show them a cartoon of someone on a telephone, and it really gets their interest. Adds some humor, too."

"Who put the goon squad in charge?" Brett said loudly enough to be heard by a dozen or so people, who immediately released some nervous laughter. Skip seemed to take this as encouragement though, and with no one willing to ask further questions for fear of answers that might trigger a laughing uproar, Skip began to walk around the room, explaining every acre of the brown paper and the findings it captured. "Ben in quality control told us that sometimes he got the same engineering change notice two or three times, so here's a pair of calipers for quality control. ECN means engineering change notice. We began to trace these lines here to see where they'd been in the system, and after we got lost for a while we just sort of drew extra lines in. It's meant to be symbolic anyway." This was getting truly horrible. I began to fantasize about the evening. I imagined a future of choices increasingly limited to brown paper or Centurions. I imagined rioters with rotten vegetables storming the building. Brett passed me a note.

"Ask him where they get the brown paper!" it read, "I dare you!" I shoved it away and made for the bathroom. "Five dollars for the tinkle!" Skip shouted after me gleefully. By the door I heard Brett deadpan his brown paper question and, hearing Skip's happy response begin, "I'm glad you asked that. It's not easy to find, and we have to keep a whole stock . . ." I walked out nearly in tears of laughter and alarm and did not go back, no doubt earning a black mark in Skip's attendance book.

By the late afternoon break it was clear Brett was having a mischievously good time. I learned with some horror that he had invited Skip to join us on our night out.

"Don't worry, that dullard wouldn't dare show up. He was passing around pictures of his family at the coffee break."

Brett joined Alan, Anton, and me at the Maison du Caviar, sans Skip, though he threatened he might join us for some clubbing afterward. Anton and Brett were discussing the merits of Parisian mistresses; I wished I could have followed their high-velocity French.

Alan had other plans after dinner, however, and he wanted to go over the Asia briefing with me now. Ever since that first BCG recruiting dinner with Morikawa, I had been in search of ever more intense caviar experiences, and this one seemed to reach a new height. Alan was in an expansive mood and encouraged me to ignore the general seafood menu and build the entire meal from selections of caviar and different flavored blini and vodkas. The beluga arrived the size of small pearls, and I was pleased to oblige.

"So what did you think of my presentation? I hope you don't mind I used you a bit there; you were really helpful. Did McKinsey ever really talk to Abegglen?"

"Of course not, unless he was giving away advice. The presentation was great. Why did you save Centurion till the end though? Why not go in strong, anchor the economics right away."

"Two reasons. One's a lesson for you." Alan neatly disposed of a collection of five vodka shots, and then pushed his plate aside. "I've got to save room for later.

"First off, there are things you should keep to yourself. You know from your visits how weak AAS is right now; nobody else needs to know that. Especially you don't need to know what we paid for Abegglen, but you should see the new house he's bought at Kanaya on Tokyo Bay—it sleeps thirty. I don't want to get stuck with the bill for that; it's important Cap picks that up.

"But I have some ideas for a new sales technique. Neil Rackham's outfit Huthwaite has agreed to help us organize a session on SPIN[1] selling, which I'd like to do in Asia, maybe Australia. What do you remember about SPIN selling?"

"Well, the acronym, and how excited you were about the process. And how it was important, for big sales, not to jump right to the solution."

"That's the key. I was using it right there at Cap's headquarters. SPIN stands for situation and problem questions, implied needs and need-payoff questions, which lead to explicit needs and benefits. The situation is Gemini in Asia and the problem is how to support it. But that's not where to focus, that's not how you get to a big solution, a big sale."

"So instead you moved forward without trying to solve it. Those numbers were really bad by the way."

"Don't remind me, please. Moving forward's the thing, that's right. We introduce implied needs of Centurion, get the implication questions going. Gee, so many opportunities we might miss, UR can't handle it, others like BCG are ready to grab it from us. So they see the problem is serious enough to justify action, and we get *them* to focus

---

[1]SPIN is a registered trademark of Huthwaite, Inc.

on solutions with need-payoff questions: what would be the benefit of solving this need? In this case, we got them to ask, and them to spell out the benefits. They concluded the sale of this idea for us."

"So it works."

"Fish in a barrel." Alan glanced at his watch, and my blini was arriving, hot from the oven, with beautiful dollops of sour cream on the side.

"Look, your beluga's going to be here soon, and I need to get going. Try not to let Anton pay, and remember your receipt. I'm going to try to get you in on the marketing executive sessions tomorrow, so check your voicemail in the morning. Don't call me! Try out some of the clock-face role plays, and think about how the SPIN selling stuff might improve it. UR's absolutely right to systematize the sales process, believe me; it's just that I know we can do a whole lot better if we try, and there's no reason to let UR own and control the whole sales process."

So the headline from Alan was to take what we can from UR and keep our own independence, at least for Asia; it was a message that would serve me in good stead, but one that Alan would find increasingly challenging in the coming years.

I had forgotten Skip by the time Anton, Brett, and I disgorged from the restaurant, but somehow he appeared as we made our way to one of Brett's favorite clubs. Brett reminded me that I had mentioned an interest in visiting the Louvre's Egyptian collections.

"I wholly approve, Lewis, I'd even join you, but I bet we won't have time. So I offer you something more Cleopatrique, and erotique"—Anton laughed at the mangled French—"something that is anyhow a damn improvement on your plans. Hello, here's Skippy!"

Skip offered hardy greetings, and something more that was thankfully lost in the din of the club's entryway. I grabbed Brett by the arm.

"For God's sake, make sure you and Anton speak to me in French, act like I'm understanding every last nuance—I won't have you strand me with the dunderhead!"

"*Bien sur*, I'll take care of it. Perhaps we can have some fun."

Skip was not the intrusion I had imagined—though it would have been hard for anyone to intrude on the floor show, which featured fabulous Egyptian New Kingdom outfits, great cabaret routines, and an endless array of beautiful women. It was certainly a new way to see ancient Egypt, and Skip seemed dutifully entranced.

Toward one of the last acts, after a brief conversation with one of the hostesses, Brett instructed me privately to go along with whatever he said and to have no fear.

He then offered us all a proposal.

"Look, fellows, we've been invited to be part of the last act; they have these great headdresses for us and everything. It just takes a minute, but it will be a once-in-lifetime experience." After much cajoling, but aided by Anton and I in the trust Brett would not really do this to us, we agreed to go down to the side of the stage.

"Right, there's just this final parade thing you see. We go on, one at a time, wearing these bits. Then once we're all on we go round in this circle, bow, and say good night. It's simple!"

The hapless Skip, of course, was to be first. With much reluctance he agreed to full regalia: a loin cloth and complicated headgear. We pretended to be fussing in preparation ourselves. Once Skip was on stage, the showgirls took control, and Brett backed us off to where he could get an illegal shot from his Instamatic.

With a little help from one of the dancers, Skip promptly found that the loincloth was not designed to stay on, and Brett secured what we were sure would be a priceless photo. The doormen seemed to have little appreciation of our efforts, however, and we were sternly told that we were lucky to come away with our camera, after a ceremonious exposure of the film. Fortunately for us, Skip missed this little setback to our plans.

The next morning Brett and I replayed the whole incident, minus the film business, to whomever would listen, and rumor quickly spread that several copies of the photo were in circulation. It just was not natural, we rationalized, for MAC and UR to be together, and we assured ourselves that our bit of fun could hardly create any more critical friction. A slideshow was promised, and by mid-afternoon, Skip broke down and begged, saying what a great time he had and all, but that he simply could not tolerate any chance that his family would see any such photo, and could he have them all back please.

With Skip utterly flustered, the remainder of the UR session proved remarkably more tolerable. Skip came back to us at every break for reassurance that we had really gathered and destroyed every copy, and that no, there would be no slideshow. Of course, if there *were* such a copy, and if by bribe or pre-arrangement, the door-man had in fact exposed an empty roll for decorum's sake, one never knows where it might show up. Note to Skip: this might be a good time to flip through the book for figures and illustrations.

CONSULTING DEMONOLOGY, TRACT 8

RED SPOTS AND OTHER RUNES CONSULTANTS USE
TO CLOSE ON LARGE FEES

1

Red-spot consultants use low-cost telemarketing professionals, pretending to be themselves, to launch a barrage of phone calls in attempt to get you a one hour visit. There are a million or more potential gateways to the purchase of consulting services in America alone, and Red-Spot consultants view it as their job to call them all. They do not waste time reading the business press for news of companies that might have consulting needs—by the time they are news it is likely too late, and if not, the background research into the crises involved will be too burdensome.

2

Red-spot consultants divide the consulting workforce into marketing executives, business analysts, and implementation officers, or some such equivalent. Pyramid hierarchies in consulting make for much aspirational strife, and those that make it to the top have a remarkable stamina for staying there and accumulating high costs. Creating parallel functions increases expertise and refocuses internal competition on interfunction rivalries rather than top management, while spreading costs and allowing wide pay differentials. Through a successive chain of dedicated sales professionals, troubleshooters, and fix-it men, consulting clients are exposed to only one area of in-depth expertise at a time, and focus on only one segment of cost at a time, creating the overall impression of getting more for less.

3

Red-spot consultants train marketing executives to confine every block of a sales call hour to specific objectives. Salespersons in consulting, or marketing executives, are trained to spot specific cues and excitable anxieties that may allow a major sale to take hold. By controlling the pace and timing for those signals to be captured and amplified, the marketing executive develops the discipline and instinct to pounce on the "red spots," the key anxiety-makers that can lead to the client's admission of need. With experience, the marketing executive will know in less than the allotted hour whether to ditch or close with his or her prospective client.

4

Methodology-driven consulting sales forces train business analysts to diagnose and amplify their client's red spots, confirming and magnifying worst fears. Troubleshooters, or business analysts, are deployed to specifically exacerbate the client's expressed concerns. Using up to ten-man teams over eight to twelve weeks, a good analysis team is able to compile, and if necessary, create, ample evidence of the client's fears. This is also seen as a good opportunity to identify areas of ready improvement that can be easily measured as evidence of later implementation teams' good progress. Direct connection between the areas to be measured and the key source problems is optional.

5

Exploding red-spot problem-solving into one- to two-year major engagements is the major objective. Taking the client nightmares identified during the business analysis phase and making them look at least more complicated if not worse is the central stratagem here. Creating and displaying as much documentation as possible, preferably on wall charts that can dominate key meeting areas, becomes a primary activity, and inviting clients to explain the horrors and complications of their individual components of the process, encouraging them to add to the detailed illustration, is considered good clean sport. Meanwhile, ensuring that a separate set of ever-improving progress measurements is maintained, on an entirely different process if necessary, becomes a silent but critical activity. For final report outs, a clean display is drawn, absent the detail, of the process wall charts, then claimed as evidence of completed streamlining.

FOR THE MORE SOPHISTICATED CLIENT, CONSULTANTS ADOPT A VERSION OF THE SPIN™ MODEL

1

Quickly cover a few background facts. Clients are easily bored by the context of what got them into the major problems they face. However important it may be to address the fundamentals that brought about the company's difficulties or challenges, the client is likely to feel these are beyond his or her personal control or may have had a personal hand in contributing to the exposure they feel. Irritation and guilt can quickly follow boredom in these circumstances, so feel encouraged to proceed in ignorance.

2:

Tag the evident problems, frustrations, or opportunities the client wants to discuss. Get the client to outline what makes him or her mad, much like the red spots discussed above. Take careful notes, but do not develop these issues with the client just yet.

3

Resist the urge to offer solutions. Do not set about trying to solve these problems in the course of the discussion, and avoid suggestions of a delayed solution or proposal, which the client will likely expect from you. Instead, expand beyond the problems or opportunities identified, amplifying their consequences and underscoring their urgency, to get the client to see the larger implications entailed.

4

Confirm that the client's needs are bigger than they realize. Show that the benefits of solving the bigger needs are bigger benefits. Once these are acknowledged, dispense with expectations for proposal document if at all possible, and get a letter of confirmation out immediately.

CHAPTER 9

DEFERRED LIVING

Stresses on the consulting industry brutally bend and twist the lives of the people who give it service. Chasing after the shock impacts of deregulation and globalization in their clients' industries, consulting firms routinely overstretch their resources in attempts to reconfigure their own businesses into multi-practice and even all-service firms. The scramble to survive, grow, and lead in the midst of these demands has led to an increasingly frenzied wave of mergers and acquisitions in the industry, leaving firms with often odd combinations of alien partners, practices, and infrastructures.

For the individual consultant, the resulting pressures to be more things to more people, to mobilize instantly to cover others' short-falls, and to immediately adjust to sometimes bizarre living and working conditions, takes a higher and higher toll. Personal success and survival in consulting increasingly requires the schizoid mix of an artist's imagination and a dullard's tolerance, a maniac's energy and a triathlete's stamina, and at times, a killer's aggression coupled with a monk's humble compliance.

With ever sharper divisions of labor, opportunities for learning and reflection, and the subsequent ability to savor the satisfaction of a job well done, have also rapidly decayed. On the front end, consultants with primary sales responsibilities are expected to make more calls requiring less time for conversion, with their own case involvements typically shallow at best. At the back end, implementers are expected to stretch out the work to its limits, reducing chances for learning from new case involvements. In between, problem solvers have time to hazard perhaps one good guess about what issues might amplify a client's own sense of needs and engagement benefits, and then move on.

Money, of course, is many consultants' answer to why bearing the inherent stresses and shallow satisfactions of the work is worthwhile. Money also can buy certain indulgences to help pad and insulate the consultant from the lifestyle's many indignities.

For many in the field, the life of consulting is simply a careful calculation of how long normal living might be deferred to assure a certain threshold of financial return. Others assume that "normal living"—sleeping regularly with your spouse, say, seeing good and guilt-free results of your own work, or having time to explain and share pride in your accomplishments with family and friends—is simply a myth, or at best a distant dream to be indefinitely postponed.

Still others, perhaps the most naïve, believe that the steadily increasing infusions of large monies, and the amplified powers of higher rank, will somehow allow a semblance of normal life to take hold, that the time, relationships, good works, and accomplishments can one day simply be bought in the course of the work. In the meantime the money is there to create the indulgences that can make the waiting more tolerable. It was into this ill-fated camp that I fell.

FLASHBACK: TOKYO, WINTER 1986

Shortly after I first started working as a consultant, at BCG Tokyo, I achieved a small fame in Japan for a lifestyle that was to be short-lived. The *Nihon Keizai Shimbun*, a kind of *Wall Street Journal* but with more depth, color of writing, and a much larger and more general reading audience, decided to open a series on young foreigners just beginning careers in Japan with a piece on me and my daily routine. The generous front-page article, complete with candid photo, described me as a leader among these "young lions." That two of my fellow expatriate friends, "Gino Manfredi" and "Pat Curran," had shared much the same background, including the same Japanese instructor in college, stints at NKK, and even similar forays into consulting, escaped the newspaper's notice, ensuring that Young Lion was a moniker I would not soon be allowed to forget.

Morikawa, himself a former journalist, had tipped one of his friends at the Nikkei that I was leading a life that had to be seen to be believed. Still riding the energy and health wave of three months' research in Hawai'i to finish my master's thesis, for much of my first year at BCG I managed a seemingly impossible routine. My day went from a long, predawn run around Yoyogi Park, to practicing with Chinese language tapes on the first subway departure, to a 7 A.M. Chinese class taught in Japanese, and then to work, late dinner with colleagues, a workout, and finally to nightclub roaming with the likes of Pat and Gino till the last subway home at midnight. I was sure the hapless pair of journalists assigned to follow me, from start to finish, would have little nice to write about me by the time they were allowed off my treadmill. But I was pleased to see they put together a favorable piece, even discussing my interests in outer space development.

This would come to a crashing end—and then get worse. Chaotic travel, casework overload, unreasonable promises to clients, and ever-expanding demands from colleagues inexorably took over. The other BCGers said that I was just growing up and would get used to doing more work and less of everything else. But I was determined that health and dignity would stay intact, and looked down on those who had clearly let themselves go.

From the first time I saw "Werner Frisch" I enjoyed a smug disrespect for him. Pale, pudgy, dark circles under his eyes, this visitor from the Munich office confessed to me that his life was fully occupied with the struggle to make manager and that his only indulgence was a substantial investment in Bavarian beers. He had no time for dating, much less a relationship. Exercise, he felt, would only be cruel infringement on his precious few hours of sleep.

Werner had come to Japan on behalf of a Swiss machine tool company, "Blohm-Reinman," to conduct a series of interviews with auto makers. Though they had never catered to the Japanese auto industry, the Swiss still produced machine tools of such adaptable elegance and power of precision that the Japanese reserved the more challenging manufacturing tasks for their use, primarily for making engine parts. Aware that domestic machine tool companies had begun to specifically target the needs of auto manufacturers and that they would soon achieve comparable quality at substantially lower prices, Blohm-Reinman were keen to preempt the domestic challenge in Japan by learning more of what the Japanese wanted in their machine tools.

Once the undisputed kings of the machine tool world, the Swiss in fact now confronted the threat of foreign competition worldwide, fed in part by major shifts in technology. Parts to be machined were once brought to the lathe or grinder, but now increasingly programmable computer-controlled robots would bring lasers and cutting tools directly to bear on the work as the parts go by on the assembly line. Such groundshifts in competition and technology were precisely the kind of crises consultants were expected to bear.

Though it appeared he had little engineering or other relevant experience, Werner had been assigned to the manufacturing practice group in Munich when this case came up, mainly because he was the only experienced consultant available at the time. Because several major customer orders were expected to be at risk there, the Swiss wanted their reconnaissance of Japan done immediately, and the BCG Munich office had obligingly committed to a round of in-depth customer interviews before contacting us in Tokyo.

"Pinault-san, we have a problem," Morikawa informed me cheerily. That he appeared amused meant it was my problem.

"The Munich office has promised a round of interviews with the automobile companies, apparently to be completed in two weeks. Some manufacturing process issue, a Swiss client of theirs that already supplies machines to the auto makers here. Nothing has been set up, of course; this is the first we've heard about it."

"We're supposed to do these? You know I'm supposed to be in New York next week. I've got a pretty full plate."

"I'll help you postpone. We're not actually conducting the interviews; Munich's sending a consultant over to us. You just have to set them up, accompany this fellow around."

"But what do I say? Do we even have any information on the case? Why isn't the client coming here?"

Morikawa looked somehow pleased. "That's just it, Lewis. If we were setting up interviews for the auto companies to meet with one of their suppliers directly, we might have a chance, even on short notice. But this is just to chat with one of us lowly consultants."

"I don't suppose you could just tell Munich no."

"I'm tempted, but that would be bad citizenship, and we have some airline privatization interviews coming up in Germany."

"And you want me to do this because . . ."

"Well, Japanese to Japanese, the auto makers will know that we know that we're being unreasonably rude according to our expectations. They'll want to see the client directly. But you have a better chance. You're an ignorant foreigner, bringing another foreigner to see them who's flown here especially. You don't know better."

I resigned myself to the unflattering truth of Mori's analysis.

"Didn't Numata have a Honda case last year?"

"Yes, he's got strong ties. I'm not saying we won't help you; we'll get you the names of some people to call. But this would be a good experience for you, and we're short-handed. You've got engineering background, and obviously the English to deal with this German, Werner Frisch. Just bring him around Japan on these calls, make an impression on the auto makers that we have a sophisticated international capability."

• • •

Setting up the interviews was more than the usual torture. Even calling in Numata's favors and working with personal contacts, I had to
make several rounds of calls at each prospect just to get a hearing.
The would-be interviewees seemed unsurprised to hear what I
wanted and were unfazed by my talking-dog Japanese: as Morikawa
had guessed, they simply expected foreigners to be rude. But my
prospects could not resist lecturing me on etiquette and several
insisted on introductory letters from the client, for which Munich
was too proud to ask. Even my usual coterie of eavesdropping colleagues seemed too embarrassed for me, to get much entertainment
out of listening to my strained attempts.

By the time Werner arrived I was exhausted. Munich had faxed
over huge volumes of material on the client's business, which I was
still trying to absorb in the midst of all the phone calls and my own
preparations for New York. I spent my spare minutes cramming technical vocabulary and trying to anticipate the interviewees' questions.
I had finally produced a full schedule of interviews, but they involved
train and plane travel all over Japan, and the logistics were nightmar-
ish. The culmination of the interviews would be a visit to Honda's
new facility on the southern island of Kyushu, where several new
machine tool orders were at stake.

Werner came to the office straight off the plane, and we spent a
first working afternoon together, going over the objectives for each
interview. I was pleased that he seemed well prepared and eager to
share the details of the case. Though dazed by the flight and being in
Japan for the first time, he also seemed to duly appreciate the work
entailed in getting everything set up.

I took a liking to Werner, in a condescending sort of way, in spite
of his overworked and overindulged appearance, and as the interviews progressed I was happy to pick up the slack and take over from
his questioning here and there. What I first took to be the effects of
jet lag, however, never appeared to wear off. Werner's energy seemed

to steadily drain as the week went on, and as he saw that I could control more and more of the interviews, he became increasingly passive, occupied with thoughts of other cases going unattended back in Germany.

The night before our trip to Honda in Kyushu, Werner showed an interest in seeing something of Tokyo nightlife. It had been a long week and I felt we were both due a reward, and I was encouraged at this spark of life and energy. I hoped Werner would put on a special show for Honda, foreseeing this might produce new casework for us both. We headed for Roppongi.

In the course of the night, I was startled to see Werner become a different person. His already serviceable English apparently became fluent with steady, large doses of alcohol. Ever more alert and energetic, Werner regaled me with tales of his life in Germany and seemed to take an increasing interest in the women around us. We had started at Henry Africa's, an oddball but homey bar rich in wood and brass, with animal heads on the wall, a good jukebox, and cheap beer. It was a favorite of the expat investment banking crowd and attracted a good many female Japanese groupies. We moved on to a Japanese sake cellar, where Werner's repeated failed attempts to get through the bartender's lack of English got us a lot of free mixed sake drinks.

Werner begged that we go back to Henry's, to meet more women, and I was cheerily compliant. On the way though we ran into my friend Pat from Asia Advisory Services and a companion he had in tow, unknown to me a secret visitor from the MAC Group come out to scout AAS for takeover. We diverted into one of the new high-tech discos, where for a staggeringly high cover charge, the drinks were free. I lost Werner there for a while, but we caught up again, and I ascertained we had both made ample use of the free drink privilege.

"Lewis, we must go back to Africa!" Werner shouted, improbably.

"But the drinks are free here! It's a great place!"

"Woman!"

"But there are plenty of women here!"

"No, no, there was a woman I was talking to back there. We need to go back."

Pat and his friend gamely decided to follow. Vaguely, I began to worry about the flight tomorrow morning. I felt a surge of sickness thinking about it.

Once on the street, I asked Werner if maybe he wanted to head back, but of course he was convinced that he had left the woman of his life at Henry Africa's. Remarkably, Werner *did* find the woman he had in mind, but it did not take long to determine she had other interests. Werner was crushed, and suddenly all his newly discovered energy seemed to leave him. He bought another pitcher of beer, and deciding it was probably a wise time to go, we escorted Werner, still cradling the pitcher, back out to the street.

While we were hustling for cabs, I realized my nausea was not just anticipatory. Just as a taxi pulled up, I heaved all over Pat's MAC friend's shoes. Werner thought this was hilarious. I shoved him in the cab before the driver could change his mind, and tumbled in after him, with only a second to make a feeble apology to Pat and his newly decorated friend.

On the way to drop Werner at the Imperial Hotel, I tried to plant the idea of an early wake up.

"I'll be fine; I'll be ready, don't worry. I had a great time. You really have a great life here, all those women. Just call me before you get to the hotel in the morning, I'll be all set. Oh, and you should really learn to control your alcohol," he admonished me, laughing.

With only the mildest guilt at missing my morning run and Chinese class, I got into a cab again at six the next morning. Recalling Werner's request, I asked the cab to pull over so I could make a call.

"Good morning Werner, how do you feel? Are you getting ready?"

"Oh yes, I just got up. I am getting ready now. I feel fine, thank you. I'll see you downstairs in the lobby in just a few minutes."

Wow, I thought, he may look like hell, but he can sure put it away and recover the next day. With the light traffic at that hour, I made good time to the Imperial and was not surprised that Werner had not made it down yet. I gratefully secured a coffee at the lobby cafe, and gave Werner another call to let him know to meet me there.

"Werner, I'm down at the cafe."

"Okay, I just got up. I will be getting ready now. I feel fine, thank you."

I was amused at his grogginess, but a little concerned at his apparent lack of progress. "You better get moving now. Just meet me here at the cafe."

Ten minutes later, I called Werner again.

"Okay, I am getting ready now."

"Werner, you're not getting ready, are you?"

"No."

"You're still in bed, aren't you?"

"Yes."

"Give me a minute, I'll be right up."

"Okay."

I had seen this behavior back at MIT, with binge-recovering fraternity brothers who could dredge up nimble lies and whole coherent conversations from the depths of sleep, to support any lie that would allow them to stay horizontal even a minute longer.

I banged insistently on Werner's door until finally he appeared.

"Werner!"

He was not ready.

Werner stood naked at the door, a mess of blubber and vomit. Soiled sheets and clothes were twisted in a swirl all around the room, like the remnants of some dissected giant snake. I walked him to the shower and ordered some coffee from room service. I was relieved to see he had a fresh suit in the closet.

"I'll be fine," a cleaner but still clearly death-visited Werner assured me, an entire pot of coffee inside him. "I just need to get some rest on the plane."

In the cab to the airport, Werner slumped against the door, never stirring from a deep sleep. As we neared the terminals I feared he might be totally unconsciousness.

"Werner, we're almost there, wake up."

"Okay, okay. Lewis?"

"Yes?"

"Do you think they have toilets at Japanese airports?"

"Of course they do," I tried to laugh, repressing sudden panic. "Driver, could you speed it up a little? Just drop us at the first terminal."

Werner bolted into the men's room, where I was relieved to see that he unleashed prodigious amounts of vomit.

"You should be fine now, Werner, looks like you got it all out of your system. Kept your clothes clean, too."

Werner smiled wanly. His face glistened in sweat, pale and sagging.

"Look, I may need your help with these interview questions."

"No problem, let's just get you there."

We got seats up front, and once settled on board the plane, Werner fell comfortably asleep, and I began to feel hopeful that we would get through this last interview fine.

As the engines grew louder with the thicker air of descent, however, Werner was instantly awake, a look of horror on his face.

"Werner?"

"I don't feel well."

"Yes, I guessed that. We'll be landing in a minute. Maybe you'll feel better after we walk around."

Werner almost made it. But seconds before touchdown, he grabbed around in panic for something to throw up in. Unaccountably, there were no airsickness bags, and in desperation he unrolled his wet hand towel and quickly overwhelmed it. I promptly gave him mine, too, but they were really not enough to hold it all. Werner had to make a sort of towel-lined bowl with his hands, in which he cupped his dripping puke. I had to fight both the urge to retch in sympathy and a great desire to laugh.

Humiliatingly, though, we were soon trapped in our front seats by passengers crowding to get out and had to wait for the entire planeload to file by in disgust before we could get up or get the attention of a flight attendant.

On the bus from the airport to Honda, I kept Werner awake. It seemed doubtful that he could still have anything in his system, but I wanted to be sure he stayed intact for the interview. I assured him I would ask all the questions.

We met the Honda facility's supply manager in one of the factory sales offices, a stark but bright, tall-ceilinged room.

"Mr. Frisch had a little too much sake last night," I offered by way of explanation and apology when Werner barely managed to murmur a greeting. The Honda man, Mr. Tanaka, the very picture of disciplined bearing, did not seem amused. We plunged on, me taking the lead in most questions. After twenty minutes or so, once we had pulled out blueprints and started to talk about Blohm-Reinman's new pumped-laser driller, Tanaka finally warmed to the conversation, and Werner joined in with sudden interest. We all got the sense that we were talking about major new machine tool sales, not just improvements to the tools to keep them competitive.

"With a handheld CNC controller, I'm sure this would be a really versatile tool. With a sliding mount, we could do linear arrays of holes." The translation work was hard but rewarded with real promise. We began a review of Honda's needs for its planned extension late next year.

"Would you excuse me for a moment?"

I cringed. Werner made a dignified enough exit from the room, but once he was out in the hall, the sound of his running steps echoed clearly through the transom high over the door. I began to speak an apology, but was interrupted by the equally clear sound of Werner's splattering and gasping, again with full echo effects.

"He's in the bathroom just down the hall," Tanaka assured me, sensing my worry about where we were hearing this from. "I'm sure Mr. Frisch will be fine."

Werner established that this would be the routine of our interview. About every ten minutes he would sheepishly smile, exit, and treat us to another chorus of upchuck. In between, rather startlingly, we made substantial progress, with Werner sometimes returning to contribute a new idea that apparently inspired him in the midst of his convulsions.

By the interview's end, Werner was finally down to empty, dry heaves, and we closed the interview with a shared sense of relief and hard-won accomplishment. Blohm-Reinman, it later emerged, won the major contract to outfit Honda's new Kyushu factory wing, based in part on "sensitivity to our needs."

I felt bad for Werner more than let down by him, but it was hard not to feel a sense of disgust, not just about the evening and the next day's copious challenges, but about the damage and constraints to his health and well being. Werner became an icon for me, a talisman warning of consulting's potential destructiveness, an image I hoped never to see in myself.

TOKYO, LONDON, AND SYDNEY, SPRING 1992

Five years later, I lay on the floor of my luxury apartment in Tokyo, secured by my generous package from Gemini. My mind struggles to achieve some kind of consciousness. Above me, looking strangely dangerous, towers the bulk of my Toshiba Big Boom, one of the largest televisions ever made for the consumer market. As I try to sidle away from the set, I feel my shirt absorb what appears to be a puddle of whiskey and cigar ash, and become aware that the man on the screen is trying to calm me down, which overall just seems more worrisome.

"Magnitudes four through five have been recorded from Yoko-hama to Chiba. Shinkansen trains continue to operate, but have automatically been slowed to lowest speeds. Aside from two reports of injury from fallen bookcases and the collapse of a *sushi-ya* in Oji, no casualties are reported at this time." I recall suddenly that my monster TV is equipped with an earthquake sensor. Sufficient jarring throws a switch to turn the television on, preset to the national news channel at high volume, which is likely to be reporting on whatever triggered the sensor within seconds. In a major tectonic seizure, I reflected, it was probably a good sign if your Big Boom was intact enough to tell you about the Big Quake.

So I had slept through a respectable seismic event, I realized. Not good. In six years' living in Japan, I had always woken promptly at even the gentlest roll of the least perceptible tremor. I must have been fairly narcotized to sleep through it, I speculated.

I was right. The whiskey and ash were remnants of my dinner. It was my habit these days to leave work "early," around seven, get some take-out *gyoza* dumplings, skip the social scene, and make my way to my painfully expensive apartment in frumpy old Sangenjaya, a bastion of Tokyo suburban integrity. I would chew and burn most of a Montecristo No. 2 while sitting atop the aircon blowers on the apartment's utility balcony. A bottle of fine Lagavulin for company, there I would reflect on failed relationships and the emptiness of my working life and of my life in general. A little later the Lagavulin would accompany me to unconsciousness, typically as I lay still clothed on the floor, trying unsuccessfully to make it through a reviewing of *Blade Runner* or *The Terminator*. "Whiskey, whiskey, *uisge beatha*, the water of life. Can there be another drink with such infinite variety, such rich complexity of smell, such devoted followers?" an advertisement had recently challenged me. I had no answer.

It was five years since my encounter with Werner Frisch, and much to my disbelief, and as I had feared, I had become him.

"I am Werner," I said aloud to the ceiling. The building gave another shake, as if in response. "Maybe worse," it seemed to say.

Throughout my four years at the Boston Consulting Group, I had tried to maintain some semblance of an exercise routine, and though many workouts were no doubt defeated by a given evening's epicurean indulgences and a Japanese high standard of drink intake, my body more or less cooperated in keeping me presentable and energetic.

Gemini and Centurion quickly tipped the balance. I discovered that I could get by on five hours' sleep, but not less. Committing psychological battery of our Philips clients, in three- or four-day, round-the-clock sessions, sometimes back to back, week after week, for nearly two years, drew me out of any healthy reality. The world was Centurion, just the mind-battery, little sleep, no exercise, and, of course, lots of money. The days in between sessions became time to seriously spend the money, making up for lost time by indulging in alcohol and anything but the Dutch diet. These became times of frantic social energy, pushing relationships with extra force and intensity to make up for sporadic-at-best time commitments.

After a while, the Centurion sessions became times to rest, oases of predictable calm in between my frantic sorties into the outside world. Like the most cynical television evangelist, I learned to conserve my emotional energies, to inflict excitement, fears, and pain, to fraudulently build hope and commitment, while remaining inwardly detached. This battlefront-to-R&R-and-back-again routine was tacitly supported by both Gemini and Philips for all the program's facilitators. Battle fatigue became a real worry, and any pretense of pre-session competitive research, intensive background interviewing, and preparation of original, tailored documentation fell to the wayside. For each session we would walk in with the same package of material, trash and rebuild our clients according to the prescribed rhythm, and then move on. Sessions were always to end at the facilitators' discretion. At first, we would occasionally extend a Centurion a day or half a day just to be sure of closure, insisting on clear project identification and commitments. By the second year, it was unusual if we did not force a wrap half a day early.

Just a few weeks earlier, I had pulled myself together enough to enjoy a week in Cambridge, Massachusetts, for MBA recruiting. Alan had made plain that he thought I needed the change of pace. The experience had mostly deepened my sense of depression.

I had felt like a Boris Yeltsin, propped up to disguise the actual chaos of consulting life in the hope of drawing more resources into the maelstrom. Throughout the interviews, I felt tempted to describe consulting life as it had become for me: a broken marriage that did not even offer the time to enjoy the newfound "freedom" of effective singlehood, an unending series of exhausting sham sessions with clients who were total strangers, a life where stimulation was much more readily found in alcohol than exercise. Friends had become things that you tried to salvage from your past, if you had time. No one in their right mind, I calculated, would take a clear look at me and see the beginnings of a new and rewarding friendship. For this reason in the past few months I had found myself both mistrusting and drawn into an affair with a woman from Singapore, a consultant who actually seemed to admire what I had done to myself. The affair became a virtual celebration of the ugliness of my life, and became the first strident signal I would try to heed that I really needed to make some major changes.

To give a slight air of professional detachment to the Cambridge recruiting interviews, I emphasized how dissolute consulting practices had become, describing what I saw as the lying, cheating, and stealing that had become a routine for the industry. The more I liked the interviewee, the blacker the picture I tried to paint. I failed in the two instances that mattered most to me. Kumiko-san, the McKinsey intern I found particularly attractive, was cautious enough to avoid my shop, but took up a job with another firm. I would later learn to my chagrin that this was because I had peaked her interest in what one well-directed person, like herself, might achieve in the midst of such chaos.

The other recruit that I did not succeed in deterring was for me the greatest irony of all, C.K. Prahalad's son. I really liked him—he seemed to have all his father's best qualities and affability, in trimmer, younger, and more openly honest form. It was as if I had the chance to go back in time and dissuade C.K. himself from a life of self-punishing, manipulative evangelism. He was not dissuaded and joined us as a summer intern.

On my return from recruiting, Alan could see that the experience had been less than energizing for me. His next tack for trying to charge up my reserves was to have me try to raise the spirits of other consultants on the Centurion treadmill.

On our way from Japan to an Australian Centurion, Alan Johnston and I had to take a long diversion to London for a one-day general progress meeting for all Philips facilitators. With Centurion, planes had become places to sleep: gone were the days that consultants on the project busily caught up on session issues. Alan had perfected the habit, always flying first class, with blinders and blanket on, in full recline and dead asleep within minutes of takeoff. It did not take me long to learn the skill. As requested, a flight attendant woke us an hour before landing.

Alan invested a few minutes to thank and make the acquaintance of the attendant, and then turned his attention to me.

"Lewis, I know we hardly have time to catch our breath before Australia, but this London facilitator meeting is going to be very important for us. 'Vanderhammen' from Philips human resources is going to be our guest, and from all reports it looks like things could get out of hand."

"Why, Vanderhammen is getting complaints?"

"No, I don't think so, at least not more than the usual whining, you know, from the Philips managers who want more sessions, or from ones who are trying to take over the process for themselves. No, the problem is with us at Gemini. I'm afraid the other facilitators are going to have some very ugly things to say."

"What, like the schedule is impossible, there's no time to follow through, there's no assurance of quality of the experience, Vanderhammen is too caught up in just counting up the number of participants and the project dollar totals?" I asked, at first meaning to be funny but finding myself caught up in my own words. "Or that we're all exhausted, that we're doing nothing but stressing ourselves and Philips to the breaking point, that we've taken two proud, creative groups of people and beaten them into cowed submission?"

Alan seemed unoffended at the insubordination. "Lewis, you're one of the most reliable and experienced facilitators we have. I'm also watching you slip somehow. You were late for the flight to that Taiwan session. Being late is one of the things that really bothers me, let me tell you, but I'm more concerned that it shows a deeper issue within you. We need to have a talk later about your lifestyle."

I almost bridled. In truth I was obviously none too happy about my life at the moment, but it seemed like my business what I did when I wasn't being brutalized at work. But I put myself in check to let Alan go on with his meeting concerns. The lifestyle issue we could take up later—and there were some peculiar things about his daily life that I would enjoy probing, I told myself.

"The United Research folks are going to be at this meeting, too. We've had a few Centurions in the States that they've run, and they're convinced they can do a better, more systematic job, and give Vanderhammen the numbers and coverage he wants."

"Oh great. The UR drones are going to make us look like wimps. They have no life anyway, and they just love headcount cuts and bloodletting. I thought C.K. banned those louts from any role without his direct supervision?"

"Well, technically Centurion's not really in his control since we acquired his company. He could complain to Timmer, Philips' chairman, but if Vanderhammen hears crybabies at today's meeting, and the ex-UR types assure him there's a better way to stay on track using their staff, there's not much we can do."

"I can't control what the other facilitators say."

"No, but we can emphasize that the bulk of the work is about to shift to Asia, and that we can continue to handle it. We'll draw resources from CMI and the old MAC team in Europe, and run it all through Gemini Japan."

"So technically we'd get all the billings. That would be fantastic for the office."

"Right. And 'Ken Murphy' and all the other Europe facilitators would probably like the shift to Asia. It would pump a little fun and exotica back into the assignment. I'd like you to catch up with your friends, blow off some steam tonight, get them excited about coming out to Asia. They miss you, you know. I've heard about your dinners and nightclub escapades when we were back here in London. It might tone down the complaints if they know you're still with the program and inviting them to join you in Asia. We'll catch UR off guard. UR won't be ready to mobilize for Asia, they can hardly handle the projected support for London and Eindhoven. I want to keep Philips in our hands, Lewis, and I need your help. I also need you to stay in shape to handle it, so later we should talk."

That night I dutifully rounded up Brett Norman, Ken Murphy, and my other Gemini London cronies who were now front-line Centurion facilitators. We decamped to the basement of Saatchi & Saatchi's swank new building in Mayfair, where a high-tech club currently enjoyed pride of place with the city's spendthrift partiers.

My wife and her family had demonstrated extraordinary tolerance in the last days of my marriage and made clear that sheer inertia, and a very Japanese adhesion to appearances, would sustain it until I broke it. Still, I was only slowly overcoming my reluctance to experiment, and I was struggling with where the affair that had begun in Singapore might still take me. Arguably, on this night I should join in the cruising for flesh, celebrating relative freedom, but I knew Alan expected me to achieve a bit more company social fusion. Tonight the club was experimenting with a new karaoke format, and looking over the list of available video recordings, I saw an opportunity to shake up the drippy crooning that had people stuck to their drinks and desultorily shuffling on the dance floor.

"Brett, I'm sure you sing."

"Not bloody likely. I get quite a few opportunities to make a fool of myself in front of crowds at Philips, thank you very much."

I turned to Ken. An Irish-American dual passport holder, Ken had the up-yours insouciance of the supremely fit coxswain too underweight for the rowing team. I knew I could count on Ken to lead the action.

"What do you have in mind?"

Within minutes Ken had five Gemini consultants organized on stage, and a dozen more seeded in the crowd of several hundred for support. Someone had just finished an unconvincingly plaintive rendition of Foreigner's "I Want to Know What Love Is."

No one on the dance floor paid us attention until Ken began to loudly intone "Oh my god it's the Americans, oh my god it's the Americans" over the microphone. The crowd grew quiet and curious. If nothing else, Centurion had instilled us with a fearless, commanding way with even the most hostile assemblies. This one seemed vaguely friendly and ready for a change of pace.

"Good evening ladies, gents, you dead Brits in your pinstripe ugly suits and faggy striped shirts" A few guffaws, a whoop. "I couldn't find a pulse out there on the floor, so we're going to try to start things up." This is greeted with a few cheers.

Though I half expected something unusually raw from Ken, the crowd is no more startled than me as he literally tears open the front of his shirt and begins a hair-raisingly primal rendition of Born to Be Wild. The hyped-up karaoke soundtrack and video, point out unharnessed babes on umuffled bikes on a wall-sized screen jammed between Gargantuan speakers, seem perfectly attuned to Ken's larger-than-life, dangerous energies.

"Get your motor running! Head out on the highway!!" Ken commands, The crowd begins to cheer and howl, and Ken, ape-man like, continues his call to the wild hanging from the stage light superstructure just above us. The rest of us know better than to compete with this, and over our own microphones Brett deadpans the lyrics in perfect Oxbridge, "looking for adventure," and I join in happily on baritone, "and whatever comes our way!" a light if crazy counterpoint to Ken's continued savagery.

As the song approaches its riotous crescendo, I become anxious that the DJ will now try to control or dampen the wild energies now threatening to run rampant. But the DJ seems to sense this would be futile, and with a look at me that says things have only just begun to get interesting, he sets the video to repeat. More consultants and random tribal celebrants from the floor come up to take over the singing. Ken drops to a squat on the floor but keeps a mike in hand as more of the masses join in. "Be American," he provides in a sinister but clear undertone. "Do drugs, take a toke. Go ahead, get shot on a motorcycle," Brett begins to narrate the video showing clips from *Easy Rider*. "Hey, you there, off with your shirt" Ken singles out an attractive businesswoman. "No, really, you can keep your business jacket on." Remarkably, she complies, and the technicians replace the video with an image of her dancing on the giant screen, flashes of succulence emerging behind tidy lapels.

The air electrifies. No longer an after-work crowd of overstressed professionals, this is primal heat unleashed, a celebration of manic energy poised on debauchery. The DJ has no intention of backing off the intensity, and "Wild Thing" blasts, with Ken and Brett singing to each other as the Velvet Underground provides the pounding rhythm. Weirdly, the soundtrack's video of Vietnam war news footage is interspersed with pans of the floor, and the camera begins to dwell on a variety of lewd acts, which are cheered by the crowd. I see a woman grab and pull Ken offstage, and I figure I have done my bit to ensure a good time.

The next day the dour Vanderhammen confronts a convincingly exhausted crowd of facilitators, and he agrees to some greater spacing of the sessions in Europe, if more coverage can be provided for the growing cascade of Centurions in Asia that Alan proposes. The ex-MAC crowd immediately agrees, with the United Research veterans caught flat-footed.

Alan is pleased with the new arrangements for Philips, but even more concerned now about my ability to handle the pace. The Australian Centurion reminds us both how harrowing these things can still be. The country manager is hostile, and continues to use BCG for projects that should contractually come under Gemini's ambit of work. The normal alcohol rules suspended, he had gotten drunk and belligerent that evening, and we had to tail him as he went room to room to harass the small groups, yelling at his subordinates, groping the women, and deriding the whole process. It was now after midnight, and Alan and I had left the hotel exhausted.

We walked outside the great expanse of the Sydney Opera House.

"Thanks, Lewis, I know that was tough. Looks like we'll get through with this one. I'm not really counting on much of a cascade of work here anyway."

"It's just hard not getting angry. He's not even supposed to be anywhere near the small groups—those are exercises in free, independent thinking. I can't believe that anything we've done here will stick."

"Well, we knew we would never have one-hundred percent success. This group is already in trouble; it won't reflect on us. But I hope you got a good look at how around the bend people can become."

We walked on silently for a while.

"Lewis, didn't you tell me you did rock climbing in college, climbing buildings?"

"Sure. It's been a while."

"What do you think about this?" Alan asked, gesturing at the Opera House.

My heart began to race a little. I took in the structure's famous steep, sweeping lines, the looping white parabolas of gravity-defying metal and glass, the complete lack of handholds.

"Well, this isn't really the kind of thing I climbed. This would be a pretty serious technical challenge."

"Come on, I want to try. We'll pick an easy part, that shorter section over there. Let's see how far we'll get."

I was speechless. The climb looked to be dangerous and, at the minimum, ridiculously conspicuous. But Alan seemed to be entrusting me with an urge to assert his own youthfulness, and I had not said no to him yet. I pointed to a section of carved stones, a wall leading up to one of the smallest cupola structures.

"I guess we should start from here." The climb up the stones was familiar, even exhilarating, but a serious physical effort. I was in a complete sweat, feeling every extra pound of beer belly I had acquired. I dried my hands on my suit jacket and tossed it down to the ground together with my shoes and socks. Alan did the same.

Breath coming hard, I coached Alan on the next step.

"The metal shell won't be easy until we get to where it levels off. Try to press the flat of your hand against these raised dimples of metal. See how they're like separate tiles? Push off them, same with your feet. Don't try gripping with your fingers, they'll just cramp and give out. Keep your body flat against the curvature all the time, and if you start falling, stay close on the shell, don't try to get up. And don't grab me, please! Just use your whole body's friction to slow down and try to grab something where the shell overlaps the rest of the building at the bottom. When you get tired, stop. Oh, and don't look down."

Alan had relatively little difficulty making progress up the shell. I struggled along, uneasy with the distance we'd gained from the ground. After a while, we lost our orientation on the giant curvature and seemed to be headed across rather than further up the peaked hump of the shell.

"This is like an Escher drawing," Alan laughed. "We keep climbing but we don't seem to be going up!"

"It might be time to head down," I hopefully suggested.

We crab-walked our way across the tiles until we came to the rim where the shell joined the top of the ground floor, which offered a reassuringly stable place to sit. We took some minutes to catch our breath and take in the great night view of Sydney Harbor.

"Lewis, you're really in terrible shape. We have a lot more of these Centurions coming, and I can't just have you crashing between sessions. I understand how we all get into that habit, but we have a business to grow, too. I need you developing Abegglen's leads and managing those cases, building us a future in Japan beyond Philips. I need you to help us get on with our Asia expansion.

"Your work is good, terrific. But I need more of it. I've seen your relationships in a tumult, you had the secretaries playing crazy games with your phone calls. It's my hope for you that things will settle down now. I have to be candid: we know you've started getting into something with that consultant from Singapore, and her boss is asking after her; he doesn't trust you. I know you hung on to your marriage mostly out of momentum. You can party hard, that's your business, but I can't have you late for client commitments, which everyone notices is starting to happen. My advice is, make up your mind. Make the jump and get married again if you want. But then manage this new relationship in a better way, and admit to yourself you're only human, and might start having affairs again. But do it in a way that doesn't hurt your new wife, the way you're hurting your old one now.

"Your appearance isn't too good, either," Alan tried to add a little more lightly. "You're starting to look too much like how our clients see themselves—you've got to hold yourself to a higher standard."

A low-flying jet curved round the harbor, probably the last flight of the night. I could just make out the passengers at the windows and envied them what I imagined to be their uncomplicated, unpressured lives.

"I want to let you in on few secrets. First of all, you've got to exercise. Do you know what I do?"

"No," I replied honestly, and not without a little curiosity. Alan seemed to be in great shape, but he kept all his personal routines very private.

"Aerobics. Aerobics with weights. Anywhere I go, I try to find a class, and if I can't, I carry these water weights with me, plastic dumbbell shells you just fill with water, and work out in my room."

The picture of Alan dancing around with his weights was not the most masculine image I could conjure; it certainly did not fit the manful, red-blooded character he assumed for clients.

"And I'm not saying don't drink. But whenever the pounds start to show on me, I just cut the alcohol for a while, and the pounds just vanish. I think we have the same body type, and with some exercise, I think this will work for you, too."

I nodded, a little inspired despite myself. I had no idea that Alan was so conscious of these things, or needed to be.

"As for this new relationship, if you get married again, the romance will fade—it always does, it's just biology, psychology. But you may have kids, and you'll have made a new commitment. This time, there will be things you can do differently. Just face the reality. Don't be afraid to make friends, find new partners. Let them know you're married, though, don't pretend you can make a new commitment. You'd be surprised how little difference it makes. Soon you'll have women in every city you fly to; you'll learn to really love the travel. But don't mess around in your own town, be attentive to your spouse whenever you're there. You'll find you love her more, and your kids will be happier for it, too."

I listened with morbid fascination, not daring to ask whether Alan spoke from experience. No doubt he was right about many of these methods and could have easily drawn them from the myriad of our divorced and divorced-again colleagues. For a moment, though, I could not help my mind jumping to the conclusion that a lot of things seemed to fall into place: Alan's early departures for assignments, his nights to himself, his staying on past assignments to pursue "follow-up leads." His wife always seemed to regard me with particular hostility, perhaps, I now reasoned, because she saw me as a representative of the vehicle that gave Alan such freedoms. Or had Alan simply seen so much of this in others that he knew exactly what to advise? Janet Johnston would be the one who really knew, I decided, and refused to think of this further.

Alan was still going on, though. "Keep the company separate from your home life. Use voicemail, and don't give out your home number. Get another line with a machine if you have to. As your vacation time builds up, use it, in big bunches. Don't resent the time you spend married again, make the most of it; make your wife really feel like your wife. Get your own special place for vacations and commit to total privacy, the absolute sanctity of the relationship and the family there."

I recalled my hostile reception in Wyoming and realized that even if Alan *was* speaking from experience, his foolproof system had its imperfections. But Alan at least had a stability to his life that I had yet to find. I was dismayed, however, at what seemed to be the choices: a UR-style death of the brain and soul, the Werner-style path of self-destruction along which I was already well along, or the frank embracing of my flaws as recommended by Alan, using the worst of consulting to make the best of my human failings.

I thanked Alan for his advice, and we started down to the ground. I asked him when his next aerobics class was, and he cheerfully invited me to come along.

"Besides," he assured me, "I'm sure it's a terrific place for you to meet women."

CONSULTING DEMONOLOGY, TRACT 9

DEMON HOSTS OF THE CONSULTING LIFE: PAIN-MANAGEMENT ARCHETYPES

1

The athlete. Fitness fanaticism is common coping strategy for surviving the overstretched consulting life. A health-minded, life-preserving response to the deceptions and pressures of the work is only natural, and with airplane confinement, rich, salty foods, and drum barrels of alcohol conspiring to achieve muscle wastage if not an early, bloated demise, intensive workouts are plainly a good idea. The difficulty, of course, is finding time and opportunity. Confined to midnight or 4 A.M. workouts, forced to suffer social abstinence among more indulgent clients and associates, and sure to draw the resentment of more rapidly deteriorating colleagues, the consulting athlete is hard put to find room for anything other than work and working out. Increasingly grim and humorless, wanting for social contact both at home and in the workplace, the athlete quickly acquires a reputation for unimaginative one-dimensionality and misses creative opportunities for major client sales and involvements. A type characteristic of many women in the industry, the consulting athlete is typically found brooding in consulting's middle ranks, filling as many administrative roles as possible to regularize workouts.

2:

The bon vivant. The consulting bon vivant's response to stresses and strains of the industry is uncomplicated. Given little time and opportunity to cultivate particular relationships or tastes, the bon vivant chooses to spend and indulge at every opportunity, making friends and sampling new relationships, cuisines, and experiences at every opportunity. Occasionally a bit of a gourmand and a drunk, the bon vivant is tolerated and even encouraged by the industry's culture for the predictable ease with which their desires and needs can be satisfied. Not a workhorse, but at times brilliantly inspired. Most often but not exclusively male, and ideally suited for random travel, recruiting, and unsavory client entertainment.

3

The connoisseur. The connoisseur, like the bon vivant, thrills to ride the waves of consulting's self-indulgent culture, but prefers to navigate his own course rather than simply drift with its random currents. The connoisseur will plan travel around ski seasons, concerts, Beaujolais nouveau, and planned affairs and adulteries in select cities. Ideally positioned for consulting leadership, the connoisseur patiently nurtures his own track record and key indulgences for a lifetime of gratifications. Almost always found among the more senior men in the field.

4

The family man. As the name implies, an almost exclusively male category. The family man lets it loudly be known that family must come first and will conspicuously both overcompensate with extra hours work, and choose key events to miss, just to show he can. A usually transient and ill-fitted species, the family man tends to either rapidly evolve into other consulting types or get summarily dismissed. Highly stressed, the family man is a frequent source of client resentment, as clients' own lives trend toward personal disruption, and is among the most distracted, unproductive, and least liked types in the industry. Ironically, the rare attempts by women to assert rights to family manhood that *are* made, with the help of implications of legal action for discrimination, are usually successful.

5

The terminator. A category roughly equally distributed between men and women in the consulting industry, terminators subsume all personal identity to the single-minded purpose of success in their consulting careers.

Unthinking and bereft of spontaneity, they are typically short on ideas and solutions, and long on reliability and stamina. Every case team needs a few around, both for execution of demanding, unpleasant tasks, and for occasional supervised display to clients. Terminators enjoy being told what to do, but require close care and supervision, showing doglike loyalty to mentors and high-billing-hour clients. Much to their bewilderment, terminators rarely ascend to top consulting ranks and do so only through fierce attachment to one or two in-house or client protectors.

6

The dilettante. A demanding model for the consulting life that requires high expenditures of energy and time, the dilettante can be one of the industry's most well-liked types, especially by clients. A successful dilettante evidences great depth and range of nonconsulting talents and interests, and brings them to bear in intelligent, creative ways to at least lighten if not usefully inform the burdens and tasks at hand. In combination with hard-working discipline and habits, the dilettante's behaviors are one of the richest, most highly appreciated cultural resources of the industry. In combination with habits of excess, however, the dilettante can quickly devolve to a merely tolerated bon vivant. Dilettante behaviors are more readily accepted in men, and tend to be viewed as an unfortunate lack of seriousness in women.

7

The supervisor. A disease best diagnosed and cured early on. Consulting is a business that benefits little from mere supervision, thriving instead on the full participation of the case team in the solution-making process. Consultants who need supervisory discipline are usually by definition not fated to be good consultants, so that supervisors become either superfluous or destructive. Consultants attracted to this model, usually men, are typically trying to hide their own inadequacies in the work and are frightening credit-grabbers. Once allowed to ascend to a certain level, however, this is a species sometimes tolerated by the culture for its desperate cunning in mobilizing others' talents and resources to get tasks done.

8

The addict. For some the idea of client problem-solving is all consuming. The dream of most clients, the addict will live and breathe the client's concerns and issues, worrying their problems night and day until a robust solution is found or created. Capable of some of the most thoroughgoing work in the industry, addicts are often frowned upon for their overconcentration on selected clients and problems, but valued for their contributions to difficult cases. As likely to be women as men, addicts rarely ascend to consulting's top ranks for want of attention to the needs of the consulting business itself.

9

The self-abuser. Unable to comfortably live with the conflicting and impossible demands of consulting life, the self-abuser will simply always try harder. Again as likely male as female, the self-abuser is characteristically worn and fatigued. Seeing his or her own inadequacies as the root cause of failed accomplishment, the self-abuser is typically unskilled at drawing on others for help. This type tends to frighten clients and colleagues alike, and can count only on sheer stamina to survive and grow.

10

The consultant. There is perhaps no ideal consulting model, but if the net forces of the industry were allowed to give shape to a composite, the consultant would emerge. The consultant would have the best possible education for both business and analytic problem-solving, say a Cambridge undergraduate education in math or physics and a Harvard MBA, and be equipped to make any intellectual challenge in business seem dead easy, given a requisite fluency in analytic technique. He would no doubt be a he, but sexually neutral in his own demands, attractive but nonsensuous, interesting but nonthreatening to clients, recruits, and colleagues, evincing a sense of romance for consulting itself. Equipped with a dilettante's range of interests but an athlete's discipline and stamina, the consultant's solutions would be creative, entertaining, and to the point. The consultant's business interests would include the success of his own firm as well as his clients' businesses. Skilled at finding tolerable pleasures in the chaos of travel and long hours, the consultant would nonetheless savor opportunities apart from consulting to reaffirm his own identity and re-create the inner self from which the consultant's energies are drawn. Low of ego, multilingual, and at ease with becoming immersed in the struggles of others, the consultant is at home in almost any environment where there is a business need. Amazingly, this composite, or something very close to it, occasionally surfaces as a real person. At BCG, for example, the youngest person there to make officer very nearly defines this profile. But it is the far more typical lack of many of these attributes that encourages firms today to divide the tasks of consulting labor, and hide deficiencies of both firm and individual in contrived stratagems and well-practiced deceptions.

CHAPTER 10

THE GREAT CENTURION

TOKYO, SUMMER 1992

BACK AT BCG I HAD LEARNED SOME HARD LESSONS ON THE SHELL CASE about working beyond my abilities, without manager and officer support, and about consulting companies' general unwillingness to turn away even the most far-afield assignments. Or so I had hoped. In my eagerness to get a break from Centurion, three years later, at Gemini Japan in 1992, I failed to see the dark outlines of a similar pattern beginning to emerge.

Foreign cigarette sellers in Japan had long contended that they were being artificially held to a maximum 10 percent share of the domestic cigarette market. After hard-fought negotiations with Tokyo's tobacco bureaucracy, Philip Morris had won the right to test this assumption. The Tobacco and Salt Bureau would allow Philip Morris to conduct an in-depth strategic study of Japan's tobacco markets, interviewing every retailer and supplier involved in cigarettes' complex distribution system. If, based on their study, they identified new ways to invest and improve their market performance, the bureau promised to assist in any needed changes and facilitate as required with domestic manufacturers.

Based on early successes with Kodak in Japan during Dr. Abegglen's BCG Tokyo days, Abegglen enjoyed a strong reputation with Philip Morris as a no-nonsense, hardened veteran of American companies' Japan market-entry wars. He also had the kind of senior acceptability needed to win Japan Tobacco's confidence in the relative neutrality of the study on behalf of Philip Morris. What Abegglen did not have, however, was a competent team handy for the task.

"Lewis, I've got some good news for you. Our next block of Centurion sessions is going to be here in Japan, with C.K. doing most of the facilitating, so that gives you almost six weeks of operation here in Tokyo. I'd like you to start off Jim's new case with Philip Morris."

Alan Johnston and I were busy watching shrimp being given a light anesthesia by way of a dip in sake at the next table. Sometime early in our stay in Japan, Alan and I had gotten into an unfortunate food gross-out contest that had yet to hit bottom. I had related to Alan one time the many unsavory things I had eaten in Asia, and he had argued that there was nothing to whine about, that all these things were no doubt healthier for me than my usual daily diet. So we had gone the rounds, first of the usual dried crickets and snake blood, then on to sea slugs and raw live lobster, and most recently horse and kangaroo sushi, one I thought Alan would surely lose. I was fairly sure tonight I would get Alan to admit surrender with the shrimp.

"Philip Morris? Kraft-General Foods Division?" I asked hopefully.

"No, I know, if you're like me this is the kind of case you swore you would never do. It's Philip Morris, cigarettes. But before you choke, let me emphasize where we're at here. Abegglen's sold almost no cases for us. Ferragamo is threatening to back off their retainer. This could be the big one—Philip Morris is all over Asia, and it would be a great catch. If we can do something on the tobacco side, I'm sure it will be a key entree for the foods group, too. Speaking of entree, what's the deal here?"

"These are shrimp. The chef's going to fry us up some veggies in the wok, and then clean it out, put just a touch of soya and sake in, and let them skitter around in there for maybe three seconds. Then you get 'em. Peel off the back carapace like he shows you, and bite in."

"They're pretty big," Alan observed.

"The trick is, once the back's peeled, bite them right there, on the back, pull their meat out. Try to keep the legs and feelers and things pointed away from your mouth and nose, because they can really get moving when you start tearing their guts out. Generally, I take a swig of sake first, numbs us both a bit, I think."

"Great," Alan leered. "I like the sake part."

"What are we supposed to do for them exactly? Don't tell me they want a revitalization program to get their morale up! Not enough smokers in Asia for them?"

"No," Alan laughed as our server approached, "This is a share-growth strategy. They have a six-percent share of the total market, that makes them the leading foreign player. So far, it seems the market's been capped at a ten-percent total share for all foreign players. Philip Morris has done some serious lobbying back in Washington, and now Japan Tobacco's under some political pressure to let the Marlboro Man get the run of the range. Am I supposed to pick these out?" Alan asked, presented with a fish bowl of live shrimp.

"That's right. Here, I'll go first. Tell me what we're actually supposed to do, then."

"Well, it may take a lot of coverage. We need to talk to all the vendors and retailers. Apparently, a lot of what determines market share is how many columns in the vending machines you see everywhere are loaded with a given brand."

"Oh, it's like beer and whiskey machines then," I said, picking out my victims. Any laws against minors purchasing beer and cigarettes would be rendered immediately ineffective by the ubiquitous presence of vending machines on nearly every street corner. The mini-keg dispensing ones were my favorite. "The beer companies come up with all kinds of bribes for store owners to give more space to their brands in the vending machines they operate."

"See, you're way ahead of the game. There are some historical distribution issues. Philip Morris has traditionally used two separate distributors for East and West Japan, and we'd need to sort out some of the efficiencies. Basically, it's a top-to-bottom distribution strategy, with some financials and projections. They want a plan to show Japan Tobacco. If they follow the plan, invest in certain increases in promotions and distribution, they want to see an overall increase for their share of the market, one that breaks the ten percent barrier for all foreign firms combined. Oooh, he's fighting back!"

I had taken hold of the first hapless morsel of my dinner. He did not seem too well stunned, protesting vigorously as soon as I had his back shell off.

"Normally they calm down a bit, long enough to get the flesh into your mouth without too much struggle. There, he's slowed up now."

I put the exposed meat of the shrimp in my mouth, and quickly incised whatever I could get away from the remaining parts of its body. A fury of legs and feelers erupted, catching a bit of one nostril, but otherwise under control. The feeling of life stolen was profound.

"Yummy," I pronounced, tossing the still-quivering remnants into the special refuse dish, adding "*Ha, oishii, genki datta,*" for the chef's benefit, letting him know he had put up a deliciously good fight.

"So let me see if I've got this right. You're saying we need to do field interviews in East and West Japan, design new logistics for distribution, develop a scheme to control and implement incentives, create promotion budgets and campaigns based on tight financials, and create measures of success or failure that the Tobacco Bureau will accept and enforce. Sounds like six to eight people, a two million dollar job over six to eight months. Maybe this is the perfect time to bring over the United Research types? They'd love all the distribution logistics."

"Well, this is the thing. Later, on a second phase, we might bring in a bigger crew. But all you described is about right, just that it's you, me, 'Sandy,' and Abegglen."

Alan tore into his shrimp, and I felt like it was me squirming in panic for dear life. Abegglen, I knew, would manage the Philip Morris contacts, but working with him would effectively be like serving another client, one who could look closely over my shoulder every day. Alan's travel schedule made any pretensions of assistance ridiculous. Sandy, a new American consultant hired through London, spoke Japanese but had limited consulting experience outside financials. That left me to do the kind of study about which I was arguably most ignorant, for the one industry I most loathed.

I grabbed another shrimp just for the distraction.

"You know, Alan, I know you think highly of me, but these Japan Centurions with C.K. won't be trivial, and distribution logistics is not really my thing. It's not that I can't sacrifice a little personal ethics for the good of the office, it's just not something I could handle well."

"I didn't think you had a problem with smoking," Alan evaded.

"The cigars are a bit of an indulgence, a mood thing with me. Ads and cartoons targeted at kids, who get vending machine access anywhere, is a lot more unsettling. What really gets me is the way smoking is positioned as a small pleasure that is supposed to make everything Japanese sacrifice for their companies' sakes more tolerable. If you can smoke, then you can put up with the long hours, suppressed emotions, fundamental unfairness, lost personal identity. Look at any TV drama."

"Look, I'm no fan of cigarettes, either, but it does sound like you're reading a lot into it. If we don't help Philip Morris it still won't stop the share increase of foreign cigarettes here. Let me make my point. This does not have to be the most brilliant study ever; this isn't some BCG intellectual breakthrough assignment. Philip Morris just needs some kind of evidence to make their case, some tracking systems, a logic for how to position their promotion funds. I know you can do it. Frankly, and I don't like putting it this way, Lewis, you have to do it."

Alan had my full attention. I let my last shrimp gasp in its own stunned state for a bit longer.

"Abegglen complains that we spend too much time on Centurion," Alan continued. It's just the excuse he needs to get off the hook for his own budget commitments to Cap Gemini. We need to show him we're committed. You and I both want to move along the expansion to the rest of Asia, but Abegglen can block this very effectively if he wants to."

"Maybe we should just pass on Philip Morris, or take on a very small phase one chunk of it, see how it goes. Meanwhile, you know we have good acquisition prospects in Singapore and Hong Kong, starting with PacRim. I could move those along, maybe the acquisition process can bypass Abegglen altogether, present him with a fait accompli."

"Okay, Lewis, here's what we can try to do. You continue with the acquisition investigation, at low speed, in conjunction with some casework. We'll split the Philip Morris stuff into phases, and I'll get you some of Abegglen's old AAS boys to help you with it. But we can't just let it go."

This was clearly Alan's last word on the subject, and we dispatched the rest of our shrimp and vegetables. A bit of history was about to repeat itself, with critical consequences.

Later, when Alan headed for the bathroom, I surreptitiously wrapped my last shrimp in a damp hand towel and stuffed in it in my coat pocket; as we walked along the Sumida River toward the main road to get a cab, I tossed the towel in. The Sumida is famously toxic, and I did not even know if the shrimp was a fresh or saltwater crustacean. But I felt a little better knowing he had at least a chance of escape.

A select few in consulting grow larger than life, inflating their presence and influence in the industry to the point where they can rise above its everyday stresses and strains. These are the gurus, super-consultants who do not fear the trend of mergers and acquisitions in the industry, but who become instead masters of exploiting them. As independent icons of power, they can comfortably focus on areas of expertise specific to their own well-defined niche and avoid the increasing pressure in the industry to feign universal capabilities. Removed from the nerve-racking game of maneuvering up the consulting hierarchy, they answer to no one but their publicists.

Consulting companies at times engineer the creation of gurus from within their own ranks. A successful veteran partner, reluctant to retire, over time becomes a potential liability. Senior consultants command such high daily billing rates that case leaders strenuously avoid them, ironically creating more and more idle time for the members of the firm with the highest salaries. While some of a firm's bonus pool may be reserved for rewarding individual performance and sales efforts, a substantial portion of the pool typically remains generically available to all members of rank, ensuring that the gray-beards get some of the highest take, regardless of billable hours.

But avoiding any exit lacking in dignity, particularly one that might draw away staff or clients, is something for which most firms will willingly pay this high price. A senior eminence can become so strongly identified with every aspect of the firm that to publicly sever relations risks destabilizing the firm itself. The consulting companies become the unwitting hostages of their highest paid, least productive staff, paying an additional price in both external credibility and internal morale if no means out of the bind is found.

Easing a senior consultant out into the public realm can offer an attractive end to their risks and high costs. New contracts reducing an officer to half-time or quarter-time status, offset by support for teaching, books, and public appearances, can become a win-win deal for consultant and firm alike. The newly designated guru typically gets a free research staff for writings, attractive office space, acknowl-edged godfather status in the form of a practice or regional office chairmanship, and complete coverage for all promotion costs. The firm ordinarily wins not only reduced costs, but also iron-clad guar-antees against direct competition, defection, or bad-mouthing, and a favorable reputation for taking care of its own. And, with luck, the newly minted guru will work hard at his new incarnation, and become a successful draw for new business and recruits.

Other gurus are self-made. Typically working up and outward from a business school professorship, the self-made icon of consulting will develop studies in the course of research and interviews, draw inferences for theories, and test these theories in side-consulting jobs, which in turn become case studies for further writing and research. Eventually, the side consulting jobs can begin to displace teaching and research responsibilities and a reenforcing combination of writing-gained referrals and learning-rich casework can be triggered.

The best of the self-made gurus become institutions themselves, complete with MBA-wielding consulting staff. Harvard Business School professor Michael Porter defined the model in the late 1970s and early 1980s, applying economic theory to corporate strategy in research and practice, founding and leading the successful boutique firm of Monitor Company, and anchoring a chain of referrals around a succession of bestselling manuals of consulting practice, beginning with his landmark *Competitive Strategy*.

As I settled into my role as manager at Gemini Japan, I learned to balance a life between the forces of both these models. I soon learned that in our relatively small outpost in Tokyo, I would effectively have no supervising officer, but instead two gurus. Alan Johnston, having opened the Gemini Japan office and fed it a train of Philips Centurion cases, became engulfed in executing the Philips work and keeping up with the politics of the global firm's ongoing merger. That left me with Jim Abegglen, who continued to use much of the fledgling office's resources for the writing of his second book, and C.K. Prahalad, keen to use Philips Centurion sessions in Japan as a testing ground for further development of his strategic intent and core competence models.

SINGAPORE, SUMMER 1992

Pat Curran and I began a restless night out in Singapore. It was my third or fourth time visiting the tightly managed city-state, and Pat's first. The woman I had started openly seeing was out of town, on another consulting assignment, which I correctly took as another bad portent for the relationships in my consulting life. We sat at the Longbar of the newly restored Raffles Hotel.

"Lewis, I've told you before, haven't I, that sometimes I feel like my whole life is spent trailing you," Pat remarked over his highly garnished Singapore sling.

"Sure, you get more poetic about it every time. We're locked in parallel trajectories, some rubbish like that."

"No," Pat laughed, "that sounds like you. I only said trailed. You really like these things?" he asked, trying to force his straw to the bottom of a glass filled with pink foam over ice, pineapple, cherries, and two miniature umbrellas.

"Not that way, no," I said finishing my beer. "If you're going to trail, do it right." I ordered us straight sling mix in yard-long glasses, with extra gin and lime juice, no ice or accouterments.

"The evidence is I am trailing you. You work at Nippon Kokan; I intern. You go into consulting at BCG; I wind up with Abegglen and the ex-BCG crowd. You go to Gemini; I wind up in Gemini. I worked on that U.S.-Japanese robot JV right after you. For a while there, I thought you were going to snake my wife before we got engaged. If you did, hell, I probably would have wound up marrying her second."

"It is kind of spooky. Are you some kind of slow-witted stalker or something? Or is it just a lack of imagination?" I teased.

Normally reserved for serious beer-drinking bouts, our yard-long glasses arrived to a good deal of ceremony and attention. Shaped like oversize test tubes with glass bulbs at one end and drinking funnels at the other, they came mounted in wooden racks and glowed like pink neon tubes. Pat dismounted and carefully balanced his yard, and took a gulp of his lukewarm, souped-up sling.

"Oh my. Dishwater, cough syrup, and a great deal of potency, in a raw ethanol sort of way. Surprisingly smooth," he adjudged, wiping pink foam from his mouth, "I like it."

"Trailer," I accused.

"Well, that's just it. If I *am* trailing you, you've got me greatly worried."

I ordered some nuts. I thought I knew where Pat might be headed with this, and was not sure this was the right venue for taking up the challenge. The Longbar is a beautiful piece of work, featuring two eponymous, enormous lengths of deeply rich wooden bars, on separate floors joined by a gigantic carved wooden spiral staircase. Mechanical pukah fans sway in unison from the ceiling, and cozy, candlelit tables and booths are scattered throughout both floors. A Filipino pop band holds forth most nights on the second floor.

"You know what I don't like about this place?" I asked, choosing to temporarily ignore Pat's comment.

"Nothing? The cute women in the slit skirts? The fawning service?"

"Exactly, all that. It's too perfect. You know, a few months ago I went to Penang, and visited the bar at the Raffles sister hotel there. It was built by the Kardoorie brothers, too, around the same time, in the 1800s. It was dirty and raggedy, with the more recent changes looking the worst, like the ratty carpet. But it's so authentic. If you want to check out the colonial lifestyle, I figure, why not go to where colonialists really hung out."

"Wasn't the Longbar always here? I thought great novels got written right here, Somerset Maugham and all that."

"No, that's just it. The Longbar used to be downstairs, almost a block away from here. It was in total disrepair, but it was real, and attracted some real characters, people who had come there nearly every day for half a century. Now we've got this, the perfect reconstruction, with modern materials, exorbitant prices, and tourists and businessmen with nothing to stare at but each other and the waitresses. You'd be hard pressed to even find a prostitute in here."

"Is that a suggestion?"

The yards by now had fully taken on the look of a chemistry experiment, with different shades of pink separating in the column, mysterious solids gathering in the bottom, and a reddish encrustation displacing the collapsing pink foam on top.

"Indeed, time to drink up."

We duly chugged our experiments, to scattered applause. Unfortunately Pat was unprepared for the turbulent gush of liquid that released itself from the bulb, once the yard was upended.

"Well, now we really need to leave," I observed.

Pat's white shirt was now a nearly uniform pink, his tie stained one shade darker. His blue blazer seemed to have absorbed the damage less evenly.

"Let's go somewhere where they might appreciate your new look."

We walked along the Singapore River, up by Clarke Quay and on toward the Next Page Pub. There seemed to be a threat of rain, the kind we would welcome in the oppressiveness of the still and smoggy heat.

"Why's it called Next Page?" Pat asked as we crossed the bridge over the quay.

"There used to be a Front Page, next to it. It was closed or burned down, maybe both. Used to be a hangout for journalists, you know, the free press and the brave little dissident crowd. Occasional drugs, a real air of trouble. Next Page is a name of protest, maybe a promise to stir up a little trouble of its own."

Next Page was brightly lit, but made cozy by a thick haze of smoke that seemed permanently settled amidst the pub's many Chinese antiques and furnishings. Screens and carvings broke up the space and lent it an air of secrecy and privacy. Seating was a mix of divans, mandarin chairs and stools, and silk cushions on the floor.

"Quite the opium den."

"Nice, isn't it? Maybe we should stick to beer here," I suggested, and ordered us two pitchers of Tiger.

"So, you're worried," I finally relented.

"Well, for a start, what are we doing here in Singapore?"

"Centurion, of course."

"Yes, the Display Components Centurion. But didn't you notice the session finished yesterday? Almost everybody's gone back to China, Japan, and Holland."

"Well, we're doing follow-up work on the projects. I've got two interviews set up for us here tomorrow."

"That's great, I mean, it's good for the billings and all, but aren't we in the middle of a new series of sessions with C.K. in Japan? You know, C.K. *Prahalad*, the guru who started Centurion, the one guy who's still serious about interview preparations and having all the competitive homework done in advance? The one facilitator who makes his complaints direct to Chairman Timmer?"

I shrugged as our pitchers of Tiger beer arrived. The accompanying glasses simply looked small and fussy, so we proceeded to drink from the pitchers.

"I mean, maybe we could rehash some stuff from the Components Division for C.K., but what about Dr. Abegglen and Philip Morris? Are you determined to get on his bad side?"

"What do you mean?"

"What do I mean! I mean, you're the case leader. You know Abegglen's not doing anything, and Alan's afraid to get caught in the details of it. Sandy's out doing a lot of offensive interviews that seem to be closing more doors than producing new data. We've got a junior Japanese analyst producing a spaghetti diagram of distribution logistics that no one is ever going to want to see. If you don't get in there and do something, Alan will make me do it, Abegglen will be on the war path, and we'll probably never get to phase two of the study."

I had a sudden image of me as Nick Fong and Pat as me, back on the BCG Shell debacle. It was time for me to share a few doubts and ambitions.

"Pat, it's possible you might get called in to Philip Morris if I leave

it, but I promise not to drag you in beforehand and leave you hanging with what I started to set up there. If you get it, it will be a fresh
case, your framework and approach."

"So you're planning to leave it? Oh my god. Does Alan know
this?"

"I expect Alan to call and raise hell any day. I haven't checked my
voicemail. But maybe it would be a good thing if I left and concen-
trated on things here."

"You mean the steel study?" Pat asked hopefully.

In an uncomfortable overcommitment of our resources, we had
taken up an all-Asia steel consumption study for an Australia iron ore
supplier. The client and the work had been introduced by PacRim, a
small conference-geared consultancy and one of our key acquisition
targets in Southeast Asia. Pat had been stuck with most of the mind-
numbing model production, while I squeezed in some fun interviews
with people like Honda to discuss their plans for replacing steel with
aluminum in all their engines and car bodies.

"Well, less the steel study than PacRim. Your spreadsheets are
looking really good, by the way. I think we have a really strong case
to show that production of steel in Japan may drop, but consumption
will remain strong. Got to love those earthquake scenarios!"

We diverted for a while into a discussion of how Pat might
manage the final presentation of the steel case. By now several new
groups of revelers had arrived, and we were crowded onto what
had once been an enormous Chinese platform bed. Though the
company was friendly, we decided to leave, still clutching our
pitchers.

We headed in the direction of the Velvet Underground, one of
Singapore's more mysterious nightclubs.

"But what about PacRim?" Pat queried a bit blearily.

"Well, you know we're planning on expanding. We seem to be
having some trouble getting Paris and Morristown excited about
supporting our acquisition plans. We've put a lot of energy into
PacRim, and both Alan and I agreed this case with them has to come

out really strong. That's why you get the luxury of spending so much time on those spreadsheets."

"Some luxury. But you and Alan are looking for some way to beef up PacRim for acquisition? Abegglen is definitely not going to be happy with the distraction."

We joined the queue waiting outside Velvet Underground.

"Well, he's going to be even less happy about what Alan and I have been thinking about. If Paris won't be forthcoming, we can up the stakes. I can quit Gemini, or take a leave of absence, and become partner and director at PacRim. I help them be a bit more robust, and glide back into Gemini by way of acquisition."

"The golden scenario! Little company in the right place at the right time! You take a huge salary cut, but make gobs back on the acquisition. You asshole, Abegglen would never let Alan get away with it. And this place looks very interesting and all, but I really don't see myself following you here. It sounds completely scary. What are your backup plans?"

Before I could answer we were ushered in, and quickly enveloped in a weird miasma of electric rhythms, high-energy pheromones, and the unmistakable tang of furtive sex. It was a dark, crowded, and complicated place, high on the list of forbidden recreations for the children of Singaporean parents. It was rumored to flaunt the drug laws—the penalty for which was death—but so far as I knew had not been raided.

The bartender refused to humor Pat's attempt to get us enhanced Singapore slings, and we instead dropped a hundred dollars on filling the two pitchers with Long Island Iced Tea, a Tootsie Roll–tasting concoction of almost pure alcohol. We settled on a zebra-striped ottoman to observe the dance floor, where some very involved things seemed to be happening with no relation to the music.

"You've done some dangerous things before, Lewis," Pat shouted close to my ear, "but mostly this sounds stupid. Tell me what happens if it doesn't work out."

"Well, for one thing, same scenario, but with BCG," I shouted back. "I know they want to start a Singapore office, and these days I'm one of the only available senior consultants who's been to Boston and knows something of BCG's traditional cultures and attitudes."

"Didn't they throw you out or something?"

"Something. I told you about Shell. After that, Boston was ready for me to return to Tokyo, my transfer time was up anyway. Tokyo made me a good offer to return, but Morikawa couldn't really help me get beyond Boston's need to have a non-Japanese manage all the fax cases. I was basically going to be a glorified librarian. The Japanese would do all the domestic cases, and I would handle all the repetitive, 'tell us about Japan and the Japanese market' components for all of BCG's global cases. This would be a very, very slow way to make partner. I had to find some other way to get back to Tokyo. That's how I found you again, and that Japanese JV, Abegglen, MAC, and Gemini."

"You mean Yoshi Morikawa, the weekly economics show guy?"

"That's right. You'll meet him soon. I set up a dinner for him and Alan. You should join us."

"Only if you're not going to get me in trouble. Right now, sounds to me like Alan will want to hand you back to Morikawa. Hey, look at that!"

We were taken aback a bit earlier to see a Chinese man and Westerner making out on the dance floor. Now, two Asian women seemed to be getting pretty seriously entwined. We paused to take in the spectacle.

"If BCG and Gemini both drop me," I eventually continued, "I have two options maybe. Southeast Asia is getting more attractive for consulting all the time, and it's a gap for almost everybody, McKinsey included. Only Booz Allen and ADL have any infrastructure here. I could work for one of them for a while, build up my own status as a guru, tracking Japanese investments into the rest of Asia. Then I could open up my own shop, and play some serious footsie with the likes of BCG, Gemini, or McKinsey. Even the accounting firms are starting to get aggressive here. Andersen and Coopers and Lybrand are on the lookout for building up some consulting talent. If they don't go for a whole company, they might at least go for me at a premium."

"I could see you as a guru! You bullshit like Morikawa, you connive like Abegglen, and you pontificate like Prahalad! Alan would never do it; he's too busy being everyone's golden-boy consultant. Everyone likes your proposal writing; they're works of art. Publish a few things like C.K., and you're on your way!"

"Thanks. You put me in high company. But maybe you're right, maybe this is the way I should go. The National Computer Board here is talking about having me as a keynote speaker. I think I'd enjoy the chance to modify some of C.K.'s work, starting with the view from the trenches."

"God, does this mean I have to start working on my obtuseness? Is my future in sermons from the mount?"

"Not yet it's not," I replied, gesturing toward the friendly female couple from the dance floor, "Look who's coming over."

Maybe these women had decided Pat and I made a cute parallel couple. We were not eager to disabuse them of anything, and when they asked us to take them downtown to Studebakers, we did not hesitate.

On close inspection, they were both attractive and likely under drinking age, and I began to suspect we were be taken along for nothing but the privilege of buying ludicrously expensive drinks. I could sense Pat would not mind.

"What do you boys do?" the less supple but more aggressively disposed of the two asked Pat.

"Oh, I'm just a business consultant," Pat promptly replied, "but he's going to be a guru."

Our evening was not destined to last long, however. Where Velvet Underground, in its high density of foreigners and older locals, seemed for a time to be given much latitude by the Singapore authorities, Studebakers, a glitzy high-tech disco import from Australia, complete with skyscraper-top vaulted ceilings and the latest pop tunes, attracted young locals and a lot of official attention.

Pat had managed to get both our new friends dancing atop one of the pedestals reserved for the professional entertainment when all the lights came up and undercover narcotics agents sprang from everywhere. Our new friends had to go, and Pat decided to follow them to the station, leaving me to my own mystic contemplations.

Things unfolded quickly, much as I had predicted. I returned to Tokyo but made arrangements to stay in Singapore, backing out of the Philips case and effectively destroying Gemini's chances at a full-scale phase two, despite Pat's valiant efforts. Abegglen was furious with Alan and would not allow him to entertain any formal agreements with me about a new afterlife through PacRim. Pat's work there for the Australian company went well. But the client disagreed with his predicted outcomes (though later validated many times over), and tensions became strained between PacRim and Gemini, especially once PacRim discovered they earned only a small share of the Centurion sessions they agreed to facilitate in Southeast Asia.

With PacRim an increasingly risky choice, but confident that Alan and I would later somehow fulfill our joint destiny in Asia, I temporarily resigned from Gemini, and I interviewed and received offers from Booz Allen and Arthur D. Little in Singapore. Booz offered more immediate responsibilities, but ADL would give me a relatively travel-free base of operations in Singapore, from which I could cultivate my own guru status and begin recruiting a base of clients and staff for later independence and acquisition.

Some of the ADL officers were rightly suspicious of my motivations, but U.S. headquarters in Cambridge openly hinted that they would like to see me running Singapore before long, and would amply pay me to keep me loyal, if I seemed worth the risk at the time. Using ADL as a base, I soon increased my public exposure, set up my own shop, and began courting both BCG and Gemini.

CONSULTING DEMONOLOGY, TRACT 10

RITES AND RITUALS FOR BECOMING A GURU IN
THE GIANT ENGAGEMENT GAME

1

Create a label. Clients and consultants alike more readily accept a guru who can be confined to a label. "*Newsweek*'s Old Asia Hand," "the Strategic Intent facilitator," or "the *Competitive Strategy* author" are safe, handy ways for clients to find, recall, and justify the use of the gurus they hire. For a guru's colleagues, labels help demarcate competitive space, identifying the bounds not to be crossed. Once established, however, labels are but a means of entry: most gurus wind up working a broad variety of case functions.

2

Establish a reusable product. Guruism requires a high degree of access and maneuverability. A standard, highly adaptable product goes a long way toward establishing early credibility and topic authority. However old and worn, a comfortable pitch and approach, be it based on a single concept or strategy, can lend a sense of historical truth uniquely held within the special powers of the guru to reveal.

3

Maximize client fraternization. Maximum face time with senior, buying clients is essential to a guru's long-term success. Usually, this comes at the expense of any in-depth understanding or appreciation of a client's fundamental needs, or of a consulting team's day-to-day challenges. Paying clients like to believe that they are enjoying a sample of the consulting guru's real life, what clients perceive to be a pattern of unrelenting indulgence. It is the guru's duty to strengthen these perceptions, affirming that the power of the mind can bring about the total subjugation of the body and its dignity.

4

Lower case costs but raise personal billing rates. To facilitate maximum client contact and create the appearance of high demand, a guru should be seen to work with the largest possible number of clients, but at a very high personal daily billing rate. The key to accomplishing this is to inflate one's own billing rate, but underbill actual hours. The underbilled hours can be one's own, or those of supporting consultants, preferably junior workers with the lowest possible billing rates, or both.

5

Identify and link to cheap resources. The next key element of a guru's budding career is finding a reliable backstop to do the actual work. Almost all clients respectful of a guru's aura and résumé will assume that the guru master commands at least equal respect from lesser consulting mortals, and that he accordingly has an army of drones at his beck and call. In reality, established firms are wary of guru leads, not knowing what unreasonable expectations or promises may have gone with the initial sale. Most gurus think nothing of plucking a number from the air as to the projected cost of a consulting engagement, ensuring further headaches for the catch-playing case team leader in establishing a workable budget.

6

Stay in the press. Business journalists are always hungry for a quote from credible sources, particularly when sound data or ready conclusions are lacking. By cultivating key business reporters and supplying them with ready-for-print quotes and the occasional substantive interview or article, a guru can create a base of favorable reviews and well-timed press releases when these become critical to important client sales.

7

Minimize travel and increase accessibility. Although a jet-setting, always-on-the-move perception greatly benefits the guru's appeal, being at hand when a client gets the whim to call or take in a dinner can be highly critical. Travel should be held to a minimum, and when it's required, should be linked to a destination that allows at least one high-visibility speaking engagement, with time generously allotted before and after the talk to allow for new and old client development.

8

Avoid exclusivity. Established firms can enjoy the privilege of assuring their clients that they will not work for their competitors, but gurus generally cannot afford the same luxury. A guru's desirability is often rooted in his or her perceived indispensability to success in a given business, and clients within the same industry prove remarkably immune to confidentiality concerns, even when core strategy and proprietary data is at stake, in the hands of a trust-inducing, must-have guru. Large consultancies are drawn to gurus for this very reason, knowing that they can deploy large teams against two or more clients with the same sets of issues, leveraging a common data base, if the guru aura of confidentiality can be extended over the whole case team.

9

Hold out for the highest bidder. Once a guru has succeeded in enticing established consultancies with their multi-client appeal and ready, high-level access, the only remaining challenge is getting the right buyout deal. If a guru has a small office and coterie of assisting staff, larger consultancies will be inclined to buy the assets of the firm, not the corporation itself, and goodwill valuations tend to fall to the wayside. Since the guru's own name is the key value to be purchased, the form of purchase should not overly concern the master consultant. But a low-ball bid should be met with determination, entailing the creation of the guru's own full-fledged consulting force if necessary. Gurus' name-brand values are remarkably lasting, allowing extended premium-building exercises in calling the would-be buyers' bluffs.

10

Accept only central, triggering roles and maximize sale credit. Once on board a major consultancy, a guru's lasting survival and peak earning power hinges on staying close to the center of major sales and getting full credit for even the most insubstantive involvements. Though the guru may never have sold more than $500,000 at a shot before, utter confidence in selling one hundred times that value is essential to creating and sustaining both clients' and colleagues' belief in the guru mystique.

CHAPTER 11

THE PROFESSIONS AT BAY

THE GRAND-SCALE INTEGRATIONS OF COMPANIES LIKE THAT OF UNITED Research and the MAC Group into Gemini Consulting in the early 1990s did not arise spontaneously. The pressures to provide a broader range of capabilities under one roof built throughout the 1980s under the weight of the external forces reshaping consulting clients' own industries. Clients found themselves under increasing strain to cope with the pervasive introduction of new technologies, the stripping away of long-enshrined regulations, and the sudden intrusion of the international marketplace into everyday business affairs. A kind of great democratization was underway that foreshadowed and perhaps even hastened the end of command economies and the first Cold War. From desktop computers to distributed networks, from airline, telecommunication, and financial deregulation, to the end of protected markets, a new wave of opportunity and a new threat to the established business order had begun to surge against the floodgates.

For consulting firms the pressures on traditional practice areas of expertise became extreme. Even generalist firms like the Boston

Consulting Group would encourage their consultants to align with one of a half-dozen practice areas after a year or two's experience: operations or consumer products, high technology or health care, financial services or mergers and acquisitions. Clients seeking to defend or newly enter a given area would take reassurance from a consultant's practice affiliation and presumed subsequent expertise. But labels could cut off the use of a given consultant on a given assignment, and few firms could afford to have dedicated expert teams on stand-by.

The convulsions of general industry also called for more kinds of expertise than consulting firms could readily provide. From accounting, tax, and legal advice, to computer information systems and foreign market intelligence, from lobbying to executive recruiting and outplacement, the range of demands on professional services exploded as large client companies shed whole divisions, merged with alien partners, and redefined their businesses top to bottom. The great accounting and computer services firms responded to the need and opportunity to offer more general consulting services and began to emerge as a direct threat to all of the traditional consulting firms—bureaucrats, organization-men's, and thinkers' firms alike.

For some, the inevitable response to the ever-growing range of client needs would be the literal merger of diverse professional services firms, creating a logical if unwieldy means of feeding growing client appetites. But for almost all consulting firms the only practical response to these demands, initially, was to just pretend that a full range of capabilities either already existed, or was unneeded or would somehow be taken care of later.

While my first years with Gemini Consulting in the early 1990s would put me on the front lines of growth by acquisition, helping Gemini to fill the ever-widening gap in client expectations and consultants' ability to deliver to them, my experience there was bracketed on both sides by more strained attempts to pretend to in-house expertise. Rapid shifts in client expectations would result in sometimes crazed responses to their needs, sometimes with fair success, but never with the confidence of working knowledge.

. . . .

One of the more extreme examples of stretched truths and utter fabrication in the name of practice group pride, in my experience, came during my own brief interval with Arthur D. Little in Singapore, a time in the mid-1990s when I had left Gemini Japan and impatiently awaited Gemini's continued expansion to Southeast Asia. ADL's Southeast Asia operations, in Singapore and Hong Kong, were almost exclusively staffed by expat Brits and had built its presence, with support from ADL London, on the back of several successful privatization cases, including the Singapore and Malaysian telecom industries. These were imperial bureaucrats dealing with government bureaucrats, genteel practitioners of a trade about to die, with the passing of the last major wave of denationalization of government industries in the region.

ADL's headquarters staff in Cambridge, Massachusetts, had been attracted to the idea of placing me in Singapore for my very American brashness, in the belief I could help extend a breath of private sector business sense into the office's lackluster performance, and bring my own MIT pedigree to bear as a proper influence on the otherwise nontechnically inclined staff there. I would be paid and supported from the States, not London, as a kind of emissary of the true faith. In return, I was expected to represent and market the services of several of ADL's international practice groups, including the steel practice.

The steel practice was not so much a practice as a small crew of economists recently hired by ADL who had worked on improving mini-mill operations in the States. Because interest in small steel operations in Southeast Asia was on the rise, and these economists were finishing up their work in America, it was envisaged that they would decamp to Asia as soon as I had helped them develop a few steel leads. With cases in the United States, Asia, and some past recent work in Europe then behind them, ADL's claim to having a major international steel practice seemed all but assured.

"Bruce Bingham" called me early one hot and wet Singapore

morning. We did not get many unexpected phone calls in our pleasant little outpost.

"Dr. Pinault, how long have you been our steel practice representative in Asia?"

"Lewis is fine, really. And it's mister, anyway, unless I can finally
figure out a way to get back to school."

"Really? Seems like everyone around here is doctor somebody."

"I can imagine. And to answer your question, since never, as far
as I knew, but I could certainly be wrong."

"Well, I have you down here in the new directory as our steel
practice rep. Your capsule biography says you worked for Nippon
Kokan, the steel tube maker."

"Well, that's true. I was with NKK about ten years ago, but I
worked as a business analyst for new marine projects, mostly heavy
engineering, that kind of thing. I toured the new integrated steelworks at Keihin a couple of times. Pretty amazing. Man-made island,
iron ore in one end, sheets and tubes out the other. Big furnaces. It's
all supposed to be ultramodern, but it still struck me as awfully hot
and dangerous—kind of like Singapore, if you say the wrong thing.
These calls are randomly sampled and monitored by the way."

"Uh, I'll try to remember that. But good enough! At least you
know what an integrated steelworks is. How close are you to
Bangkok?"

These kinds of questions were common. From the United States
and Europe, the assumption ran that any office in Asia could handily
cover work anywhere in the region, most likely on a same day trip,
like Boston to New York or Washington. That it was seven hours or
more from Singapore to major cities like Tokyo, Beijing, or Bombay,
and much more for airports without connections, did not usually
occur to project managers based in the West. Bangkok however actually could be done in a day, depending on auto traffic once you were
there.

"Not far. We cover it occasionally and have a new job coming up
there soon, the city waterworks I think."

"No kidding. What are you doing with the waterworks?"

"It's a reengineering job. I can't believe we sold it, actually, there were thirteen bidders, almost all with more in-house expertise. I was tossed the proposal writing task basically as make-work. I really got into it—you know, I used to be with BCG and Gemini, and I guess I felt I had something to prove, that a little private sector energy could go into a government proposal. I pulled together this rag-tag team that helped outline almost the whole plan right there in the proposal, it was a real giveaway. But we got it, a multimillion dollar monster. Sad thing is, of course, that a simpler solution would be just to shut off the water to their damn golf courses, a million gallons of water a day for each one, which just goes to make the Japanese business tourists happy and which poisons the groundwater with fertilizer anyway."

I sensed I might have gotten a little scary and offtrack.

"Well look, Lewis, I have a presentation to make there in a few weeks, and I'm wondering if you could help me a little with the logistics and help me work the crowd."

Yuck. Escort services for visitors rarely turned out productively. Bangkok was sown with land mines for the would-be visit manager: demands for the rare, lewd, and exotic could get out of hand. Oh well, a duty for the homeland, I reasoned.

"Yes, well, sure, let me know the dates. Try to bring a little library of steel materials we might use as handouts. We'll set everything up from here. Look forward to seeing you and all that."

At least the change of pace would be welcome. Singapore remains but a blip on the consulting map, but is a place of occasionally very special charm. The Chinese majority make a fascinating study in a possible future path for managing mainland China, and the Malay and Indian minorities add a disproportionate richness of cultural depth and texture. It is both a future-looking and a wary place, which has led to the unnecessary loss of some great architecture and diversity of lifestyle, but pockets of charm and originality persist.

My health had slowly begun to show signs of improvement, courtesy of the American Club gym and the more languid pace of life in the literal backwaters of international consulting. My second marriage, however, had emerged to be something of a colossal mistake. I had traded consulting stress for violently taxing domestic scenes. Most of these revolved around my unworthiness, which seemed centered on the fact that any personal or family attraction my wife had felt for me had been rooted in the soullessly successful consultant I had been, not the exit-minded new person I hoped to become. ADL Singapore, despite the rank and pay, seemed a self-inflicted demotion, and my talk of starting something on my own or jacking out entirely soon created intolerable levels of tension.

Even doing my best to avoid confronting the homefront, after a few months of soap operas at the colonial-style club scene, hanging out in Little India and the Victorian era quaysides, and frequenting the handful of really fine restaurants and the only two nightclubs with an edge, Singapore can become very, very small. I started to look forward to Bangkok's unruly masses, overt sexual tensions, choking pollution, and the sights of elephants and mopeds fighting for space among cars gridlocked for miles.

I would get more of it than I knew.

Two weeks before Bingham's talk, we were on the line again.

"Look, Lewis, there's no reasonable way to say this, but I can't make it. We have a new proposal here at National Steel, and we're all over it; it's very hot, competitive as hell."

"I'm really sorry, Bruce. I think you might have gotten a lot of mileage for your practice out of the visit. I'll work on all the cancellations, maybe we can find something similar for you elsewhere in the region in the next couple of months."

"No, no. No cancellations, except for me. We've been booked at this thing for almost a year, all the investment banking steel analysts and experts are going to be there. *Metal Bulletin's* doing this huge piece on it. We can't miss this chance; our credibility will be totally shot."

I started to get a very bad feeling.

"Are you planning to send someone else, Bruce?"

"We really can't from here. Lewis, I'm sorry, but we've got to ask you to cover. I'll send you all the materials; we can have a couple of teleconferences and drill everything. You can charge all your time to the practice, take a week to get up to speed, more if you need it."

I knew I would do it. There was even a certain perverse thrill that went with pretending to have any understanding of this at all. But I had to at least try to be rational.

"Bruce, really, you've got to be kidding. 'Peter Lynch' and all those other steel gurus are going to be there, like you said. And from what little reading I've done so far, mini-mills are all the rage now. They're going to tear into the presentation, whoever gives it. The questions will be murder."

"You'll do fine. I'll coach you on everything. When you can't answer, just have them get back to me."

Reluctantly, I agreed. I received a faxed copy of Bruce's presentation that night. It was full of arcane process diagrams, unfathomable vocabulary and calculations, names of companies and products I had no idea existed. I nearly puked.

I began leaving constant messages for Bruce, which were invariably never returned, unless at some weird hour when only a voicemail capture was possible, and then only to say we'd talk later. I was sorely tempted to drop the whole impending fiasco, but knew that my unsympathetic local managing director would delight in the failure of the time he felt I'd already wasted, and I did not want to lose my only line of support back in the States. I would simply be a good soldier, I decided.

I flew to Bangkok on the last flight the day before the presentation, only half prepared to pull off the sham. When I arrived, I was surprised to be greeted at the airport by a *Metal Bulletin* reporter.

"Dr. Pinault, I hope you don't mind, Mr. Bingham called to have us pick you up."

At least he bothered to call someone, I reflected. My reporter friend was a very pleasant-looking woman with a huge satchel of documents and recording equipment. She looked more Chinese than Thai, but some million of Thais are Chinese by ancestry, I recalled.

"My name is 'Francine Ong,' I'm from Singapore. I came up on the same flight yesterday."

I liked this news. Instinctively, I began to think that a dinner with this woman might be a highly compensating adventure, once we were back in Singapore. Perhaps even tonight. I was, of course, I paused to reflect, currently married. As Alan had predicted, I had slid from one marriage to another, and not very successfully. Briefly, my Singaporean wife had appeared ready to start a new life in Tokyo and find a new job, while I continued to work at Gemini. There had been amiable discussions about assisting in the divorce, and, rather bizarrely, on her recommendation, I employed the U.S. divorce lawyer she had found for a married man she once dated. But at the end of the day her family insisted she remain in Singapore, and I, no doubt subconsciously seeking an urgent escape from consulting life as I had known it, had agreed to drop Alan and Gemini and move to Singapore with ADL. As Alan had foretold, it was not long before my interest wandered, but I had done little in the way of following his practical advice.

"I have my equipment with me; I thought we might do an interview in the car."

Suddenly, the prospects of ever seeing Ms. Ong again seemed less pleasant.

"Actually, I'm pretty keen on getting some rest. We could just do some background, I suppose, but maybe you should wait until after tomorrow's presentation for the interview; it will give you a lot more to go on."

I managed to make my way to my room without incident. As I opened the door the phone rang, and I lunged for it.

"Lewis, glad I caught you."

"Bruce!"

"Yes, look, I'm really sorry it's taken us so long to catch up, but I'm sure you're all set, just wanted to check to see if you have any questions."

I was apoplectic. I had left more than one person hanging in my day, but this evidenced a degree of sangfroid that I would only acquire with further practice.

"Bruce, if you want me to do this, you're going to spend the next three hours on the phone with me. We're going to go over every slide, and you're going to help me answer any conceivable question that might arise. If you don't, I'm going over to the *Metal Bulletin* reporter's room, we're going to get drunk, and I'm going to sleep in. She's looking more attractive than you by the second, which is easy because apparently I'm never going to see you."

"Okay, okay, don't panic, I said I'm sorry. Okay, you can have the three hours, as long as you like, I'll explain the whole process and our whole study."

"I don't *want* you to explain them to me, Bruce, seriously, it's too late. There's no hope of my understanding. I just want to be able to make the right noises when people ask. That I can do. And don't ever do this to me again," I added, partly in petulance for the *Metal Bulletin* woman I would never properly impress.

We then spent a bizarre few hours going over the material, with my checking the pronunciation and emphasis for key items in the presentation, but never questioning their consequence or meaning. I wrote down possible answers to questions that made no more sense than the presentation itself.

By the end of our conversation I felt much better, but I could sense that I finally had Bruce worried.

"You know, Lewis, I know you'll do fine, but I'd understand if you just got sick or something. You've already done your bit; they all know you're there and everything."

Now I felt ready. Just to show Bruce he would get the protection and coverage he didn't deserve, I was ready to go and determined to dazzle the audience.

"Good night, Bruce. *Dr.* Lewis signing off."

The next morning was a deeply satisfying exercise in theatrics. I tried to ease my own tension by telling the audience that as a substitute speaker I was about to learn what my grandmother's vaudeville ventriloquism profession must have been like, but not a soul seemed to comprehend the concept. I plunged on, giving a breezy, authoritative run through all the presentation material, perfectly timed, doubt and certainty expressed in all the right places, excitement and enthusiasm delivered with utter authenticity.

The *Metal Bulletin* woman fairly glowed. Even the famously critical Peter Lynch looked friendly.

"Lewis, that was a really helpful review of mini-process applications. But how well would they work here? Who are the key players that might help interested investors in Southeast Asia?"

Bruce had prepared me on both these questions, the first because of my own prompted curiosity. I gave a full-length review and handily disposed of the audience's other, easier questions.

Then I got a scare.

"Dr. Pinault, could you give us just a few examples of mini-mills in the Asian region that might be suited for the kind of approach you've modeled? Who are some of the players today that might begin looking more closely at this?"

Yikes. I did not even know the name of a single small mill in Asia, much less which might make use of the dynamics I had just explained in blind ignorance. An Alan Johnston trick-of-the-trade inspired me.

"Well, I would love to share some examples with you, but frankly, several of these are our own client situations under development now. Under a more formal arrangement, however, I could disclose some of the names and even details of their operations, with their agreement, of course."

In a few days I would learn that I had just made a sale for Bingham.

I got off the stage as quickly as I could. I felt as if I had been possessed, speaking ancient tongues in complete demonic control. Peter Lynch came up to say good-bye.

"That was either the greatest pinch-hitting job I ever saw, or the greatest bullshit artistry ever." He clapped me on the shoulder and began to walk off. "I don't want to know which."

Neither did I.

I did know I would not again pretend to expertise, and headed off to find *Metal Bulletin*.

CONSULTING DEMONOLOGY, TRACT 11

CLIENT BEWARE: CONSULTING SPELLS FOR TRIGGERING
GLOBAL PROFESSIONAL SERVICES SALES

1

Consultants seek to make clear that they do not have inconvenient conflicts of interest. While attorneys, auditors, and even investment bankers confront heavy internal regulation and some external regulation and scrutiny in the course of their work, consultants ride free, with virtually no accountability for their actions, beyond getting paid or not. In the course of building one-stop shopping for professional services, consultants become a natural, relatively risk-free wedge for aggressively introducing a full gamut of more technically complicated services.

2

Global firms are prepared to position every member of the team as a consultant and have every consultant prepared to avow any needed practice group affiliation. When strained for manpower and talent, consulting firms can very effectively draw on their enlarged nonconsultant ranks to fill out the team. Using the mainline consultants as the opening wedge, other professionals can be brought in to play as consultants themselves when the client's appetites focus on the size and quantity of the core consulting effort. A qualified attorney may know more about international joint ventures, for example, than her consulting cousin, but there is a world of difference in introducing her with a consultant's business card and title, as consultant who happens to carry legal qualifications, than as just another lawyer looking to exact transaction costs from a deal. Every member of the team is likely to have capsule biographies prepared to attest to experience in any practice area, making liberal use of others' case experiences.

3

Consultants maximize perceptions of themselves as innocent advice givers. Consultants continue to bask in the perception that they are ***consigliore***, counselors hired to give congenial advice. Like children, they are not perceived to be ultimately responsible for their actions. In giving an outline for strategy and general problem solving, consultants may enlist countless other skilled professionals, and bring them all under a warm blanket of low performance expectations.

4

Global consultancies purvey information systems strategies with abandon. While information systems continue to require years of intensive training to master, and conforming a given system to given client's needs remains largely a sophisticated art form, trust in generalist consultants runs high enough to piggyback the principle of an enormous systems sales on the back of a general consulting engagement. Expert-to-expert sales, with technology consultants selling to client information officers, are generally discouraged.

5

Global consulting houses highlight that accountants and lawyers are risk-averse by nature. Clients continue to be attracted by the unpredictable character and charm of the presumed-to-be adventurous consultant. With a wave of the hand, consultants can invoke the necessity of a some deeper technical expertise as a necessary but boring, naturally resulting component of their own work. The fact that such work may well be ten or a hundred times the consultant's cost need not be confronted till far into the engagement. When the client's own maximum risk threshold is approached, the more risk-averse members of the team are then invoked as an assurance of disciplined control.

6

Global houses trample accountants' natural mistrust of consultants and their instinct to protect clients. In a large merger of consulting and accounting talent, the accountants stand to gain from the consultants' profitability, but not from their skills or referrals; no one will switch accounting services just because they have engaged a given consultant. The reverse is true for the consultants, however: returns on accounting manpower are unattractive, but the accountants' goodwill with clients can represent a gold mine of new sales opportunities.

7

Consultants are routinely used to diversify projects sufficiently to justify multiple sales to the same competitor set. Consultants will routinely work for clients in the same industry, share and rehash examples of one client's work with another, and take a given engagement for use in a proposal with that client's closest competitors; all such instances are glibly defended by assertions of differences in the nature of the assignment. Sales of the same strategic information systems or accounting package within the same competitor groups are less likely to get noticed under the cover of diversified consulting strategies.

8

Consultants' high client-hiring eligibility is used to further infiltrate and penetrate the sale site. In extension of the McKinsey approach to seeding client sites with their own alumni to better anchor future sales, professional services conglomerates infiltrate the management ranks of their largest clients with strategy consultants. Increasingly, under the influence of consulting propaganda that information systems are key strategic differentiators for a client's future success, the decision-making power for the highest-budget strategy-and-systems assignments rests more within the CEO and corporate planning groups than with the information managers themselves.

9

Reengineering assignments are targeted for maximum systems, accounting, and legal impact, to ensure highest group billings. All reengineering work, under whatever jargon it is labeled, tends to point toward hyper-complexity, inefficiency, and breakdowns and bottlenecks at precisely the points in the system that will entail the highest billings to fix. Faulty junctures at the intersections of different vendors' information systems can be ideal for the consultant, becoming the rationale for trashing multiple systems and replacing them with new ones under their firm's control. Lawyers are set to pursue vendor failings, claiming more experience than the client's in-house counsel in such technical cases. It does not matter that no win is likely, it is still good fees and a means of showing that the consultant is confident that there are things that are seriously wrong.

10

Consultants' experience in flexible, extensible fee structures is used to price the whole larger deal. Pricing a strategy engagement has always been an art form, one enabling its master practitioners to expand task definitions to neatly encompass the last ounce of available manpower and lap at the exact threshold of client budget tolerance. Information and accounting systems have an unfortunate transparency to their task definitions, resisting ready expansion, and the dollar-for-output costs of each micro task are almost unavoidably general knowledge. For these reasons alone strategy consultants are typically put in charge of technology sales. Leaving it to the selling professionals to scope the work and regroup the tasks in a way that defies early technical scrutiny is a typical ploy, for example letting "Management Resources Planning Module II Reporting Cleanup" become "Enabling the Revitalization Platform." Including high-billing-rate consultants on every technical task sub-budget, in a show of strategic integration, ensures they get out of the way and share their budget excess to enable the work to really get done, with plenty of inflated fees to go around for all the consultants.

CHAPTER 12

ZIRCONIUM PROPOSALS

SINGAPORE, WINTER 1994

MY INTERIM EXIT FROM GEMINI JAPAN, AND MY SUBSEQUENT WORK WITH Arthur D. Little in Singapore in the early to mid-1990s, was very much a journey back in time to when consulting was a more genteel profession. Isolated from the consulting mainstream, with only one other neighboring competitor, and staffed almost exclusively by senior British expats and junior Malay Chinese, ADL Singapore stood as a staunch defender of a bygone era. I had entered a world where consulting relationships were carefully cultivated for years, usually over gentlemen's club dinners. Book-length proposals would be meticulously researched and beautifully prepared, for reading at a prospective client's leisure. Protracted negotiations and engagements were the norm, and so long as the office's high overheads (colonial homes, outrageously taxed personal cars, and of course, club memberships) were met, a not-too demanding trickle of new business— business almost always drawn from the consultant-dependent government sector—would be viewed with great satisfaction.

Regional travel was viewed with disdain. ADL Australia and Hong Kong could be relied upon to cover much of the rest of

Southeast Asia, with the exception of Kuala Lumpur in neighboring Malaysia. I had been half forced on Singapore by ADL's senior management in Cambridge, Massachusetts, where I enjoyed a high cachet as an American familiar with both the Far East and the consulting industry's most trendy products and latest competitive upheavals. That ADL and I shared an MIT heritage was also a key element of my hiring. Though it was correctly anticipated that I would be a bit of a loose cannon on the orderly decks of the H.M.S. *Singapore*, there was a plain expectation at headquarters that I would breathe new life and private sector dollars into this overly exotic outpost.

Local management had a different view, one that came closer to the mark. In their hiring due diligence, ADL had talked to Morikawa back at BCG, among others, and confirmed that I was a consultant of higher appetites and capabilities, a worker accustomed to on-the-edge, fast-paced assignments across a strong mix of clients and functions. That my impatience with opportunities at both BCG Tokyo and Gemini Japan had led me to ADL Singapore reportedly did not surprise Morikawa. ADL Singapore inferred correctly that after stirring things up a bit, there was a fair chance that I would go away, conveniently confirming to headquarters that Singapore should be left to the more patient colonialists.

I would soon learn that local management saw other advantages in my being around as well. Under pressure to increase travel to provide more regional coverage, to formalize a new operation in Kuala Lumpur, and to change the business mix to represent both more private sector clients and better development of international ties to other ADL offices, Singapore had plenty of dirty work for me to do. In trying to find out what ADL Singapore *did* do, it quickly emerged that the entire ten-man outfit seemed to spend two-thirds or more of its time perfecting the art of proposal writing.

ADL's prim managing director, complete with rail-thin physique and handlebar mustache, was "Richard Williams." Richard had succeeded to the directorship by attrition, but he was no less proud of his post. His predecessors, another pair of Brits, had discovered new lives:

one, uncharacteristically brusque and energetic, had been snatched up in Andersen Consulting's Asia expansion, to head strategic services in Kuala Lumpur; the other, finding both comfort and capital in his highly developed network of local connections, moved on to the even more relaxed pace of executive recruiting, allowing him to virtually live at the local club.

"Lewis, we have a query from our German friends I suppose you should have a look at. Seems a client there wants to conduct a pan-Asia study of automotive opportunities. I'd say it's your cup of tea."

That Richard really spoke like this was an unending source of amusement to me, as though he was performing a Monty Python skit just for my benefit.

"Terrific. Should I give them a ring? They might already be at work now."

"Oh, no need for that just yet. We should go over this rather carefully; they seem to expect rather a lot. I suggest we discuss this over a bit of lunch."

I knew this didn't mean the downstairs sandwich shop.

"Tanglin Club or the Raffles?" I mustered in as businesslike a fashion as I could.

"Tanglin Club, excellent. Give them a ring, would you? We'll put it on my number."

A Singapore institution for well over a century, the Tanglin Club is a snug, secure holdout of colony life. Once the bulwark of civilization for rubber plantation and tin mine owners operating in what is now Malaysia, it became a place to safely drink to oblivion and sleep the night over, eat the foods of home, or sample the best of local cuisine. In an atmosphere redolent of the great and the tragic in British imperial history, its members thrive on familiar companionship, shipshape service, and utter exclusivity. I usually tried to avoid lunch there for fear I would stay through to the night.

We sat in the huge main dining room, in a half-booth. With two-story-high ceilings paneled in oak, as were the walls, it was a very quiet place for lunch, in which two diners could feel securely lost and apart from anyone else, with little danger of being overheard.

"So Lewis," Richard began, "the essential issue with these Germans is that they need an all-Asia, intensive study on something about which we know essentially nothing, for a measly seventy-thousand U.S. dollars. I can only think that they're comparison shopping us with some market research outfit."

Richard picked daintily but systematically through his mulligatawny, a viciously spiced Indian black pepper soup. I had the same, well doused in lemon, and joined Richard in alternately cooling down the fires of the broth with generous gulps from a large pint of Tiger draft. Even Morikawa would have trouble speeding through this lunch, I reckoned.

"We've only got this fax?" I asked, gesturing toward the document Richard had placed on the table, which he seemed reluctant to share with me.

"That's it, plus a phone message to look it over and reply by their week's end. Have a look. You won't see much, but there is a great deal they want. That was an outstanding talk you gave at National Computer Board, by the way, excellent publicity."

"Thanks," I replied, somewhat suspiciously. Richard was not much taken with the mass mobilization, revitalization work I had adopted from C.K. Prahalad. I gave the short fax a careful review.

"What are stamping presses?"

"Exactly. Apparently, these are the devices that shape sheet steel into automotive bodies. Surprisingly high tech, very proprietary. I asked around a little—it takes a lot to take a flimsy bit of steel and turn it into a solid but aerodynamic Mercedes body. Point is, however, that's all I know, after an hour's worth of phone calls. The idea that we would find all of Asia's press makers, sort them, grade them, and suggest something about their suitability for partnership or takeover, on a few weeks and seventy-thousand dollars, is ludicrous."

"I think I might agree. Maybe we should just tell that to ADL Germany." I toyed briefly with relating my adventures with Werner at

BCG Tokyo, but concluded Richard would not appreciate it. "Maybe they could lend us a hand, send somebody out through some other engagement or training or something. Maybe there's more budget than we know, we just have to ask."

Richard seemed to absorb this for a minute before rejecting the notion. He neatly finished his soup, mopping up with a bit of fluffy *naan* bread.

"No, I've seen this kind of thing before; I think they're just trying to exploit what they perceive to be a cheap resource and keep the main force of the work for themselves. If there is more budget, no doubt they'd want it. But maybe you're on to something. There's certainly a way to test this."

"Not another one of your proposals?" I fairly groaned.

"Not my proposal, *your* proposal," Richard answered, clearly pleased with himself.

In the few months I had now worked at ADL, I felt I had done little else except proposal writing, great tomes that Richard seemed to spend as much time revising as I spent writing. Richard was keen that I subject my proposals to his detailed review, on the excuse that I needed to learn how the style of the firm's approach to casework differed from my prior experiences. Most of the cases were very small, hardly worth, in my judgment, the time we spent on them. Most of them actually sold, and I still had not determined to my satisfaction whether this pleased Richard or not. I had the odd sense that actually taking the time to do the work, rather than write about it, seemed somehow impure to him.

Richard and I were more peers than boss and consultant, and I bridled a bit at the prospect of another major proposal production. I had to admit, though, that under Richard's tutelage I was becoming a master proposal draftsman. Since Williams's only strategy to prevent my displacing him as managing director appeared to be burying me in proposal work, I was not too worried about finding some alternate path to making the most out of ADL. But it would still be several months before I could begin courting BCG and Gemini.

"Okay, okay," I relented.

"Right, then. Let's have another pint, shall we? And don't get me wrong, I understand what you're saying. I suggest you go the whole way, like you said. Size the entire task properly, and bluntly demand whatever it takes to do it. We can probably swing your visiting Germany to present the proposal."

I recognized this as an extraordinary gesture for Richard, who believed in promoting the stand-alone merits of a well-written proposal. Proposals were meant to be read, Williams was fond of saying: if they needed to be flogged in person then they were poorly written. In regard to proposals, Richard reminded me of the reluctant shoe salesman at Philips.

Our entrees arrived just as a gaggle of Indian women took over the dining room.

"Ah, the Indian wives club," Richard winced.

Many of India's wealthier classes had thrived under British rule and found safe havens for their wealth and extraordinary lifestyles in enclaves like Singapore after India's violent transition to independence and socialism in the 1950s. Now well settled into this little city-state, these itinerants spawned bevies of bored, moneyed wives, proud to wear their gorgeous saris over improbably exposed bulges of unsightly flesh, bedecked in pounds of gold and jewelry.

Richard began to mince his *meegoreng*, a dish of spiced Chinese-Malay noodles and vegetables that was once standard fare for thousands of tin mine workers. I started in on my Szechuan chicken, made with dozens of enormous toasted red chilis. The chilis were served mainly for decoration, but I had found myself becoming addicted to their taste.

"You seem to be losing a bit of weight," Richard commented, watching me gasp through my chilis. It was true. The beers seemed to disappear in Singapore's tropical heat, and I had taken to highly spiced foods that seemed to make up in intensity what they lacked in mass and quantity. These days I ate for taste, not for a sensation of fullness. And in a work environment where travel, or "trips outstation" in the persistent colonial jargon, were rare, I actually had time to work out. I had taken to exercising at the American Club, the Tanglin's much less exclusive rival across the street. What the American Club lacked in atmosphere it made up for with its excellent, socially lively gym. I had even started to harbor hopes of starting a healthy relationship.

"That would be good. There don't seem to be many borderline health wrecks like me here. Everyone seems either pretty thin or just astonishingly gross. You mean it about going all the way with this proposal?"

"Yes, and I'd like you to involve 'Brad Wong' as well. He'll help you with the proposal, and he's been making a lot of noise about getting out of Singapore. He's a good chap." Brad Wong was indeed a good chap, an Australian-educated mid-level consultant with the panache of a McKinseyite or BCGer. Fluent in Mandarin as well as local Chinese and Malay dialects, and a star Monash MBA with a taste for luxury and big dealing, it was not hard to see why he was chafing to get out. Brad had told me that he confronted Richard earlier in the week, threatening to quit if he was not put on my next case.

We finished our entrees and moved on to selections from the club's gigantic cheese collection, one of the greatest dangers to my tentative physical recovery. I included a bit of fruit, and got coffee rather than port. Satisfied, I ran my estimates of the numbers by Williams.

"Brad Wong is a pricey resource. I noticed you just upped his billing rate this week."

"Yes, well, between you and me, he can be a bit insubordinate. It was fire him or give him what he wants, so up went the money."

I politely chose not to reveal what I knew of Brad's demands to be on my team. It was a characteristically elegant maneuver by Richard to buy up a bit of Brad's loyalty at the expense of my managing an already difficult case budget proposal.

"Eight-hundred and fifty thousand," I announced, having scratched through two napkins and the outline of three phases of work.

Richard seemed very pleased. At more than ten times the asking price, with this I did not doubt that he believed I would be wrapped up in the proposal for weeks, and then lose both it and Brad's misplaced loyalties, not to mention a good deal of face.

"Right then, cheerio. You best get busy!"

Just a few months later Brad Wong and I sat in the back of a chauffeured car, uncomfortably far south of Beijing and still going. The stamping press case had indeed sold. With Richard's unrelenting appetite for detail and solid construction, and Brad's strong sense of the tasks likely to be required, I had written one of the most comprehensive consulting proposals of my life. Unexpectedly, I found myself liking the drafting process, in part because I was bored with my only other case in hand, a features-and-attributes trade-off study, or conjoint analysis, for a Singapore to Kuala Lumpur luxury bus service. Bad enough that they wanted to plow through the forests of the Malay peninsula with a new highway, I had groused to Brad, but we have to design a diesel polluting bus fleet service to ensure the damage.

At the moment, though, Brad was probably wishing he was back on that highway. In short order we had found not only a target partner for the Germans in mainland China, we had identified a smaller Taiwanese press maker to act as broker, helping with translation, standards, and quality. Mueller, our client, had been thrilled and delighted with our proposal, and my presentation had seemed to sit well with Mueller management, just because I represented expertise in a geographic area that they found difficult to imagine, much less do business with. But though it was the largest private sector case yet sold by ADL Singapore, we won only half our eventual million-dollar asking price, and the negotiated agreement had left Brad and I working hard and racing to keep up with a very aggressive schedule.

We had missed our once-a-day flight from Beijing to Jinan and, borrowing the car and chauffeur from the transaction lawyers we had hired under the proposal, we were now barreling our way deep into

China's hinterland. We hoped to make Jinan in eight to ten hours of hard driving.

Brad and the driver had been going at it in Mandarin for some time, with a speed and intensity that completely lost me. My key language value on this assignment, it emerged, besides a degree of serviceable German, was in speaking Japanese to the Taiwanese partners. They had poor English, but graceful Japanese courtesy of their country's fifty years occupation.

"What's going on?"

"He's just nervous."

"About not making it on time?"

"No, it's just that he's never driven outside Beijing before. Beijing people love Beijing. To them it's order, the center of everything. They pity people who have to waste their time outside and are afraid of what's going on there. Thing is, I think he might be right."

"About being afraid?"

"I'm afraid so," Brad laughed.

"Does he at least know where he's going?"

Disturbingly, Brad felt the need to interpret this question.

"He says yes, if the roads are still where they're supposed to be."

In half an hour or so I understood what the driver meant. Manicured roads and boulevards had long since given way to meandering lanes through small towns, punctuating two-lane high-speed roads. The traffic had shifted from taxis and sedans to almost exclusively goods and military trucks.

We came up to a roadblock, where a group of men wearing army jackets but no other recognizable uniform elements crowded around a small fire.

"Bridge ahead. This road's out, need to go around. Pay toll," Brad translated.

"Is this for real?" I asked. "They didn't stop those trucks ahead of us. If the road's out, where are they going? Are they really army? Maybe they're going to rob us on some side road," I added less than helpfully.

After a long bout of translation and discussion, Brad offered me the driver's wisdom.

"Maybe army, maybe not. A lot of them have been selling off their uniforms. The road is probably fine, but he thinks *we* won't be if we try to ignore them. Better to pay toll."

"How much?"

"Ninety *rénmínbì*."

This was about a dollar. Frightened to reveal that we had a few thousand times this in cash, I hurriedly urged the driver to pay and move us on. If it was an ambush they could have it, I figured, I just didn't want to be killed for my shoes.

This was a pattern that would begin to repeat more and more frequently. Roadblocks, market goods and vegetables we felt compelled to buy, spare gas and oil loaded gleefully into our trunk. Weapons were often in sight around these seemingly innocent dealings, which encouraged our generosity, and soon we fit in quite well with the surrounding goods trucks.

"So who's going to lead the discussion at these talks," Brad asked me.

"Well, assuming we get there in one piece and something like on time, you and I will. Mueller's international manager, the Taiwanese, and the lawyers will all be there, but we're the only ones convinced a mainland-Taiwanese partnership will work. The Jinan folks will be very skeptical. The Germans are going to have their intellectual property rights concerns. The Taiwanese want lots of escape options. Not easy. You do it."

Alan Johnston could not have done it better. I was beginning to perfect an ability to cultivate a certain energy-conserving laziness, like a fit but seemingly slow panther, and turn it into a consulting virtue.

Brad was ready. He outlined his opening presentation strategy and asked me for some creative latitude in translation, to which I readily agreed. We began to peel our third or fourth oranges from our huge bags of loot.

"So, how are you going to explain how you look," Brad asked with deceptive casualness.

I had become the object of a complete physical makeover, something most of my acquaintances were too embarrassed to mention, however much of an improvement might be in evidence. Kusum Goklani, a friend from the American Club gym, had helped me accelerate my weight loss with diet and exercise coaching, and then I had begun to make more daring changes. I lost the part to my hair, and brushed and slicked it back. I had work done on my teeth, skin treatments, and a long list of helpful prohibitions. I had begun to transform into someone who looked like he might be enjoying, rather than sacrificing, his own life—a risky strategy for a consultant.

Kusum was an extraordinary expat for Singapore, an American of Indian birth whose beauty and vibrancy provided remarkable and amusing contrast to the members of the Indian wives club. Her young twin daughters, fresh out of college, created quite a stir among the Indian crones and the general expat community alike. Sharing their mother's striking beauty and high exuberance, the three were often mistaken for a traffic-stopping trio of sisters. Sasha, one of Kusum's daughters, had additionally suggested I sport a half-growth of beard, and I now looked as much rogue and pirate as tortured consultant.

"Well, people seem afraid to mention anything about how I look. But if I'm asked I'll tell them the scruff makes me feel more relaxed, healthier, more centered. I noticed people seem to find me more accessible now, they seem less fidgety to get away."

"That's just because I'm trapped in this car with you," Brad jibed.

We were now close to Jinan but caught in a traffic jam from some darker, evil dimension. A hillside rose from the major river separating us from Jinan. We knew there were no other ways across for dozens of miles. Zigzagging up the hill's switchbacks for three miles or more, a standstill display of heavy trucks and military gear seemed to define the largest, most immovable traffic jam of all time.

An energetic exchange between Brad and the driver ensued.

"It's okay," Brad assured me, as our car began a dizzying ascent off the road and headed straight for the zigzag of trucks, with the apparent intention of cutting straight through and across it. I was convinced that an axle would break any moment, and began to wish it would happen, to spare us getting shot as soon as we crossed the next section of road.

We pulled up in front of one of the largest trucks, having bypassed several hundred cars on our first off-road traverse.

"Give him one-thousand *rénmínbì*," Brad instructed.

I complied, and marveled to see our driver brazenly walk up to the truck driver, shove the money at him, and walk away. Soon after our driver was seated, I was astounded to see the truck back into the car behind, forcing it and one more vehicle several meters back down the road. A space was thus cleared for us, and we crossed over through the resulting gap, diving off the road again on the other side. We continued on our way, repeating this system almost to the top, until the slope became too steep for us to negotiate.

We arrived in Jinan a mere two hours late. "Reinwald," our Mueller client, seemed too relieved to see us to care.

Brushing my face with his knuckles, "*Was machst du denn da?*" he queried of my appearance, as Brad had predicted: what are you doing with yourself there?

"A lovely woman's idea," I answered succinctly, and Reinwald seemed immediately approving. The Chinese made no comments, with Brad later charitably explaining that all Westerners looked alike, namely, ugly.

The joint-venture discussions went well, with a complicated ownership structure permitting the mainland Chinese to distance themselves reasonably comfortably from their erstwhile Chinese cousins. Reinwald was enthusiastic, but dropped a stunning hint that Mueller was very happy to pay for Brad and I, but not for all the supposed supervision by ADL. It was an invitation for us to strike out on our own, and I began to place some calls with Gemini and the Boston Consulting Group.

CONSULTING DEMONOLOGY, TRACT 12

THE CONSULTING BOOK OF THE DEAD: HOW TO READ
AND PRICE A CONSULTING PROPOSAL

1

Overall length. Most firms would ideally prefer to give a client just a one- to two-page letter, rather than a detailed proposal, to serve as the contract for an agreement. A simple letter can save the consulting company hundreds of hours of high-risk billing time in preparation, speed a favorable decision before competitive entries might come into play, and avoid later liability for overly specific commitments. But short proposals are missed opportunities for clients. Full-length proposal documents are a good indication of the quality of product and thinking that a given team at a given firm has to offer. They can become highly useful in familiarizing other managers within the client company with the needs and expectations for the engagement. They are also a source of good ideas, a way of forcing some early thinking about the project, and a means of quickly surfacing any misunderstanding of the mission or its details. In competitive situations, there is also a mercenary but no less real value in drawing the best ideas from all proposals and putting them in the hands of the winning consultant, one of the reasons consultants are most reluctant to give speculative proposals full treatment. Finally, for comparison shopping and final negotiations, full-length proposals are highly desirable for clues and details as to what tasks can be accomplished, by how many consultants, of what billing level, and over what period of time.

2

Graphics versus text. The use of graphics versus text can be a good clue to the relative importance of the assignment to the consulting firm and to what a consulting company really plans to offer on a given engagement. A select few original graphics can do much to enhance a narrative-style proposal, lending logic and clarity to the issues treated and processes proposed. The use of generic graphics, however, is more likely filler than anything that will improve understanding. Worse still, proposals made in presentation format, making use exclusively of graphics, are usually little else but a rehash of past proposals, and a weasely means of avoiding specific commitments.

3

Situation understanding. Any good proposal should provide a sufficiently in-depth recapping of the client situation that calls for the consultant's involvement. It should show an accurate understanding of the problems the consultant proposes to engage, and capture the issues in terms that newcomers to the situation will find reasonably easy to comprehend. A client should be able to read this section and feel that their own understanding has been clarified and improved. If this section is missing, inaccurate, or reflects a mere parroting of the client's fears and complaints, the rest of the document should be read with caution.

4

Outline of Tasks. A simplified outline of proposed tasks should immediately follow the understanding of the situation, and neatly address the issues raised in that section. A misalignment that shows up here can indicate superfluous or underpowered tasks, or a poor understanding of the issues overall. A simplified outline of tasks can also be used as shorthand for how much money each major task and subtask is likely to entail, creating a useful negotiating tool for both client and consultant.

5

Approach description. In the approach description all tasks proposed should be described in reasonable detail. It is a safe assumption that if a given task's description is missing or vague, the consulting firm has little specific idea about how to do the work proposed. Weak or missing approach descriptions are an important warning that the consulting firm has first made a decision about what they believe the client is willing to pay, and then found a team and means to expend the target price. A more honest proposal will involve the actual case leader in laying out the needed tasks against the key issues first, selecting the right available people against those tasks second, and creating a budget against estimates of case duration third.

6

Phase commitments. Proposals that break up the work into discrete, separately priced phases provide important checkpoints and exit strategies for the work. Later phases of the assignment may be subject to many unknowns, and it is fair for the client to see at what points along the way an engagement might be wrapped up early, expanded, or internalized. Pricing estimates should be provided for all phases, however. Too often a low phase-one price is used to bait a client into larger engagements or to make one firm appear more cost-attractive than another.

7

Team biographies and commitments. An area of highest reluctance for almost all consulting firms, recruiting biographies that represent a true commitment of a specific portion of a given individual's time are hard to come by. So is accuracy in the biographies. A consultant's biography will typically consist of a series of bullets that synopsize past case assignments. These cases may or may not have been ones that the firm itself conducted, and even if they are, the consultant may have had only the most glancing involvement in the case. The most attractive-looking biographies are included in all proposals, even if the person may only be available for a 5-percent commitment or not at all.

8

Pricing clarity. Preferred pricing by consultants involves a lump sum, distributed over three to four payments, with the largest payments pushed to the front. Longer assignments may feature a large up-front portion followed by monthly fees. Expenses are usually treated as an addition, as generous percentage of fees (from 20 to 35 percent). Breakdown of pricing by phase, task, individual, and projected expense may be highly desirable but is rarely won. But even if the consultant will not agree to place it in the proposal, gaining an understanding of individual billing rates can help determine how best to use different consultants' time over the course of the engagement, as their skills and competencies become known. Consulting companies like to use new, cheaper-rate recruits on long engagements to create budget slack and internal training opportunities; the client should learn what he or she is paying for.

9

Boilerplate. Most proposals will come with standard wording regarding liability and confidentiality. The legal absoluteness of this section is vulnerable in many respects—for example, signing an agreement per the standard wording to limit consultants' liability to fees paid does not really limit the damages a client might later seek and successfully win. But wording worth examining closely is that relating to use of client materials and consulting work product. A disturbing amount of material derived from work with one client will routinely turn up on work with another, even on work for competing companies in the same industry. Use of the client's name for promotional purposes is another element that should be, but is not always, featured in this section. Most clients prefer not to involve in-house lawyers in examination of consulting proposals because of potential delays and unwanted visibility, but a lawyer should at least look at the boilerplate general provisions section of any proposal, even those from the most reputable firms.

10

Closure. A thoughtful, personalized closure is a healthy sign that the case leader has gone through the entire proposal and feels an appropriate sense of completeness about the document. The closure should invite questions and suggest alternatives, setting a tone for the case itself in terms of accessibility and accountability of the case leader for the entire team.

CHAPTER 13

COLONIZING CONSULTING

SINGAPORE, FALL 1995

It's the 2.00 a.m. security shift change at the Gateway Building towers in Singapore. I wait at the bottom of the parking level escalator for the recording video cameras to pan in my direction, and sure I am now on film, begin a noisy ascent to the security desk, grumbling about the hour, time zones, and unreasonable home office management. This is nothing new to the guards on duty, and they commiserate as I complete sign-in procedures.

I see that the camera is now approaching the apex of its turn away from the escalator, and with a distracting drop of my documents file, the guards bend to help me as three ADL staffers dash past the camera to the stairwell entrance by the elevators.

"Next time at this hour, you can just park here by the front entrance," one of the guards helpfully suggests.

"There won't be a next time," I reply truthfully.

I make my way on to the elevator. Brad Wong and two other local staff are by now, I assume, a few flights up the stairs. Their thirty-story climb will not be pleasurable but will go unnoticed by any monitoring devices. I code my way through the front doors by ADL's reception desk, and, lights still out, do a quick check by flashlight to ensure all offices are unoccupied.

From our practice drills I know it will be a good twenty minutes before Brad and our accomplice analysts will arrive. I unlock my own office and remove a half-dozen heavy-duty trash bags, stored in my desk last week for this occasion, and begin to unpack my shelves. There are over fifty bound documents relating to Mueller and recent background work for Mobil Oil, none of which I want in Arthur D. Little's hands. I pack the Mobil material neatly into two pilot-style briefcases, and unceremoniously toss the Mueller materials into a splayed open trash bag on the floor. Next, I begin to carefully sort other ADL case materials from library reports and multi-client stud-ies.

Hearing a gentle knock by the rear access door near my office, I open it to reveal a sweaty Brad and company.

"God," Brad wheezed, "I wish the air con was still going."

"I thought about ordering up overnight air con for us, but I fig-ured that would be too much. Wouldn't want to get in trouble for improperly charging it to a case number."

"Very funny," Brad remarked, looking worriedly at the growing mess in my office. "Okay, boss, what do we do first?"

"First, a few lights. When the guards pass by they expect to see signs of my working. But none of you pass by the entrance doors. You have the key to Richard's office?"

"Right here. 'Viki' gave me the whole lot of spare keys when I asked for mine today. Just remind me to put it back after you're done, would you?"

"Okay, I'm on my way to Richard's. 'Frederick,' 'Clay,' you guys can finish off my office. Put all this library stuff back, exactly where it belongs and all the case materials into the group inviolate files, all chronologically sorted like they should be. Leave Richard no clue what I've been working with lately. Jumble up all those annual reports with the others; they go in those file boxes. They were always a mess anyways."

"What about your desk?"

"It's been completely empty for days. The correspondence files we need are already at home, and I bought ADL a brand new hard drive for my computer last week. You've cleared your computers already?"

"All set."

"Okay, I'll meet you back here in a few minutes."

Inside Richard's office I was in unfamiliar terrain. I wanted specific files, proposals, case documents, and correspondence, and these would be dispersed in a variety of locations. Fortunately, in his plenitude of long days lived in the office, Richard had neatly labeled and arrayed everything I needed. Many labels unexpectedly begged for attention: "personal correspondence," "credit cards," "vacation planning," "home leave," "hobbies," "Deirdre," "snakes." I sorely wanted to inspect. "Deirdre," snakes, hobbies? Were these related? At fortynine Richard remained a lifelong bachelor, and his personal life was shrouded in much mystery. I successfully resisted temptation. Already uneasy enough with our enterprise, Brad would be mortified to learn that I violated Richard's closely guarded privacy.

I found what I needed, surgically removing folders and labels to better frustrate any early comprehension of things gone missing. With a quick fingerprint dusting more for effect than real concern, I locked up Richard's office and returned to my own.

It had been reduced to empty shelves, a barren desk and table, and several bulging trash bags.

"Okay, good work. You two to the inviolate files and the library, bring everything back to us in the copy room. If you have any doubts about what's left in your own desks, now's the time to think. Everything should look normal and lived in. Any questions about Mueller and Mobil, just say I asked for them, which is the truth.

"How's everybody feeling?"

"Good."

"A bit villainous."

"Like Peter Sellers in that museum break-in."

"Well, I'm glad everybody's having fun. Brad, who's Deirdre, and why does Richard like snakes?" I teased.

Brad went ashen.

"You promised you wouldn't go into Richard's personal things!"

"Don't worry, I didn't, but his filing system begs for exploration."

Brad's color improved.

"That's the girlfriend, I think; he's only mentioned her to me once. Something very long and complicated."

We made our way to the copy room, dragging the heavy trash bags.

"What about snakes, though?"

"That's a tough one, but I think I have a clue. You know Richard lives in one of those converted black and whites, those old colonial Dutch homes, still surrounded by jungle. Very creepy, full of ghosts. I don't think any Chinese would live there very long."

"What about them?" I asked, clearing the heavy-duty shredder.

"Well, last year Richard comes home one night, gets ready for bed. Ever share a room with him?"

"Once, yes, not too pleasant."

"So you get the picture. There Richard is in his little brown briefs, doing his nightly calisthenics, deep into the rituals of his nightly routine. He pulls back the bedsheets."

"A snake!"

"A black asp, utterly deadly, but Richard doesn't know that yet."

We begin steadily feeding the shredder, a tedious ten sheets at a time, fearful of breaking it.

"He chases it all around his house. He finally corners it, but doesn't know what to do. Of course he calls Viki, who promptly tells him to call the police. They have a special snake patrol, with capture lanyards, net bags, anti-toxin kits, the whole lot."

"And they got it?"

"Yes, but Richard was more scared by the reaction of the patrol than by his first encounter with the black asp. He could tell by their fear and caution that he had a really dangerous guest, and nearly threw up recalling his antics chasing it around the house. Ever since, Richard tells me, he's taken an interest in knowing his snakes, bought some guidebook or something."

"Gee, if I'd known, we could have left a plastic snake under his desk."

"Hilarious for you, maybe, but then he'd know it was me," Brad replied, choking on the growing cloud of shredder dust.

The work became tiring, and the overheated shredder motor, stale air, and clouds of paper particles combined with the inevitable adrenaline crash to make for a really bad smell. Frederick and Clay dragged up three more unwelcome bags of documents.

By about the time we had destroyed nearly everything from my office, the shredder finally died, half gorged on a description of the Taiwanese stamping press industry. Frederick looked at Clay expectantly.

"We're getting a little nervous. There's a big dumpster on B2 by the freight lift. Maybe we could just bury these deep in there?"

"Okay, that's probably better than some parking lot camera showing us loading up the trunk, even though there's no video hook-up on those. We're down to pretty innocuous stuff now anyway. Just give me a second back in my office; you work on unjamming the shredder."

Everyone was getting a bit giddy, and from the hall I could hear Brad relating Richard's snake story. Back at my now completely emptied office, I placed a single sheet of paper on my desk and signed it. As far as I knew I had the only key to my office, and on a perverse impulse I left the key atop the paper, shut the lights, and closed and locked the door.

"Okay, let's get the hell out of here!"

We shut everything down, checked the corridors for security, and piled down the stairs with the remaining trash bags. We began whooping it up, tossing the bags from one floor to the next, trying to hit each other with them.

"Snakes, snakes!" Clay began to shout, and this became a chant all the way down to about the third floor. From there we proceeded more quietly. The stairwell ended at the ground floor, and I exited and made my way to the elevator banks, to summon a lift and trigger the characteristic "ding" that would announce that someone had just descended. From there I walked to the security desk, while my accomplices waited in the stairwell, prepared to drag their burden to the B1 dumpster.

"Working hard, sir?" the security guard commented approvingly. The other guard was absent, probably on patrol.

"Oh yes," I replied. As I hoped, no one had been in or out after me, and I recorded my sign-out as a mere thirty minutes after entry, when in fact it had been three hours.

"You know, I think I may just walk home tonight. Would you be so kind to unlock the front door for me?"

"Certainly, sir," the guard replied, apparently grateful for something to do.

I caught a glimpse of bulging bags and running bodies as the guard busied himself with the locks. Just as I walked out, I slapped myself on the forehead, pantomiming tired forgetfulness.

"Oh no, you know what, I left some documents in the car. I should probably just drive home after all."

"Very good, sir," the guard replied amiably.

At the car I found my companions already inside, huddling down on the floor and giggling like schoolchildren. We sped off to new lives and careers, and a place among the blackguards of Singapore consulting history.

LONDON, SUMMER 1996

About a year later I sat with Alan Johnston in his commanding office at the new Gemini Consulting building in London. We had much to catch up on, and I had a partnership at stake.

"Good to see you again, Lewis. What do you think of our new office?"

"Intimidating. It took me fifteen minutes to get past reception and convince them that I could see you, even with an appointment. I don't see too many familiar faces, either. Neil and Ken are still here, aren't they?"

"Yes, but they're both on assignment on the Continent, banking work. There'll be semi-permanent offices for them when they're back; we kind of hot-seat it here now."

Gemini had institutionalized its blending of MAC and United Research lifestyles, and the main interest here was clearly impression on clients and security. No midnight office evacuations here, I imagined.

"You're looking good, Lewis. I hear you're engaged," Alan continued.

Alan himself looked slightly piqued and overweight, but otherwise the same. I suspected he was about to go on alcohol abstinence again. My own appearance had indeed changed. Temporarily liberated from working for others, except for my handful of clients, my freelance consulting permitted me a long-forgotten control of travel, eating, and sleeping habits. Sasha made sure I made the most of this, and my first ambitious exercise program since college, with her encouragement, showed good results.

"That's right, Sasha; you may have met her."

"Who could forget the Goklanis? Stunning, and smart. The mom's a looker, too. Sasha and Sabena work for you now, I heard, and the father's a client or something."

"The dad and I have always been friends, met him first, actually. Ramesh is not actually a client, but he's been a key referral for others. And I've trimmed back the staff; Sasha's the last to go, but not too keen on the joys of consulting anyhow."

"Mmm, she really *is* smart. Well, now that you seem to be out of the acquisition target game, the staff would only be liabilities for you."

I took in a good look around Alan's office. A total refurbishment of the building was completed before Gemini took it over, and the best of its Edwardian-era details seemed to have been preserved. A large bay window was the centerpiece of the office, its tidy white lattices framing a full view of the Thames River and its southern bank. A small but apparently working fireplace graced one end, and Alan's favorite partner desk from the old office filled out the other. Framed photos of his Wyoming ranch and some unusual semi-erotic *ukiyoe* woodcuts adorned the walls. Having spent much of the last year paying high rent for anonymous serviced-office spaces in Singapore and Hong Kong, I viewed it all with not a little envy.

"Well, the Boston Consulting Group didn't work out. An old rival dredged up a bad case from five or six years ago, that fiasco with Shell I told you about one time, and he got enough mileage out of that to delay my hiring as partner. The idea, at their suggestion, was that I would leave ADL, set up my own shop, and position myself for acquisition as a firm."

"Not a bad scenario, and you would be good for them, too. We might have done the same if you hadn't welded your name onto the Abegglen enemies list. What happened?"

"Well, I soon learned that my chief merit to them would be as a feeder agent, screening the small fry, with the presumption that once I came up with anything big, I would hand it over to them. They were in no hurry to make an acquisition, and I never got any of the referrals I hoped for. I heard a rumor they were recruiting from Stateside staff to set up independent operations in Singapore, which now turns out to be true. So one day I found myself with the opportunity to compete against them on a mid-size proposal, and I went for it. Neither of us got anything, but it pretty much burned the bridge."

"Well, Lewis, the bridge with me is still intact, and we know your work. Your friends here still have an interest in you. 'Sarjit Singh' is going to try to get Gemini Asia going again, and we've talked for a while now about how to bring you back in."

"What's the state of Asia since you came back to London?"

"Sarjit's got a good proposal to Cap Gemini to build a base from India through Southeast Asia, independently of Japan and Abegglen.

The Centurion work has calmed down; we manage it from here again. Jim's sort of struggling along, but the old UR team and the Cap computer consultants are getting some good mileage out of the office for their own work. I don't think it's an environment that either of us would like."

Sarjit was an Indian holding dual citizenship in Britain, a regular from the days of my adventures with Neil and Ken. One of the brightest sparks at Gemini, and a darling of C.K.'s, he should have become partner by now. I began to suspect complications in securing my own partnership in re-joining Gemini.

"You know, Alan, I'm not trying to sell you a bill of goods here. I'm not asking you or Gemini to buy me as a firm, or buy my assets and a modest client list, like AAS and Abegglen. You just get me. But I've proven out my dimensions as partner. Sales volume, hit rate, billibility, skill sets, the works. I'm a known quantity: you know my capacities and weaknesses, which buttons to press. I don't want to invest my energies in the politics of positioning for partner review after I'm hired. Let's just do it now, get it over with, and we can move on."

"You make a good case, Lewis. And you're a good case for partner in and of yourself. Not just the person I've known, either," Alan said appreciatively, as if really looking at me for the first time.

"You've grown up as a consultant, gotten past the indulgences. Freelancing was a brave move, and anyone who's known you can see it's helped you grow. And I can see Sasha's given you some balance, some motivation for health. But growing is about keeping the capacity for challenge, too."

"You want to tell me about Sarjit?"

"Sarjit's had his frustrations, Lewis, and I think he's on to something very exciting. Together with you I think he could build something really fantastic and make a bundle doing it."

"It's another one of these semi-independent company things, isn't it?" I asked, feeling the immediate partnership prospects begin to slip from my grasp.

"Gemini is ready but it's not ready. We only just managed to create a rationale for the company in Japan, and the board, Paris, and Morristown are not eager to go through the Abegglen-Centurion convulsions we did in Tokyo. For the rest of Asia, the company is looking for some committed managers and partners, with the right language skills and dedication to the region, to put their own stake into Gemini's growth there. People like me scare them, and people like you scare them. They don't want amateurs like me, who inevitably get pulled back, in my case for the boys' schools and Janet's boredom. And not people like you, because you not only know your strengths, you're quite mercenary about them, apparently ready to go to the highest bidder."

I made to protest on both counts, but Alan put up his hand to let me know he wanted to go on.

"Sarjit has found the right play. He's been frustrated in his own bid for partner. Too long in C.K.'s shadow, basically, no time to develop and demonstrate sales and clients of his own, despite tremendous capabilities. So the deal is this. He, and I hope you and maybe Ken and a few others, start a company of your own, with a small amount of your own equity in it. Gemini will put in a substantial stake itself. We'll call it Gemini Ventures or something similar, so you get some brand name cachet and spread the word for us, too. You build up the case work, starting with some of Sarjit's leads in India, or yours in Southeast Asia, too, if you like. Anything gets too big, you pass it up the chain to us. When the time comes, we buy you back, and you know you'll be rich."

I was intrigued, but much of this sounded unsettlingly familiar, and I told Alan so. He was silent for a few moments, then phoned his secretary for some coffee.

"Lewis, what was it like to leave ADL? How did you do it? How did you make those first few months work?"

This was an interesting and moderately alarming change of tack. Alan would have heard any number of rumors by now, and I decided this would be a good time, as it always was with Alan, to be frank and honest.

"Leaving was reasonably dramatic, and fortunately for me, well prepared. Both headquarters and most especially my local managing director made clear that they were in no hurry to make me partner, I was just too valuable as a workhorse who would follow orders. I had two clients that had a lot of praise for my work and the need for extensive further consulting services. Neither one wanted to pay high fees, though, especially when they knew they were only really buying my time, not any other added benefits of the firm."

"Who were they?"

"One was Mueller, one of Mercedes-Benz's costliest suppliers. They make the large stamping presses that turn out steel auto bodies. Very high tech, very proprietary."

"Right. You mentioned them to me in your voicemail. It is interesting that they supply one of Cap Gemini's shareholders, I agree it might be an interesting angle."

"The other was Mobil. I'd done a regional plastics study for them. I asked them both how they would feel about me, and the same team that had done their work at ADL, continuing the work independently, at a substantially lower price. They were both immediately enthusiastic. As I developed the idea with them, I asked how they felt about bruised feelings at Arthur D. Little, and the fact that ADL would retain competitive information about them and their interests. Mueller in particular were surprised it was an issue, and asserted their contract rights to all the casework product as their own proprietary material. When we got down to the wire, they instructed me to take all the work product with me, and give it to them or destroy it, but to leave nothing there. They were even concerned that ADL would use it against them in casework with one of their competitors, just out of spite."

"So that's what you did. How did you time it?"

"It was fairly dramatic. I waited for a session with the senior VP for Asia, visiting from Cambridge headquarters. I demanded a schedule for my promotion and bonus expansion, and predictably, he only hemmed and hawed. Late that same night, I came back with a few others ready to defect with me, and cleaned out everything in my office, and then some. I trashed everything relevant to the Mueller and Mobil cases that I couldn't use. For effect, I returned everybody else's documents and case materials to the inviolate file and the library. My office was spotless. I went through everyone else's stuff, including the managing directors, and removed anything that belonged to my clients. And to be a real prankster, I put the only key to my own office on top of my resignation letter to the VP, the only thing on top of my desk, and locked the door."

"Jesus, Lewis, you can't do anything like anyone else, can you? Lawsuits?"

"Almost. I got some very nasty letters from ADL's general counsel. I never went back to the office, but the others were back at work the next day like nothing happened. They tell me there was a real fit when they finally noticed, through the smoked glass wall of my office, that I'd cleared out, and then they couldn't get in. They almost called the police, thought they might find a body or something. Over the next few weeks, things got worse. Staff began to leave, the clients didn't return calls, and then Mueller wrote to say no thanks, we're working with Lewis now. And finally the managing director realized his own office had been penetrated.

"Then it was war. ADL does work worldwide with Mobil, and they called in the big guns. My client's boss put pressure on him to stick with ADL, and he caved. I had to do one of these Checkpoint Charlie things with the documents I had, and handed them back over to ADL. But Mueller stood by me. I found a spunky lawyer and we made clear that this was a case of clients' rights and my iron rice bowl. Singapore sometimes has an undeserved reputation for being all pro-corporation, but when it comes down to it, the right to enjoy the dignity of your work is a big deal there, and well respected by people and government alike. ADL made a mistake, threatening to keep me from practicing the job that I was most skilled to do. This counterbalanced whatever I had signed in my initial contract, and I finally got busy doing the work."

"I heard you did really well."

"Too well. Things moved too fast. Soon I was faced with the choice of hiring about thirty-five people, for whom I had no idea whether I could sustain work, or sticking with about five, which was more responsible but no way to grow. That's why I trimmed back, and that's why I'm here now."

"Lewis, this is exactly where Gemini Ventures comes in. No lawsuits, no legal fees at all, we take care of all the set up and admin, you just put in some token equity. When the workload gets too high, you have all of Gemini to lean on. When it's too dry, you have us for referrals. You work with people you know; you're not training up some novice team. Then, when the time is ripe, we buy back your share, and you're rich, with all the benefits of a Gemini partner and more."

It did sound good. What I could not tell Alan was that I found it very hard to think far beyond my future as a partner. He was right, of course, I had matured as a consultant. I had become efficient at sizing the work, taking on the right level of commitment, and sticking by it. I delivered good work, and had evolved into one of the most persuasive salesmen, facilitators, and recruiters in the business. Having found the critical balance to sustain both health and a partner-level career without burnout, I was about to hit peak earning power, and might be well advised to park in this inviting slot and just let it happen.

But though I was driven by a strong desire for completion, for partnership as the rationalizing culmination of a lot of craziness and deception, I was increasingly plagued by doubts about the nature and impacts of my work, and a sense of time lost and other pathways closing. I needed to make partner at some primal level, so that I could finish this one thing and make a choice to move on, if I then wanted to, and if there were indeed choices. I had not yet achieved the detachment to consider quitting the business *without* becoming partner. But I was too impatient to nurture the kind of complex path to partner that Alan was offering through Gemini Ventures.

"Alan, I know this is a good deal, but it's really not what I want to do. I've used up my interest in independent, or semi-independent enterprises. I want back in. I want to earn my partner stripes in the good-old fashioned way. I'll give you good service as a partner. You'll at least have as good a guarantee of service as you get from anyone, probably more."

This was true. Once in, and while I philosophized about my life choices, I was certain of doing reasonable work, and would have no interest in joining competitors for higher compensation, which is more than could be said for many others. But I could see that Alan looked troubled.

"Lewis, this isn't an easy thing to say," Alan began.

In a flash, I realized that Alan's hard sell on Gemini Ventures had more to do with it being my only option, not an interesting option.

"Abegglen?"

"Abegglen. Look, Lewis, he's really had it out for you since Philip Morris. I don't even know how he got wind of your interest in re-joining, but he's made a hell of a stink about it. I think he sees your exit, and return to London soon after, as a personal betrayal. At some level, he's covering up his own inadequacies, but he put the blame for Gemini Japan's stagnant performance squarely on you, and he won't support your re-entry now."

"But I don't understand—why do we need it?"

"Well, he has a degree of charm with Cap Gemini, and they're worried about what his leaving the Gemini circuit might do to our still shallow reputation in the marketplace. The other thing though, Lewis, is that to make it work I would have to put you straight on some casework in Europe, fill your billing cycle right away. I'd have to keep you away from Asia and Abegglen. You would wind up on this bank case with Ken, most likely. It wouldn't be the kind of partnership that you remember."

"Any other options?"

"Well, we can try a few intermediary things. Have a look at the banking work; I think you'll be convinced it's not your style. Sarjit has a new case coming up with Chase in Hong Kong, maybe you should do some work with him on that, as a Gemini subcontractor.

We'll get you some namecards and everything, the client will see you as a local specialist. We could give you top-end rates. Hell, you'd make more than a partner with bonus, and it would give you and Sarjit the chance to get to know each other again, talk the Gemini Ventures work through. And Abegglen won't be around forever. Do a good job with Chase, and we could re-institute your Asia partner bid."

We said our good-byes. Alan seemed genuinely sorry not to have me back. We had started an adventure in Asia that involved the best of consulting's colonization of new geographies. While the U.S. and Europe struggled through brutal mergers and acquisitions, and the industry there moved inexorably to mega-scale, technologically intensive casework, Asia remained a place where smaller scale work and traditional strategy tools, not to mention CEO schmoozing and fine dining, still held sway.

I had a different kind of fine dining experience awaiting me. Sasha and I had arranged after my meeting with Alan to meet at Gordon's Wine Cellar, down the Thames from Gemini. This exquisitely cozy, Roman-arched basement wine bar has been going in one form or another since the 1300's. Buried deep below London's most ancient streets, the tunnels serving the cellar have been converted to candlelit havens for savoring fine wines, cheese, and the best pub food, with the tunnels' dankness and occasional dripping more than compensated by the warmth of the happy bodies always pressed into them. A place too historied, organic, and human for serious business types, Gordon's was the perfect place to discuss my waning interest in consulting.

"How did it go?"

Even in the dim candlelight Sasha's elegant, exotic appearance attracted not a few stares, among them my own. I marveled that emerging from the wreck of my past marriages I had found this woman who so effortlessly held my faith and every attention. If all that consulting ever gave me was this one uncritical love, I reflected, it was surely worthwhile after all. I surfaced from my reverie, savored my first glass of a fine Rosemont, and indulged in the view.

"Not great, exactly. Alan wants me back in the fold and has given me a couple of options, but kind of everything but the direct Asian partnership I'd like. I could go with another startup, something they're calling Gemini Ventures, or maybe join a case in Europe, an on-site analysis and diagnostics assignment, one of those things where you go in to pump up more problems and more business."

"You don't sound too happy about it. What happened? Is that it?"

"Abegglen seems to be what happened; he's still hot and bothered about my abandoning him to Philip Morris. Nothing I can do about that, really; he's not a man to make peace with. Like Patrick always said, once on his bad side, that's it."

"So what do we do now?"

"Well, Alan has this thing with Sarjit Singh—you met him."

"The one who you said looks like C.K. Prahalad's son?"

"That's him. I can subcontract with Gemini to help Sarjit do a new market expansion project for Chase Manhattan Bank in Southeast Asia. The money's good, and like Alan said, Abegglen won't be around forever. And maybe Sarjit and I would want to do something with this Gemini Ventures thing, though right now I'm exhausted with the startup/takeover game."

Sasha filled my glass and we said nothing for awhile.

"Lewis, let me ask you something," she said presently.

"Anytime."

"How many consulting cases have you been happy with?"

"What do you mean by happy?"

"I mean, happy about the outcome, about what you're actually doing, the changes your creating."

"You mean, cases where I think the results are for the good?"

Sasha nodded.

"Well, none."

"None?"

"None, zero. There have been quite a few cases where I really liked the clients I worked with, and I was happy that I made their work easier, maybe their lives better. But there's nothing in the end results that makes me proud. That HDTV case for the Pentagon would have been a good outcome, a major act of industrial policy to build a new city, great for efficiency, and managing impacts on the environment. But Congress killed that. No, let's see. I've helped the world get more concentration of banking and insurance power, more cars, more diapers, more gadgets. I've identified new resources and peoples to exploit, and new means of getting at them. I've helped companies steal from each other, prostitute themselves, rape each other. No, I can't say my consulting life has been one for the good."

"Then maybe you shouldn't be over-investing your energies in something like Gemini Ventures, or making the sacrifices of moving to Europe. When would we even get to see each other? I know you'd like to make partner with one of the big firms, and maybe that will still happen. Maybe it's time to look into other things. But for now the subcontracting may be a way to bide the time and put away some resources. I don't love you for your consulting accomplishments, you know."

I did not know it at the time, but my life had just taken a profound turn.

HONG KONG, WINTER 1996 AND SPRING 1997

And so I settled in Hong Kong and fell back to the work I knew well, the programmed deception, without the benefit of an immediate partnership. Gemini was fairly desperate to convince Chase Manhattan of both the attractiveness of Southeast Asian markets and the depth of Gemini's expertise there. That both were nonexistent were mere inconveniences for me to address.

Based on a series of working visits, my mission was first to persuade Chase management that Indonesia's markets for consumer banking products were not only attractive but reasonably stable and robust. Chase had recently merged with Chemical Bank, and as a result the new bank had inherited two separate infrastructures and two widely different views of Indonesia's future. I picked the side most willing to bet on Indonesia and used them to explore possible partners and avenues of development for credit cards, personal and automotive loans, mortgages, and investment products.

My presentation seemed convincing enough, and Gemini was soon engaged to do an intensive study of Indonesia, Thailand, and Hong Kong for market penetration and development. Only Gemini did not see it that way. In what would be my final and most surreal exposure to the business propeller model at work, I watched in fascination as a team of business analysts descended on Chase Hong Kong to diagnose and amplify our clients' concerns. Within weeks the emphasis was a on a new product that Gemini wanted to push, an electronic stored-value cash card, proffered by another of Gemini's clients. The idea was to get Chase Hong Kong to see this as the solution to their development needs in Southeast Asia, ensuring years of Gemini implementation work and dual client efficiencies.

Not surprisingly, Chase had little interest in this pitch within a pitch, and grew increasingly concerned about Gemini's lack of on-the-ground knowledge in its key target cities, Jakarta and Bangkok. Within a few months they decided to sever their links with Gemini on the case, much to Sarjit's disappointment. But since I was the only consultant who had actually lived in the region, rather than flown in from London and Morristown, Chase asked me to stay on as an independent, and Alan approved in the hope that I might yet bring Chase around to Gemini.

Chase had other plans. I had gradually let slip my actual disenchantment with market prospects in the region, and had helped design a staged entry for Chase that would commit first to only one product, a co-branded credit card. Using one of Chase's proven alliances in the credit card market, such as Shell in the States for a gasoline co-brand, Chase might best test the waters with a drown-proof product, I advocated.

My cautious recommendations would be well embraced by Chase senior management (and later vindicated in the ensuing regional market crises). To implement them, however, Chase encouraged me to find and recommend a capable consulting firm with a large enough established presence in the region to get the work done. It was not long before I found "John Jameson" and Coopers & Lybrand Hong Kong.

Coopers had taken the giant accountancy's path to consulting, using well established offices, deep client relationships, and extensive regional presence to support a rapidly growing, and almost wholly externally acquired, base of local consulting talent. I was impressed that Jameson had put together a team of Financial Institutions consultants who were intimately familiar with the banking and insurance markets of Asia, and who had the right relevant knowledge and experience, as well as the requisite languages and common sense understanding needed for this kind of case.

We put together a large engagement, one which would make Gemini or any consultancy envious. As the intermediary between Chase and Coopers, I anticipated a certain perverse enjoyment in managing a team of consultants from the paying client's side. But soon I learned there was not too much to manage. Coopers was incredibly structured and organized, I discovered. Accustomed to working as a smoothly functioning machine, and utterly familiar with both the product and systems requirements at hand, my great beast of a team proved both tame and efficient, and more facile than me in use of technologies and communications.

To coordinate between Chase and Coopers team members dispersed from New York to Hong Kong, Singapore, Bangkok, and Jakarta, we set about weekly two-hour conference calls that became a highlight of Wednesday mornings at Chase headquarters. Soon known as the "John and Lewis Show," these weekly reports of progress and joint trouble-shooting sessions were marvels of productivity, and were as likely to be conducted from a traffic-stalled taxi in Bangkok or the comfort of my own bed in Hong Kong. Laptops and document e-mailing smoothed transmission of Chase's U.S. co-branding expertise to the local markets, and Cooper's emphasis on simply doing a great job, as opposed to strategizing expanded sales, produced a concentration of effort that bore solid results.

After some months of this it became clear that there was little else for me to do except step out of the way. Offered both a Chase vice president's slot for Hong Kong and a Coopers directorship and partnership, I felt a certain cleansing irony that after working so hard at self-promotion and the internal business angles of consulting, a partnership would finally fall into my lap from trying to mind the client's business.

I accepted Coopers' offer without hesitation. The staid banking lifestyle, particularly one based at Chase's consumer services facilities in Hong Kong's Northern Territories, could not be a wise choice for me, I reasoned. And the moral merits of calculating how many thousands of new bankruptcies we would create among the region's struggling middle classes were for me at best questionable.

With an odd sense of thrill I realized that accepting Coopers' offer and becoming partner meant that I could finally quit consulting. I had so internalized the norms of the industry, so ascribed my own sense of worth and personal progress to consulting's standards of success, that I could not look beyond consulting as a whole person until I had ticked off this last achievement. Perhaps ever since that first recruiting dinner with Morikawa when he visited me in London from BCG Tokyo, I could accept nothing less than the top of the consulting hierarchy. Now that freedom was at hand, I embraced my new job with deep calm and purpose.

I was also encouraged enough by the honesty of Coopers' work to believe that I might enjoy it, and even reconcile away the loss of any future contributions I might make to science and the law. But two forces combined to finally have me make good on my own anticipated consulting self-destruction.

As a new partner I was positioned with Coopers to lead their strategy practice in Shanghai. One of the first leads I cultivated, together with some of Coopers London's seniormost executives, was the Bank of China, the holy grail of financial institutions consulting.

Breaking the deadlock of a long series of failed attempts to create a scale engagement there, I captured the Bank's interest with a proposal for process facilitation. Though I tried unsuccessfully to steer their energies elsewhere, I discovered to my horror that the more I made the work sound like what I had done with C.K. Prahalad and Philips in the Centurion program, the more Bank of China liked what I had to say. Programmed enthusiasm and anxiety, linked to the creation of specific projects, in a cascade of revitalization sessions, held unaccountable appeal for this client. I began to have visions of countless sessions with the Bank's many tens of thousands of employees scattered throughout China, cajoling and harassing, scaring and manipulating until the numbers began to look favorable, like some kind of new cultural revolution.

I did not want to be part of this new red guard. The case helped me recognize that I would not likely escape my own past in consulting, that the unattractive things about me which somehow made me an attractive consultant would inevitably keep surfacing, unless I quit. The other factor which led to my decision was Shanghai itself. I had not visited the city in some years, and was astonished at the thickness of coal-burning dust that choked the city. A degrading influence on any life there, and a specific health hazard for Sasha, the dust highlighted the explosion of consumerism and development that has overrun this city once known for its great charm, intellectual iconoclasm, and complex culture. Where once exploitationist interests in the first half of the twentieth century added dimension to this metropolis, in the 1990s Shanghai became an inhuman expansion of steel and concrete, poisoning itself and the surrounding countryside in an attempt to feed China's newly triggered grosser appetites. This was not the beast I wished to feed.

There was no "gotcha" satisfaction to leaving Coopers as there had been with ADL. This was not an exit of drama and pranks, but a protracted discussion of lost financial opportunities (Coopers was about to merge with Price Waterhouse), fast exits from Shanghai after Bank of China, and serving China from Hong Kong. Fortunately, in retrospect, no alternative posting was suggested which I might have felt obligated to take.

With remarkable equanimity, aided no doubt by acknowledgment of the large caseload of Chase work that I had dropped in their laps, Coopers accepted my resignation. I, the exemplar of the Consulting Demon, was free at last of my own consulting demons.

CONSULTING DEMONOLOGY, TRACT 13

MODERN MAGIC FOR SURVIVING THE CONSULTING STORM

Consulting's global weather system is changing for the worse. Shifting economic climate, e-commerce and unstable technology environments, and increasingly interdependent business ecologies contribute to a chaos of stormy unpredictability in the industry. No consulting career begun now, even with the most established firms, will finish the way an exiting partner's professional life does today. A select variety of survival strategies have so far succeeded in riding out the storm.

1

Cheaper, Better, Faster. For most consultants there is little time to think about how to survive, and the instinctive response to external threats is pursued with vengeance: do more of the same, just push harder. As a firm McKinsey has succeeded with this strategy for decades, famously urging its consultants on to higher and higher levels of adrenaline, stamina, and machismo. This deepening of the trenches to prepare for the next assault, however, tends to dispense with creativity, encouraging instead a reliance on ritual and rote performance. McKinsey's evolving alliance with technologist Andersen Consulting is a telling indication that more-of-the-same strategies, even when practiced by the established masters attracting clients who *want* more of the same, may not long endure.

2

The Guru Way. Consulting's accelerated changes and extensive transformations have all but erased authentic claims to guru status. In more than a decade, no single new practitioner has emerged, a lá Clay Henderson or Michael Porter, who has so much to offer both clients and consulting peers, and who so thoroughly alters the field with each major case or industry publication, that the industry itself rushes to adapt around him. There is no longer any individual font of ideas shaping the business. A senior consultant today would be fortunate to have one idea associated with his name, like C.K. Prahalad's Strategic Intent-Core Competence frame, and it is more likely that that single concept becomes detached from the name, like Business Reengineering has from Michael Hammer. But the myth of guruism can persist in the business press, and in this there may be an avenue of survival. The casual business reader is made to believe that a given author's views have wide currency among their peers, and a book will attempt to conjure the impression that a would-be guru has legions of client followers hanging on every utterance. In reality there is no longer any such beast. Once free of the grip of their self-aggrandizing professors, freshly minted MBAs discover that no single senior consultant can be of real help unless he is intimately involved in the immediate job at hand. Clients similarly learn that no one individual, with the breadth of active experience to stay current on all the changes critical to their business, would have the time to get close to their own issues and needs. The era of the knowledgeable team has arrived, and to aspire to guruism, while not necessarily impractical, is to aspire to mere fakery.

3

Discovering, Nurturing, and Protecting the Niche. Consulting niches are likely to proliferate with the industry's continued expansion. A given product, approach, or focus will become increasingly important to achieving any kind of differentiable identity in the field. Defining and securing niches will also become a critical part of brand name development as mergers and acquisitions continue to blur client understanding of a given firm's attributes. But for the individual consultant the development of a given niche involves high specific risk: the niche may prove short-lived, or quickly be overwhelmed by better-resourced imitators. The most favorable outcome is likely to be buy-out and absorption of the individuals defining the niche. As the Borg in *Star Trek* are wont to say, your assimilation will contribute to our uniqueness.

4

Independence. For many clients the core contributions of consulting to their business, namely objectivity, problem focus, and cross-industry perspective, will continue to be ably provided by the sole practitioner. The independent consultant who focuses on a small group of clients, and heavily invests his or her time in addressing those clients' needs with fairly priced, proven concepts and services, will be rewarded with a regular base of good-paying customers. As large-scale consultancies grow ever more dominant, working for only the largest clients with any in-depth sensitivity, smaller clients or those with more modest spending expectations will be increasingly drawn to the sole practitioner. Pressures and temptations to expand one's staff and client base, and to become absorbed in new product and concept development, remain the greatest threat to the individual consultant's more modest, and generally more honest, practice.

5

New Client Development. This is perhaps the hardest and most danger-ous survival strategy to pursue, and one that absorbs a great deal of many firms' energies. Converting a client that has not used consulting services before involves many upfront costs and risks in the proposal making pro-cess, and once engaged, the risk of mismatched expectations rising to the fore is substantial. But firms remain attracted to first-time conversions, because they are less likely to directly involve competition from other consultancies, often involve work that is easy to fix, and because in their ignorance first-time buyers may accept outlandish fees. Once engaged, however, fresh clients are hard to keep; large firms make it a practice to prowl for the recently converted, using underbidding to bring them into their own fold. Fewer and fewer of the unconverted remain, forcing new-client strategies away from the mature U.S. market.

6

Colonization. Ensuring a long life for the successful consulting mindset requires moving on to more fertile ground: China, India, and Southeast Asia will continue the bankrolling of rampant consulting growth for some time, and firms with scale and savvy are fast building their presence in these regions. Here all the benefits of new client development are in force—easy work, less competition, and client ignorance of proper pricing—with fewer associated risks. Less experienced, lower-cost staff can be entrusted to do the work, and mistakes are likely to go unnoticed or be more readily for-given. Paranoid about data sharing, and unaccustomed to outsiders pene-trating characteristically family-style operations, once Asian clients permit a given consultant entry, they are likely to remain intensely loyal.

7

Conferencing and other Subsidiary Services. The growing scale and concentration of top-end consulting firms is now creating a host of sub-sidiary services that become new businesses in and of themselves. From travel agents to recruiters, conference organizers to specialized publica-tions, and geographic intelligence units to translators and interpreters, a growing number of support services have turned their attention to dedicated service of the consulting industry. A few experienced consultants with an entrepreneurial bent have spotted this as an opportunity in itself, becoming expert herders of talent, from secretaries and production artists to project engineers and process facilitators. As more consulting firms move away from a centralized office model for their business, such services will likely become even more critical.

8

Subcontracting. Subcontracting's parasitic existence has become increasingly attractive as more and more large firms use this as a means of controlled growth and expansion. Testing for acquisition and hiring opportunities through the use of subcontractors, as well as using their contacts to fish for new client opportunities, large firms also make intensive use of subcontractors to expand their profiles and capabilities. Most larger firms think nothing of putting subcontractors and their case experiences into the consulting biographies of their client proposals, and some will even claim geographic presence in a country or city where a subcontractor is in fact their only link. For the subcontractor, business between engagements may be hard to find and manage—taking on new commitments can block the feed of future work—but the attractiveness of not having to invest in the sales process, and being assured a steady, often very attractive pay, can more than compensate.

9

Size Strategies. Strategies of scale remain the preferred approach for the top consulting firms. The largest engagements entail the highest efficiencies. The expensive sales process is best leveraged by large sales of long duration; better training of larger teams follows from big, extended cases; more time and opportunity are provided to emplace proprietary products that can lock in a given client for several successions of cases. To handle the largest engagements, of course, a firm must wield vast numbers of on-call personnel, and thus intense pressures for merger and acquisition now re-shape the industry. The firm with the largest number of bodies can justify the largest stand-by force for new engagements, and the highest advertising, recruitment, and promotion budgets. Here the former accountancies bring great power to bear. What they lack in experience, the newly created powerhouses of tax and accounting heritage, like PriceWaterhouseCoopers Consulting and the Deloitte & Touche Consulting Group, achieve in ready-made scale and infrastructure.

10

Technology Advancement. The core consulting survival strategy of the new century is the advancement and control of new technologies beginning with e-commerce. The largest, most crucial clients will increasingly differentiate themselves through the competitive use of technology, be it in customer service, distributions and inventory control, manufacturing process, or supply sourcing strategies. Somewhat surprisingly, this is a leap that even the largest, most capable firms are not yet prepared to take. The most ambitious firms in this area, like Andersen and Gemini, prefer to focus on general computer software solutions, where a high ongoing service component can greatly stabilize and augment fees. Others recognize the criticality of technically expert knowledge, like ADL, Booz Allen, and the newly formed Deloitte Consulting, but do little more than highlight its importance to their clients, in the hope that at least seeing the problem will earn them a role in engaging it. The strategists who embrace the role of technology, as McKinsey may through Andersen, may have the most to offer their most influential clients; those that appear to eschew it, like BCG (an irony, given the scientific and analytic biases of its founder), may find they are permanently outdistanced.

HEROES FOR THE ZEROES

Mass-market advertising for consulting firms was an unthinkable gaucherie when I joined the industry in the 1980s. When it first emerged among the accountancies' fledging consulting forays, by the more established houses it was deemed to be a sure sign of organizations wanting in professionalism. As the practice becomes more widespread today, from airport billboards to popular newsweekly inserts and internet banners, I find these advertisements and public pronouncements offer good clues to the perceptions and practices consulting companies will seek to control in this new century.

The powerful but untested newcomers to the field seem to be spending the most, in rather desperate attempts to wish away the competition, through mimicry of the very things in others that they claim make them unique. Many seem to draw on Gemini's decade of high-visibility investment in the integration of process, technology, operations and strategy. That everyone else in the field from Andersen to PriceWaterhouse Coopers is doing the same does not bear mention. Knowledge, the buzzword of the moment, manages to secure at least a non sequiter name drop in the text of many ads, now that ADL has got such good mileage from it. For good measure, even in the same copy, firms are often presented under different names, say as XYZ Consulting and the XYZ Consulting Group, enabling experimentation with the potential cache of "Group" that seems to have worked so well for BCG and others.

For me, these universal, we-do-it-all campaigns represent an amalgam of everything, and an identity of nothing. But the investors behind these large-scale efforts know that scale and concentration are on their side. With the right infusion of technology and expertise, surfing the first waves of e-commerce, they may well prove to be the top players of the new consulting century, where objectivity, focus and perspective mean less and less, and where the consulting behemoths will inevitably subsume more and more of their clients' corporate sovereignty.

Another sign to watch for the growth-grasping perversities of consulting in the Twenty-Zeroes is in the industry's advertising for recruitment. Professional journals for doctors, lawyers, psychologists, scientists and engineers will continue to fill with ads designed to drain these professions of their talent, inviting young degree holders in particular to leverage their impressive credentials and experience, and readily convert them to consulting skills. For these new Heroes of the Zeroes, the money, the challenge, the high-achieving colleagues will no doubt be touted in new and cunning schemes of expert seduction. That the money is unfair gain from society and client alike, the challenge to avoid the norms of law and non-destructive living, and the achievement that of survival, reckless of all costs and consequences, will then as now require a certain demonic focus and appreciation.

Today Yoshi Morikawa continues his association with the Boston Consulting Group, securing the title of office President, unique in the BCG system, to counter his long-denied Administratorship. He remains busy with both Japanese television and politics, and works hard to differentiate himself from rival Kenichi Ohmae of McKinsey, who harbors all too similar ambitions.

Mike Garrity gave himself as much distance from consulting as possible for awhile, helping a Japanese racing boat company set up in Hawai'i. He then returned to California, where he does specialized technology consulting for a small firm.

Brett Norman, Ken Murphy, and Sarjit Singh, the core of Gemini London's work force, left consulting when it became apparent that their prospects for partnership could only be sustained through a long series of on-site assignments, which gave them little room for their own client development.

Pat Curran continues to live in Abegglen's shadow at Gemini Japan, surviving but achieving little notice back at Gemini Paris and Morristown.

Brad Wong left consulting for his family's tire manufacturing business in Malaysia, which he reports is less exciting but less stressful. Frederick opted to stay with ADL, and after some initial chastisement, continued to thrive there for some time. Clay traded his silence for a business school reference, and recently graduated with his MBA from UC Davis. Richard Williams finally relinquished his grip on ADL Singapore, and was reportedly on the lookout for ways to stay active at the Club. No consulting firms have picked up his unequaled administrative skills.

At last report both Prahalad and Abegglen had new books in the works. In an era where Japan's threat to his vision of global business transformation, C.K. may have lost some of his energy, but no doubt new threats will emerge to sustain his peculiar brand of urgency. Dr. Abegglen continues to rank among the foremost analysts of Japan's complex interpenetrations of Asia; it is hard to believe he is not selling some client on this expertise right now.

Alan Johnston remains a central icon of Gemini London, re-configured like many of his peers as an e-commerce expert. No doubt he will soon be tapped, with some reluctance, to head Gemini's overall, integrated consulting operations. I believe Alan would prefer to stay at the next tier down, to best enjoy his lifestyle of self-directed travels, but I imagine Gemini, aware how keen Alan is to survive at all costs, will maneuver him to the place and role of their choosing.

As for me, I am about to complete my J.D. with emphasis on Space Law, and am progressing toward my Ph.D., incorporating both Planetary Geosciences and Future Studies, focusing my interests on resource issues for the international settlement of Mars. I enjoy my work as a researcher, and recently I made my first, and controversial, presentation on asteroid origins at Johnson Space Center. I received numerous compliments about my presentation style; I hope to one day earn more for the content of my work.

Combining a bit of all the threads of my life, I recently contributed to the Third United Nations Conference on the Peaceful Uses of Outer Space. There, as a Space Generation Forum delegate representing young space professionals from around the world, I was thrilled to help shape, together with nearly 200 of the most talented and ambitious space enthusiasts from every area of the planet, new policy for promoting the progress and benefits of space exploration. Satisfyingly, the Conference was held at the same UN facility in Vienna I interned at back in 1982, where I missed the last such Conference just as I left for my first job in Japan. Using my consulting background in a way I have not felt for many years, I was especially pleased to help organize and facilitate some of the small group meetings among my fellow delegates.

Sasha and I continue to grow and thrive together, and I am enjoying the first marriage in which I can have real faith and hope. I needed to overcome some serious issues of maturity and self-control. But somehow achieving this has been made simple, through her love, and my welcome distance from the consulting industry.

I am asked occasionally to take on consulting assignments, and about my interest in joining a large firm once again. It usually takes me but a second to assure that consulting belongs more in my past than in my future—though I heard last week that Price Waterhouse Coopers was now working with the International Lunar Exploration Working Group. Perhaps the demons are not done with me yet.

INDEX